SUITING UP FOR SPACE

D1034417

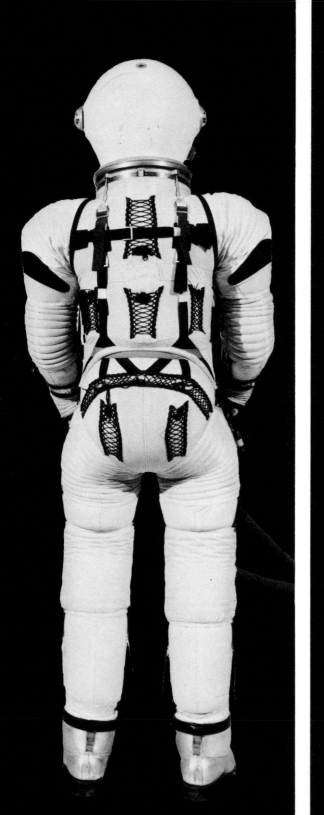

SUITING UP
FOR SPACE

The Evolution
of the Space Suit

LLOYD MALLAN

The
John Day Company
New York

For their cooperation
beyond the call of duty,
the author salutes
Dr. Charles L. Wilson,
Chief Medical Advisor,
Life Support Systems Program Office,
Air Force Aeronautical Systems Division;
and Dr. Edwin G. Vail,
pioneer space-suit scientist,
now in the Space Systems Department
at the Hamilton Standard Division
of United Aircraft Corporation.

The John Day Company, 257 Park Avenue South, New York N.Y. 10010
an Intext publisher

Published on the same day in Canada by Longman Canada Limited.

Library of Congress Catalogue Card Number: 75-89308
Printed in the United States of America
Designed by The Etheredges

CONTENTS

ACKNOWLEDGMENTS

Warmest appreciation is due to the following persons for their more than generous aid in supplying the author with important research material and/or photos from their private files.

At the Aeronautical Systems Division, Air Force Systems Command, Wright-Patterson Air Force Base, Ohio: Dr. Charles L. Wilson, Lieutenant Colonel, Chief Medical Advisor, Life Support Systems Program Office; J. Donald Bowen, Project Engineer and Group Leader/Pressure Suits, 6570th Aerospace Medical Research Laboratory; Mrs. Lee Rock, Project Engineer/Pressure Suits, same Laboratory; Philip Pollock, Historical Division; Lieutenant Colonel John J. Whiteside, former Director of Public Information; Robert M. Quayle, Public and Internal Information Division; Robert Maltby, Chief, Public Information Office; Carroll High, Assistant

ACKNOWLEDGMENTS

Chief, same office; and Airman First Class James L. Fishback, same office.

At the Hamilton Standard Division of United Aircraft Corporation, Windsor Locks, Connecticut: Dr. Edwin G. Vail, Space Systems Department; Thomas W. Herrala, Assistant Preliminary Design Engineer, Advanced Systems/Space and Life Systems; Charles A. Anezis, Public Relations Director; Francis G. Real, Senior Public Relations Representative; and Rudolph Schiffer, Public Relations Department.

At Headquarters, National Aeronautics and Space Administration (NASA), Washington, D.C.: Margaret Ware, Audio-Visual Branch.

At the NASA John F. Kennedy Space Center, Merritt Island, Florida: Mel Snyder, Public Information Officer; Jack King, Deputy Chief, Public Affairs; Dick Young, Public Information Officer; Ed Harrison, Public Information Officer; Darlene Hunt and Diana Boles, Public Information Secretaries.

At the NASA Manned Spacecraft Center, Houston, Texas: Howard Gibbons, News Operations Manager, Public Affairs Office.

In the Office of the Assistant Secretary of Defense for Public Affairs, the Pentagon, Washington, D.C.: Lieutenant Colonel Robert A. Webb, USAF, Chief, Book Branch, Magazine and Book Division; and Major S. R. "Kirk" Kirkpatrick, USAF, Magazine Branch, same Division.

At the School of Aerospace Medicine, Air Force Systems Command, Brooks Air Force Base, Texas: Colonel Timothy Glasgow, former Director of Information.

At Headquarters, Air Force Systems Command, Andrews Air Force Base, Maryland: Dr. Harold Helfman, Office of Information.

At the 6571st Aerospace Medical Research Laboratory, Air Force Systems Command, Holloman Air Force Base, New Mexico: Dr. Harald von Beckh, Chief Scientist.

At the David Clark Company, Worcester, Massachusetts: Mr. David Clark, founder, now retired, a pressure-suit pioneer.

At Grumman Aerospace Corporation, John F. Kennedy Space Center, Merritt Island, Florida: John L. Vandegrift, Manager of Public Affairs; Gena Theriault, his hard-working Girl Friday.

At the Bendix Corporation, John F. Kennedy Space Center, Merritt Island, Florida: Bill Lyerly, Public Relations Director.

At the General Electric Company, Apollo Support Department, Cape Canaveral, Florida: Eugene (Gene) J. Folkman, Information Development and Planning Manager.

At Arthur D. Little, Inc., Cambridge, Massachusetts: D. Reid Weedon, Jr., Senior Vice President; and Carl A. Hiester.

At the Massachusetts Institute of Technology, Cambridge: Michael Hugh Salamon, student/Mathematics and Physics: for his helpful suggestions in Chapter Seven.

At the Lockheed Missiles & Space Company, Cape Kennedy, Florida: Milton Jay Salamon, Senior Publications Engineer: for supplying numerous pertinent technical papers and reports.

At Litton Industries, Inc., Beverly Hills, California: Colonel Barney Oldfield, USAF (ret.), Corporate Director Public Relations & Advertising, International.

Special mention should also be given to Helen W. Schulz, former Historian of the Historical Office at the now defunct Air Matériel Command, Wright Field, Ohio, for her diligent and accurate research into the early years of full- and partial-pressure suit development.

L.M.

Chapter 1

BALLOONS AND BOILING BLOOD

The first person on earth to prove that the human body could survive in the hostile regions of outer space was a colorful young daredevil from Dorchester, Massachusetts. He later died unsung in an insane asylum.

Both events had a common base. For according to most physiologists of that time—the early 1930's—only a madman would expose himself to the deadly environment of airless space. Without the weight of air to pressurize it, the body would blow up like a balloon. The water vapor and other gases in the body would expand wildly and then swiftly leak away, trying to fill the vacuum that surrounded it. These scientists also pointed out that at a height of 63,000 feet above the ground, air pressure is so low that water starts to boil at a temperature of 98 degrees Fahrenheit.

That is approximately the normal temperature of the human body. Since the content of human blood is almost three-quarters water, the blood would burst into a turbulent stream of raging bubbles. Death would be instantaneous and inevitable.

Such ominous scientific predictions did not appear to frighten young Mark Edward Ridge of Dorchester, Massachusetts. He was impelled by some inner drive to do outrageous things. His aim was to soar 17 miles above the earth—sitting in an open, entirely unprotected basket of a balloon. This altitude was about 27,000 feet higher than the level where blood begins to boil.

Mark Ridge was considered variously to be a psychotic, a man of great courage, and a visionary. One way or another, public opinion did not bother him. He was convinced that a suit of protective clothing could be designed that would keep him alive and warm in the lethal near-vacuum and coldness of 90,000 feet.

Underneath his apparent derring-do, according to one famous psychiatrist, was a kind of death wish, a strong desire to punish himself by facing death. Karl A. Menninger, co-founder of the Menninger Clinic, included Ridge as a footnote in the 1938 book *Man Against Himself*.

Quoting from a story that appeared in the March 19, 1934, issue of *Time* magazine, Dr. Menninger stated: "Mark Ridge . . . insisted upon testing a 'stratosphere suit' he had designed by having himself shut in a steel tank packed with dry ice at a temperature of minus 100° F. 'Daredevil Ridge, 28, has long been willing to risk Death for Science.' Of course," continued the psychiatrist, "more discreet and no less courageous examples of this fill the pages of medical history, but in these instances the benefits to society outweigh the purely autonomous impulse to take a long chance with death."

It could be said that Dr. Menninger was being unfair to Mark Ridge—if one were to believe Ridge's own stated motive for his planned ascent into the stratosphere. The young Massachusetts daredevil claimed that he wanted to perform the experiment for the benefit of national security and the scientific progress of military aviation.

On the other hand, at the age of twenty-five, three years before he stepped into a steel tank filled with dry ice, Ridge became front-page news by performing a meaningless stunt. He jumped out of an airplane while flying at 2,000 feet above the Charles River in Boston. Of course he had a parachute, but he didn't open it until he was at least halfway down to the frozen surface of the river.

At the time, January 16, 1931, there was a Massachusetts law in effect prohibiting anyone from "leaving the cockpit of an airplane to perform a feat of daring." Maybe Ridge didn't know about

Section 53, Chapter 90, of the General Law. In any case, after he
landed on a sheet of ice in the Charles River Basin and Berkley
Street, he was immediately arrested. Ridge was shortly released,
pending a trial.

Then he disappeared. Seventeen weeks later, on May 22, the
East Boston police received an anonymous telephone tip as to Mark
Ridge's whereabouts. When they found him, Ridge refused to admit
his identity. There were reports that he had been in the Boston City
Hospital in the interim. According to another account, he had been
negotiating with a motion-picture company about a spectacular stunt
job in the movies. But nothing ever came of any stunt-job offer,
since Ridge never did appear in a motion picture. At his arraignment
in court the following Monday, he was given a suspended sentence.

For the next two years little was noted in the public press about
Mark Edward Ridge. He was working quietly but insistently behind
the scenes to fulfill a new "itch." Now he wanted to explore the
stratosphere. This new itch was inspired by three Europeans who
had twice dared to invade that unfriendly dominion of the sky—and
done it successfully—in a balloon.

Auguste Piccard, a Swiss physicist, headed both stratospheric
expeditions. The first flight was made on May 27, 1931—just two
days after Mark Ridge received his suspended sentence in the East
Boston District Court. Piccard and Charles Knipfer reached an
altitude of 51,777 feet in a flight that took seventeen hours from
Augsburg, Germany, to a glacier near Innsbruck, Austria. On the
second record-breaking balloon flight, Dr. Piccard's companion
was Max Cosyns. They reached a height of 53,152 feet on August
18, 1932, and were forced again to land on a glacier in the Alps.

The Piccard assaults on the stratosphere were accomplished in
a hermetically sealed and pressurized gondola. Mark Ridge wanted
to be different. He wanted to ascend to an even higher altitude in
an unsealed open basket. To do this and survive the flight, he knew
that he would need a space suit. But the space suit was then non-
existent.

By the time he had reached the age of twenty-seven, Ridge was
vigorously pursuing a campaign to get himself into the stratosphere.
He talked with physiologists at the Harvard Medical School and
wrote numerous letters to outstanding scientists asking for their
advice and help. Among these were such Nobel Prize winners as
Dr. Robert A. Millikan and Professor Albert Einstein. Later he
managed to convince the president of the Massachusetts Institute
of Technology that his cause needed support. Dr. Karl T. Compton
of MIT took his case directly to the Chief of the Army Air Corps.
But no support was forthcoming.

Mark Ridge was continually frustrated by the United States

government. Both the Air Corps and the Navy at first listened sympathetically to his pleas for aid. But after consulting with their advisors, they began to consider him either a crackpot or a publicity seeker—or both.

His first disappointment came from the Navy. On May 1, 1933, he addressed a long letter to the Honorable Claude A. Swanson, Secretary of the Navy.

Enigmatically, he did not sign the letter himself, but only typed in his name. Beneath his name was the signature of William J. Perry and beneath that was the typewritten title "Secretary." Perhaps Mark Ridge felt that this approach would impress the Secretary of the Navy.

The letter began:

Honorable Sir:
The writer is contemplating an ascent into the stratosphere in an open basket type balloon to an altitude of 12 miles or more for scientific research work. To overcome low barometric pressures and the intense cold while on said ascension the apparatus to be worn must be tested for perfection in action and must be used with all precautions which our existing physiological knowledge shows to be necessary.
Professor Philip Drinker, respiration expert at the Harvard Medical School, who has been cooperating with the writer on the construction of said apparatus, informs the writer that the decompression chamber at the Harvard Medical School is not suitable for my test, as low barometric pressures could not be simulated such as I shall encounter at high altitudes.
The Experimental Diving Unit, Dept. of Construction and Repair, U. S. Navy Department at Washington, D.C. informs the writer that they have a decompression chamber that can simulate an altitude of 67,000 feet which is ideal for the writer's needs; also that they would be pleased to cooperate if the necessary permission was secured to use same.

Mark Edward Ridge, twenty-seven-year-old daredevil from Dorchester, Massachusetts, is shown here as he posed in street clothes, on November 29, 1933, for a news photographer sitting inside the London altitude chamber where the following day he successfully tested the world's first space suit to an altitude of 90,000 feet.
Blood begins to boil because of low pressure at 63,000 feet if protective clothing is not worn.

Courtesy London Daily Mail

At Cambridge, Massachusetts, on March 8, 1934,
Mark Ridge entered a tank filled with blocks of dry ice
to test the insulating qualities
of an aluminum-lined suit he had designed.
Purpose was to wear this suit under a space suit for ascent
through the stratosphere in an open-basket balloon.

Other portions of the letter emphasized Ridge's background of scientific knowledge and the "untold importance to the Navy Department" in permitting this test of a suit to protect fliers in the stratosphere.

The letter was passed from one Navy bureau to another for comments. On May 10 the chief of the Navy's Bureau of Medicine and Surgery evaluated Ridge's request and wrote a letter—classified confidential—to the Chief of Naval Operations (the Technical Section). This letter was not declassified until January 4, 1963— nearly thirty years later. Ironically, Mark Edward Ridge had died less than nine months earlier.

The text of the letter was brief. It follows in full:

1. It is stated in the subject-named [Ridge] request contained in Enclosure (A) of reference (a), that Professor Philip Drinker of Harvard University is cooperating in the construction of apparatus in connection with the proposed flight of Mr. Mark E. Ridge into the stratosphere and that valuable research data will be obtained relative to the physiological effects of atmospheric conditions in the stratosphere.

2. A representative of this Bureau discussed this matter on May 8 with Professor C. K. Drinker, also of Harvard University and a brother of Professor Philip Drinker. He was informed that the latter is not cooperating in the undertaking for the reason that it is being planned primarily for publicity purposes rather than for scientific research and, in any event, the personnel [Ridge] would not be competent to properly conduct such research. Professor C. K. Drinker strongly advised that the Navy Department not lend encouragement to this project.

3. This Bureau concurs in the paragraph 3 of enclosure (C) to the effect that the proposed research work may involve certain hazards to personnel in which it would not be advisable for the Navy Department to be involved.

Mark Ridge was not even faintly aware of what had been happening behind the curtain of military protocol when on May 12, 1933, he finally received an answer from the Secretary of the Navy. In two short paragraphs it acknowledged receipt of Ridge's request to use the decompression chamber at the Washington, D.C., Navy Yard—and flatly refused to let him use it.

However, the Acting Secretary of the Navy, W. V. Pratt, made the mistake of "explaining" why he was flatly refusing Mark Ridge: "The Navy Department considers the subjection of individuals to abnormal pressures a distinct hazard, because of the unusual respiratory conditions." This statement, of course, was lifted directly out of one of the official memos. All it accomplished was to infuriate Ridge—who immediately wrote to his Congressman, attaching copies of his request to the Navy and its curt reply.

The Congressman was John W. McCormack of the House Ways and Means Committee. Representative McCormack went to bat for Ridge by requesting that the Secretary of the Navy reconsider the negative decision. The Acting Secretary's reply stubbornly repeated the contents of his letter to Mark Ridge. McCormack forwarded this answer to Ridge, who became even more infuriated.

On May 18, 1933, Ridge sat down and typed the following strong statement to the Navy's Bureau of Construction and Repair:

The letter in answer to Congressman McCormack, seeking cooperation of the Navy Department, to allow Mr. Mark E. Ridge permission to use divers' decompression chamber at Washington Navy Yard, has been received by writer, also a reply from Office of the Secretary.

It is due to the existing prevailing ignorance, that the Navy Department believes that the writer shall be in a hazardous position, if he is subjected to such an abnormal pressure, because of the unusual respiratory conditions; to the contrary, the writer shall be perfectly safe with the apparatus he is to use, and that all physiological precautions may be taken, the writer would subject an animal to said test, prior to making it himself. . . .

Said test from an aeronautical standpoint will allow our Pilots to reach a higher altitude in an open cockpit plane, instead of being enclosed in a sealed cabin ship.

The writer shall sign any necessary papers to absolve Navy Department in case of casualty; said mention of casualty sounds ridiculous to writer, as he is well aware of what he is attempting to do.

It shall be appreciated that contents of this letter are given due consideration in the interest of Science.

The letter, this time, was signed by Ridge himself.

Back came the briefest answer of all from W. V. Pratt, Acting Secretary of the Navy:

Your letter, addressed to the Bureau of Construction and Repair of date 18 May 1933, has been given consideration by the Department, which still abides by its adverse decision as covered in letter of 12 May 1933 addressed to you.

Since Senators are generally more highly respected than Representatives in Congress, Ridge next called on the Honorable David Walsh, Chairman of the Senate Committee on Education and Labor. He followed up the meeting with a letter to the Massachusetts Senator. The letter shows very clearly that Mark Ridge really understood the scientific aspects of human survival in the stratosphere. It also shows that he was either deluding himself about the cooperation of Dr. Philip Drinker, Harvard's famous inventor of the iron lung, or else the doctor was misleading him.

Ridge's letter took up the Navy's reluctance to submit an individual to the hazards of the stratosphere:

The answer to that is: If it were required to go much above 40,000 feet; and to a barometric pressure below 130 mm [millimeters of mer-

cury]; it would be necessary to enclose the airman in an airtight dress, somewhat similar to a diving dress, but capable of resisting an internal pressure of, say, 130 mm of mercury. The dress would be so arranged that even in a complete vacuum the contained oxygen would still have a pressure of 130 mm. There would then be no physiological limit to height attainable.

Due to prevailing ignorance, of best method to suitably overcome low barometric pressure, the Navy is wrong in not delving deeper into what the writer proposed to do and learn something that will benefit it in military importance, as well as aid Humanity.

Professor Philip Drinker, respiration expert at Harvard Medical school, inventor of Drinker Lung, that saved so many lives during Infantile Paralysis epidemic, the last word on respiration, has designed suit the writer is to wear on ascension; the decompression chamber at Harvard is not suitable for test, as barometric pressure desired can not be reached; the Navy, having the only suitable chamber, it is imperative that permission be granted, not for any personal reason of the writer, but for medical science; the writer must know whereof he writes, with the only two respiration experts in the world to substantiate him.

In all previous correspondence of Mark Ridge that the author has seen, there is no mention of any "respiration experts" other than Dr. Drinker. Nor is the second expert named in this communication to Senator Walsh. The mystery may be thinned a little when it is considered that soon afterward Ridge began a correspondence with professor John Scott Haldane in England, who was then the world's foremost authority on respiration.

The letter to Senator Walsh was dated June 8, 1933. On June 10, the senator sent it to the Secretary of the Navy, along with his own request of "what reply I can make to him [Ridge]."

On July 5, 1933, the Senator received a letter from Admiral W. H. Standley, then Acting Secretary of the Navy. His second paragraph began:

For the third time, reconsideration has been given to our refusal to allow Mr. Ridge to use the facilities of the decompression chamber at the Experimental Diving Unit. . . . The Department fails to see that the representations made by Mr. Ridge in the enclosed letter afford any basis for modification of its opinion. . . . Refusal of his request is therefore in order.

Admiral Standley suggested that Mark Ridge approach the U. S. National Bureau of Standards, since it had a "metal chamber which can be operated under partial vacuum to stimulate rarefied atmosphere at high altitudes, and possibly it will be able to handle the test for Mr. Ridge, if he will enter into the necessary arrangements therefor." But I could find no record indicating that Mark Ridge ever approached the NBS for permission to carry out his experiment in its vacuum chamber.

He did approach the coroner of Boston, Dr. T. Leary, for advice.

Dr. Leary recommended that Ridge consult the eminent physiologist John Scott Haldane, who had urged, years before, the use of a pressure suit to fly at high altitudes. Dr. Leary's simple suggestion started a chain of events that led to the world's first successful space suit.

Mark Ridge immediately wrote to Dr. Haldane, in care of the British Royal Society, and not long after received an encouraging reply. The great English scientist was interested in the young American's desire to test himself in an altitude chamber at very low atmospheric pressure.

Since 1892, according to his equally famous son, John Burdon Sanderson Haldane, Dr. J. S. Haldane had been experimenting with human subjects in a "small airtight chamber . . . lined with aluminum foil" at the University Laboratory of Physiology, Oxford. In 1907 the elder Haldane had developed a method of stage decompression for deep-sea divers that made it possible for them to ascend safely from the depths to the surface of the sea.

The invention of stage decompression to prevent divers' "bends" —more aptly known as caisson disease, a paralyzing, painful, occasionally fatal result of excess nitrogen bubbles in the blood stream, caused by too rapid a change of pressures against the body—was stimulated three years earlier when Professor Haldane first met Sir Robert H. Davis. Sir Robert was a Doctor of Science and member of Siebe, Gorman & Co., Limited—a pioneer firm in the development of deep-sea diving suits.

As Sir Robert put it many years later, "I first became acquainted with Professor J. S. Haldane in 1904, and the association resulted in the production of Safer, Deeper Diving, Better Breathing in Irrespirable Atmospheres and High Altitude Breathing techniques."

For almost a century and a half, Siebe, Gorman & Co. had been producing suits for divers. The firm's founder, Augustus Siebe (1788–1872), was the original inventor of the closed diving dress —a suit that was pressurized with air or a mixture of air and other gases, at pressures that matched the changing pressures encountered against his body as a diver descended through different levels of water. The deeper a diver goes, of course, the greater is the surrounding pressure.

The conditions surrounding a man as he flies higher and higher are exactly reversed: the pressure against his body becomes less and less. But the principle governing the protection of life is identical with that applicable to the diver: he must be pressurized in a way that maintains his normal bodily functions.

Augustus Siebe, then, laid the foundation for development of a space suit. In fact, Sir Robert Davis, who ultimately became president and director of the firm, was responsible for placing the firm

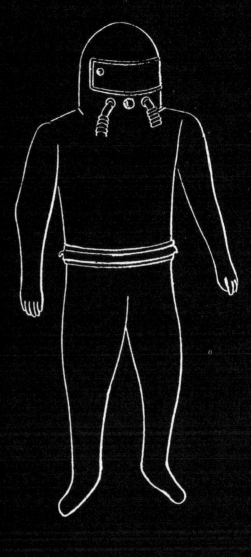

*Patent drawings of
the Haldane-Davis space suit
are shown here.
Inner lining of suit is at right,
outer suit at left.
Design for world's first space suit
was adapted from diving gear.*

Courtesy Dr. Charles L. Wilson, Lieutenant Colonel, USAF

in a position to build space suits. His research installation at the firm's Neptune Works was operating some twenty years before the company ever produced a space suit.

In a private communication with Dr. Charles L. Wilson, a leading physiologist of the U. S. Air Force, Davis stated on February 12, 1963:

In our Works we have all facilities, which I installed over fifty years ago, for testing men in deep water, in connection with decompression problems; at High Altitudes; in poisonous atmospheres; in High and Low temperatures, etc., etc., and we have been experimenting for many years in these conditions of work.

Professor J. S. Haldane naturally had access to these facilities for experimentation on respiration problems. About a year before the facilities were set up, during 1911, Haldane led an expedition to Pikes Peak in Colorado, where he studied the effects of low atmospheric pressure on himself and others. Following the study he proposed the use of an oxygen-pressurized sealed suit for ascent to high altitudes. He even sketched out the requirements for building such a suit. By 1920 he had published his classical work, *Respiration,* in which he elaborated in detail on the requirements.

So everything was ripe for a space-suit test when Mark E. Ridge wrote to J. S. Haldane in the summer of 1933. Ridge, as it turned out, did not have the space suit that Dr. Philip Drinker had allegedly designed for him. Yet he was eager to be his own guinea pig in a suit test at low barometric pressure. His final goal, of course, was a balloon flight high into the stratosphere.

While he was corresponding with Professor Haldane, the balloon record established by Dr. Auguste Piccard and Max Cosyns was broken by the Russians. Reportedly, on September 30, 1933, three Soviet balloonists—K. Godunov, G. Prokofiev, and E. Birnbaum—penetrated the stratosphere to a height of 60,695 feet in a Red Army balloon christened *USSR.* This exceeded the Piccard-Cosyns altitude by 7,543 feet. It was also only 8,055 feet below the target of 13 miles set by Mark Ridge for his own flight.

Again, however, the altitude record was made in a sealed, pressurized gondola—and not with a space suit in an open basket. Nevertheless, it spurred Ridge to increased endeavor to be tested in a suit. He proposed that Professor Haldane build such a suit for him. Haldane turned the request over to Sir Robert Davis. Together, in less than a month, they produced a modified diving suit designed to work in outer space.

Ridge promptly left for England, at the invitation of John Scott Haldane, Professor of Metallurgy, Gasses, Liquids and Respirations at Oxford University.

On November 16, 1933, Mark Ridge donned the space suit
designed and built by Haldane and Davis. He was sealed into the
low-pressure chamber at the Neptune Works and waited, somewhat
apprehensively, to see what would happen. But his chance had come
at last—even though this was to be only a preliminary test of the
suit.

The chamber was evacuated of air until the instruments indicated
that the pressure was equivalent to that at an altitude of 50,000
feet. Everything worked perfectly. Ridge suffered no ill effects.
After they brought him down to sea-level pressure and helped him
out of the Haldane-Davis space suit, he was questioned by re-
porters. All he would give them was the simple answer: "History
has been made."

History was indeed made exactly two weeks later, on November
30. Mark Ridge stepped into the same chamber wearing the same
suit. The airlock was slammed shut and fastened. This time they
were going to take him up to the limit of the chamber's altitude.
It would be far past the atmospheric level where blood begins to
boil. A leak in the suit would cause death within nine seconds,
twelve seconds at the very most. That was too little time for enough
air to be pumped back into the chamber to save him.

Even Professor Haldane was apprehensive about this "flight." He
remarked afterward: "I felt worried all the time, in case Mr. Ridge
should have symptoms of this effervescence of the blood.

"At 3:58 P.M. [Greenwich Mean Time], Mr. Ridge entered the
steel chamber. The door was closed and the purges started," continued the professor. "In five minutes he was at the equivalent of
twenty-six thousand feet. In thirty minutes he was at eighty
thousand feet. And in fifty minutes [4:48 P.M. GMT]—he was at
ninety thousand feet.

"After a few minutes he was brought down—none the worse for
the experience."

Simply but graphically, Professor Haldane had described an
epic moment in the history of manned space flight. Mark Edward
Ridge, at the age of twenty-seven, had become the first person
on earth to survive the hostile, lethal conditions ever present at
the edge of space and beyond, dressed only in a suit of protective
clothing.

When Ridge emerged from the steel chamber, his first words
were: "It was Dr. T. Leary, Medical Examiner of Boston, that put
me on the right track." He claimed that he had felt no discomfort
whatever while wearing the Haldane-Davis suit in the near-vacuum
of 90,000 feet.

The London *Daily Mail* praised "the industry and ingenuity of
Sir Robert Davis . . . and his son Mr. Gorman Davis, [who] with

the cooperation of the firm's staff were at once concentrated on making an entirely new type of apparatus in less than a month."

Although Mark Ridge had not actually flown to the top of the stratosphere, it is worth re-emphasizing that he *had* survived the *identical* conditions that exist there. The Royal Air Force was immediately interested and requested that the new suit, along with scientific data on the "flight," be placed before the Air Ministry for evaluation.

The excitement was connected with a fact that Ridge had, all along, intensely believed and promoted—that pilots dressed in protective clothing could safely fly at unprecedented altitudes in open-cockpit airplanes. The military advantages of this were obvious, since there would be no need for the heavy equipment demanded to pressurize a sealed cockpit.

Ridge tried to persuade the Air Ministry to lend him an openbasket balloon that he could take up through the stratosphere while wearing the Haldane-Davis suit. He himself had designed an insulated garment to be worn under that suit as a protection against the extreme stratospheric cold. But the Air Ministry refused his request, although it commended his daring pioneer experiments in the altitude chamber. Its reason was logical: a balloon must drift helplessly with the winds—and the winds might carry it far beyond the frontiers of the United Kingdom. If this should happen, the Haldane-Davis space suit might fall into the hands of a potential enemy of Great Britain.

A rumor which has never been factually established was that Mark Ridge's disappointment at being refused a balloon flight by the British government was so great that he approached the newly established Nazi government in Germany.

If this story is true, then apparently he was also turned down by the Nazis—who, not much more than a year afterward, began a concentrated effort to develop a pressurized high-altitude suit.

Back in the United States, Mark Ridge doggedly pursued his dream of flying through the stratosphere in an open-basket balloon. Now, after his successful chamber test in England, he was *certain* that he could safely establish a new kind of altitude record for balloons. But the problem was to find a balloon. The kind he needed was extremely expensive. Nobody he approached would finance him. The attitude he often faced was: Well, your stratosphere suit may keep you alive with breathable air, but what's to prevent you from freezing to death?

It was true. His ride in the British altitude chamber was a test only of a steep drop in air pressure. There had been no equivalent drop in temperature. The chamber had not been temperature-controlled during his "flight."

Ridge's next step, obviously, was to prove before the world that he could withstand the deep cold of the higher stratosphere. As was already noted, he had designed an insulating suit to be worn underneath the Haldane-Davis pressure suit. Now he concentrated on finding someone to produce it for him. Since aluminum foil was a necessary material for the insulating suit, he finally found his man in Samuel Ring, a Boston dealer in aluminum-foil products.

Ring worked with Mark Ridge until they had evolved a garment that outwardly resembled a pilot's coveralls. Inside, however, it was made up of six layers of aluminum foil and six layers of cotton cloth, alternately placed one on top of the other. The suit incorporated coverings for hands and feet. A full head covering was put together in the same way. For full face protection a chamois mask was used. The mask had three holes: two for glass goggles and one for an oxygen hose.

With the suit completed, Ridge was able to persuade the Liquid Carbonic Corporation of Cambridge, Massachusetts, to set up an experiment for him. The company produced dry ice, which is solidified carbon dioxide and therefore very cold. The company executives agree to line a steel tank with slabs of dry ice so that Ridge could step inside the "icebox" and test the insulating effectiveness of his suit. The executives felt that they would not only be helping scientific progress but would also get favorable publicity for their product.

On March 8, 1934, Mark Ridge climbed into the steel tank, where a thousand pounds of dry ice surrounded him. He was breathing pure oxygen from a small O_2 bottle that he carried. Despite this precaution, the carbon dioxide gas that was boiling off the dry ice got to him. Before the lid could be closed on the big tank, he waved for help.

It wasn't the suit that had failed: it was the oxygen mask. By the next day, Ridge and Samuel Ring had repaired the mask, and Ridge was all ready to go again with the test.

But when they approached the head of the Liquid Carbonic Corporation, he slammed the door in their faces. The national newspaper publicity about the previous day's "failure" had annoyed him. It was not the kind of publicity he wanted for his company. So again Mark E. Ridge was frustrated in his goal to reach the stratosphere. Yet he would not give up.

Within the next two years, a famous round-the-world flier named Wiley Post designed his own space suit and flew with it to the edge of the stratosphere in an unpressurized airplane—again proving the contention of Mark Ridge to be correct.

Ridge began a new campaign. He persuasively presented his case before the internationally respected Karl T. Compton, physicist and president of the Massachusetts Institute of Technology. Dr. Compton, on March 25, 1936, wrote a rather strong (for a cautious scientist) endorsement of Ridge's case to the chief of the U. S. Army Air Corps, Major General Oscar Westover:

We were visited by a Mr. Mark E. Ridge whose address is 110 Draper Street, Dorchester, Massachusetts, with a letter of introduction from Professor A. E. Kennelly of the Harvard Engineering School and quite a portfolio of supporting letters from such people as Einstein, Yandell Henderson of Yale University, and especially Sir John Haldane and Sir Robert Davis of England. The latter three men, as you know, are scientists interested in the physiological effects of high altitudes and related phenomena.

It appears that Mr. Ridge served for some time as an assistant and a sort of laboratory "guinea pig" for Haldane in a number of experiments. These, with reference to Mr. Ridge, are described in one of Haldane's recent books. They have to do with tests of a special suit for balloonists or aviators to enable them to operate at very high altitudes. With this suit Ridge has remained comfortable for a period of several hours in a low pressure chamber at 17 mm. of mercury and at the temperature of carbon dioxide ice. As I understand it, the suit is heat insulated by aluminum foil and is provided with a small stream of oxygen entering at the helmet.

In the interest of accuracy, I wish to intervene here. Mark Ridge never spent more than a few minutes at an atmospheric pressure of 17 millimeters of mercury, which is the equivalent air pressure at about 90,000 feet of altitude, according to Dr. John Scott Haldane himself. Nor did Ridge ever spend "several hours at the temperature of carbon dioxide ice," as the reader must know from preceding paragraphs. But apparently Ridge was a very persuasive person, since he convinced the great Dr. Compton of these "facts." Nevertheless, Mark Ridge cannot be blamed for his exaggerations. In his own deteriorating mind, he undoubtedly believed every word he said. And what he said was *based* in truth.

Ridge says that the Army aviators and scientists in England believe that a suit of this type, rather than the sealed gondola, is the answer for high altitude flying, and Ridge understands that the suit is now in experimental use by the British Air Force [which it was]. He thinks that they have gone with it up to 50,000 ft. in airplanes, although he is not sure of the figure [which was approximately correct—see Chapter 3].

Ridge has the backing of Haldane and Davis (as evidenced by recent letters) in an attempt to arrange for a high altitude open-basket balloon flight as a test and demonstration. He feels confident of reaching altitudes very far exceeding those of the closed gondola ascents. The British are unwilling to carry out a test under present European conditions. . . .

Apparently Haldane (who recently died) and Davis, who designed and probably had patented this suit, are willing to let Ridge use it in a trial flight in this country if one can be arranged, and that was Ridge's purpose in calling on me. The only possibilities that I could see were, first, that the National Geographic Society might be willing to have its balloon used again next summer for an open-basket flight carrying Ridge and his suit, or second, that the Army Air Corps might have some interest in looking into the matter.

Neither Hunsaker nor I know enough about the situation to know whether this is an old story to you and whether it is likely to be of interest. It would seem that the space devoted to it in Haldane's book and the interest of Yandell Henderson in the matter were <u>pretty good guarantees that there is something really interesting involved</u>. [Underscoring mine.]

General Westover hastened to answer the president of MIT:

With reference to the suit for flying in high altitudes, as presented to you by Mr. Ridge, you are advised that his idea is not an entirely new one, as you may recall that Wiley Post on his recently attempted stratosphere flight across the United States wore a similar suit.

You spoke of the possibility of Mr. Ridge making a trial flight in this Country to test the suit and in connection therewith, you are advised that the balloon used in the National Geographic Society–Army Air Corps Stratosphere Flight was cut up and made into book-markers and distributed by the Society to its members a few months ago.

Such was the luck of Mark E. Ridge. Even the concept of a bookmark took precedence over his dream.

Yet the odds against his maintaining sanity did not stop there. General Oscar Westover had forwarded Dr. Compton's letter to the chief of the Matériel Liaison Section at Wright Field near Dayton, Ohio, for evaluation and comment. At the time, the Matériel Division supervised all research-and-development projects of the Army Air Corps. Its opinion on whether or not Ridge should be given a chance to prove himself would normally be the ultimate word to AAC Headquarters. The division *did* offer that chance, but General Westover chose to ignore it.

The evaluation and comment on Dr. Compton's letter by the Matériel Division culminated in a report that concluded:

If Mr. Ridge's suit is available, it would be well to give him an opportunity to demonstrate his suit here at the Matériel Division before starting the construction of a suit similar to [Wiley] Post's. Laboratory tests should be followed by a prolonged flight in the rear cockpit of an airplane flown by another pilot at high altitude.

The remainder of the report discussed the difficulties that Wiley Post encountered with his own high-altitude pressure suits. It was these negative aspects that General Westover preferred to emphasize in a second letter to Dr. Compton, which he wrote on April 13, 1936, the same day he received the Matériel Division's report from Wright Field.

General Westover concluded his letter thus:

I appreciate very much your interest in bringing this matter to the attention of the Air Corps, but under the circumstances and from a consideration of all the factors involved, I cannot see that the Air Corps can have any special interest in Mr. Ridge's contemplated flight.

Mark Ridge had *almost* made it this time—insofar as the technical people at Wright Field were concerned—but because of a misunderstanding or a too hurried reading of the Matériel Division report by General Westover and/or his staff, the situation became more bleak than ever. Now Ridge had lost the influential support of Dr. Compton and the Massachusetts Institute of Technology.

He turned again to Sir Robert Davis of Siebe, Gorman & Company. On August 28, 1937, he wrote to Davis proposing a new attack on his problems.

No doubt you believe I have given up my endeavours to secure a backer. Well, I practically did, as far as securing one for a million cubic foot balloon, as the price the Goodyear people want is prohibitive.

But with the new method used by Piccard of using sounding balloons, matters look much brighter. I have talked with manufacturers of sounding balloons and they inform me that 125 of their No. 700 type sounding balloons would take me to a 17 mile height. The initial diameter of [balloon] bag on ground is 48 inches; the maximum diameter is 20 feet, or its bursting point. The weight of [each] bag is 1½ lbs.

What I am endeavouring to do at this time is to secure 125 of said bags, also 17 miles of steel piano wire and the necessary number of bags to support said wire.

You will no doubt wonder why the wire? Well, with said wire it shall be wound around a drum or winch of a donkey engine, and one end made fast to suitable connection in the ground, the other end to the 125 balloons. As the balloons ascend, the wire will play out from winch or drum of engine, and at various points along the line the necessary [extra] balloons will be attached to wire to support it.

At the highest point, which will be 17 miles [89,760 feet], the engine shall be reversed to reel in line and to detach balloons along the line.

Sir Robert privately considered Ridge's sounding-balloon proposal "a fantastic idea," even as Ridge himself had remarked in a different context.

Ridge's optimism about finding a financial backer for his new idea soon was transmuted into leaden pessimism, but he fought on anyway. A year later, on December 7, 1938, he approached Louis Johnson, then Assistant Secretary of war:

You no doubt know Mr. Johnson that England has the altitude [record] for airplanes with an open cockpit. Accomplished with pressure suit designed after the one writer tested.

Sir Robert informs that considerable improvements have been made of the original dress.

Our government needs that pressure dress. It is ours if the writer can obtain financial aid to make his stratosphere ascent.

Consider for yourself, Mr. Johnson, how important a pressure dress will be for bombing purposes during war, also for scientific research.

We may not have a plane at this time capable of reaching a ten or more mile height. But if England can design such planes, so can this country.

Consider the chances of hitting a pilot dressed in a pressure suit, with the hitting of a pressure proof cabin plane. The sealed cabin plane offers a much greater target.

If a bullet should puncture the pressure proof cabin the occupants would die like "rats." But on the other hand if they were dressed in a pressure suit what harm would be done as long as the bullet didn't hit a vital part of the plane.

Hoping that you can see the importance of such ascent being made, and that you can help me in its accomplishment. Respectfully yours.

Assistant Secretary of War Johnson received this plea on December 13, 1938. Over the signature of Major General E. S. Adams, Adjutant General, an answer was mailed to Ridge on January 5, 1939:

High altitude suits for individuals may have an application for scientific investigations of the stratosphere, such as the proposed flight by Polish aeronauts scheduled for June, 1939. However, such equipment for universal use by military personnel is not considered of sufficient military value to warrant the expenditure of funds for the development of this type of equipment at this time.

By the end of that year, the Army Air Corps had begun an intensive research program for the development of pressure suits. Mark Ridge could not have known this: the project was classified secret.

Just before he broke down mentally, Ridge made a final, desperate effort to fly his dream balloons. On January 22, 1940, he wrote to President Franklin Delano Roosevelt. The brief letter, written in longhand, is in the National Archives.

Dear Mr. President:

As our nation is in a state of hasty rearmament, the writer feels it important that you, Mr. President, as our leader, should know of a means of conquering space, of the vitalist [sic] importance to our Air Forces. The physiological possibilities of said means have been proven beyond a shadow of doubt by the writer and his colleagues Sir Robert Davies, inventor of the Davis Submarine Escape Apparatus, and the late eminent Professor John S. Haldane of respiration fame.

The British Air Ministry further proved its practicality by securing the world altitude record for heavier than [air] aircraft with said means.

Endeavors to date, by the writer, to obtain cooperation from the proper agencies in this country, to show the tremendous military and scientific importance of means referred too [sic], have been futile and highly discouraging.

It is felt, that, when the eminent Professor Albert Einstein is ready and willing to convey his opinion as to the desirability, possibilities, and scientific importance of said means being utilized, the men of our nation who guide our destiny should look into the matter whole heartedly at this time.

With kindness [sic] wishes to you, through these trying times, I am, sir, Respectfully yours.

Rubber-stamped on the first sheet of the letter after its receipt at the White House was: "Referred For Acknowledgement / Signature / Secretary to the President."

So ended a strange, visionary, and heartbreaking odyssey. From then on Mark Ridge convinced himself that he really had a stratospheric pressure suit in his possession, hidden away in a secret place. He talked to a feature writer of the Boston *Globe* about it— and was believed. In the Sunday editorial and news feature section of the *Globe* a story appeared, attesting to this, on July 6, 1941.

The following year he was admitted to a mental institution. For the next twenty years—except for one brief interlude, when he escaped—Mark Ridge remained in one or another of the institutions surrounding the Boston area.

While in one of these, he called the *Globe* and told a reporter that he was offering himself as a guinea pig to be sent aloft in a captured German V-2 rocket to be launched from the Army's then White Sands Proving Ground in New Mexico. He hoped to reach an altitude of 75 miles, or 396,000 feet!

That was in May 1946. The last story ever printed about Mark Edward Ridge by the Boston *Globe* appeared in its April 16, 1962, editions. It was an obituary. The "Air Demon," as he had been acclaimed by the London *Daily Mail*, was dead at the age of fifty-six.

Mark Ridge was a tragic figure who met frustration almost everywhere he turned. But he was every bit as visionary as the more successful Wiley Post.

Chapter 2

FROM TROPOPAUSE TO STRATOSPHERE

Wiley Post had his problems too, but they were of a different nature. Like Mark Ridge, he was intensely motivated to fly through the dangerous regions of the stratosphere. Unlike Ridge, he wanted to do it in a heavier-than-air flying machine. Wiley Post felt that the lighter-than-air balloons were obsolete, that the successful future of travel in the skies—from both a military and a civilian standpoint —was dependent on the airplane. To Ridge, ultimately, the space suit became an obsession—an end in itself. To Post, it was a necessary "evil"—the only means available then for safe exploration of the vertical frontier.

Again, like Ridge, Post faced multiple defeats. But these were technical defeats, which were finally conquered. Flying in an open-basket balloon requires only a minimum of control on the part of the aeronaut. He can just sit there most of the time, without a need to move his arms or legs. Controlling an airplane is a different matter. The pilot must be able freely to move his fingers, hands, wrists, elbows, shoulders, knees, and feet, to operate the complex of controls. A pilot's pressure suit therefore has to be mobile.

The goal of Wiley Post was to design such a suit. When he conceived the idea of a pilot's pressure suit in 1931, Post was not aware of the Haldane-Davis suit—which, indeed, was then only an idea. He had no background in the biological or medical sciences, even though he very well understood the physiological hazards of low atmospheric pressure.

Writing in the October 1934 issue of *Popular Mechanics* magazine, Post very graphically demonstrated his awareness of the hazards:

To fly at extreme altitudes, you first must have oxygen and on top of that pressure to force it into your lungs and to keep down the tendency to bleed all over the entire body. The thirteen pounds differential pressure at high altitudes [he was talking about a height of 50,000 feet], compared with sea level, affects every cell in the unprotected body. Blood vessels in the eyes may rupture and cause permanent blindness. Heart action is affected, and other serious changes may result. Therefore, for all serious altitude flying, which we are coming to sooner or later, it is necessary to maintain pressure around the body by sealing off a space and pumping air into it. . . . My idea is to employ a suit, something like a diver's outfit, which the pilot can wear, and which can be blown up with air or oxygen to the required pressure. Such a suit does not weigh much and is flexible enough to permit normal handling of controls.

The last sentence is a concise, prophetic description of the space suits worn by today's astronauts. Yet from the time those words of Wiley Post were published, it took more than thirty years of stubborn effort to develop space suits that matched his description.

Wiley Post was a farmer's son who hated farming. He was born on November 22, 1898, on a farm his parents had established in Van Zandt County, Texas. Through childhood and adolescence, he avidly followed the flight experiments of Wilbur and Orville Wright as well as those of the other pioneers who soon came on the scene. Quite literally, he grew up with aviation.

By the time he was approaching age fourteen, the Post family decided to move to Oklahoma. His teacher at the rural school in Oklahoma many years later told a reporter: "When I prevailed upon Wiley to improve his grammar, the boy remarked he wasn't much interested in that study as he wanted to be an aviator—an unusual ambition at that time."

Post decided to become a mechanic—a skill that was then comparatively well paid—so that he could earn enough money to realize his earliest ambition, flying. He set to work raising cotton until he had saved up enough money for automobile mechanics school. By the time he reached sixteen, he was back in Oklahoma with a mechanic's diploma and a job in a garage. At seventeen he began working at the Army Signal Corps flying field near Fort Sill, Oklahoma. But he was never given a chance to fly in an airplane.

Post's first chance to get into aviation didn't come until the summer of 1925, when he bluffed his way into a regular job as substitute parachute daredevil in a flying circus. Part of his earnings immediately went for flying instructions.

He made his first solo flight that same August—after only one hour and forty minutes of dual instruction in a Jenny. Now he decided to go into business for himself. So he borrowed a parachute and rented airplanes, along with their pilots, to put on shows throughout Oklahoma.

After making ninety-one jumps as an itinerant daredevil parachutist, all without injury, Post decided that this was not the quickest way to make sufficient money for the purchase of an airplane. His rental fees and other expenses were too high to leave a good margin of profit.

Thus in the late autumn of 1926, he found a job at Seminole, Oklahoma, as an oil rigger. During his second day of work, he was pounding a link pin into a thick iron chain when an incandescently hot chip of metal flew out from under his heavy hammer. It struck him directly in the pupil of his left eye.

The doctors were unable to save the eye, and it was removed by a surgeon.

This would be a devastating blow to most individuals. But Wiley Post found in it a philosophical consolation. He was paid eighteen hundred dollars in workmen's compensation. At last he had enough money in one lump sum to buy an airplane of his own.

Although he had no proof that he would be able to pilot an airplane with only one eye, he started looking around for a good purchase possibility. At Ardmore, Oklahoma, he found a Canadian Jenny that had been wrecked. Post looked it over and figured that he could easily put it back into flying shape. The *Canuck*, as it was called, cost him $240. By adding another $350 for repair materials, he had a first-rate airplane for just under $600. There were almost no labor costs, since he did most of the mechanical repair work himself.

He didn't want to trust his one eye on a trial flight, so he asked Art Oakley, a pilot friend, to take up the *Canuck* and check it out. The airplane flew perfectly. Post, with some apprehension, then got into the pilot's seat and took the plane into the air himself. This was only his second solo flight, but it was enough to convince him that the loss of an eye would be no handicap.

From May 1927 to January 1928, Wiley Post logged seven hundred hours of flight time in the *Canuck*. Then he sold it—at a profit of $110.

By August 1928, he was applying to the Department of Commerce for a commercial pilot's license. The medical examiner was amazed to discover that Post's depth perception with one eye was better than that of most pilots with two eyes. The rest of the physical examination showed that Post was in excellent condition and well qualified to pilot an airplane. The doctor recommended that the Department of Commerce issue Wiley Post a commercial license.

Since Post was the only one-eyed licensed transport pilot in the United States, a special waiver had to be written into the flying laws to grant him a commercial certificate. Each year, as he was re-examined, the waiver had to be renewed.

It was a ticklish situation—but it made Wiley Post probably the most cautious pilot in America. He flew with extreme care, because he was afraid that the slightest accident—even if it was not his fault—would cause the Commerce Department to rescind the waiver.

Just over a year before he was granted a commercial pilot's license, Post got married on a moment's notice. He had been stunt flying in West Texas to earn a living. On June 27, 1927, he was at the town of Ardmore making preparations for a stunting exhibition above a pasture when he saw a familiar face in the crowd of onlookers. It belonged to pretty, seventeen-year-old Mae Laine, a young woman he had known when they were children in Texas. She waved and he smiled. Then he climbed into the waiting airplane and zoomed off the ground in a curving climb that ended in a loop. He came out of the loop upside down and proceeded to perform a series of rolls, falling leafs, side slips and a variety of other loops.

When the show was over, Mae Laine come over to congratulate him. He learned that she now lived in Sweetwater, Texas, and offered to fly her home in the back seat of his airplane. En route, a malfunctioning magneto forced them down in a meadow near the town of Graham.

As they were walking into town, they spotted a sign: JUSTICE OF THE PEACE. They looked at each other, nodded, smiled, strolled up to the house behind the sign, and knocked on the door. When the justice appeared in the doorway, they told him, almost in chorus: "We want to get married." There is no record of what they used for a wedding ring. But their courtship was probably the swiftest one on record anywhere.

The impetuous Wiley Post soon discovered that he could not support a wife by stunt flying—or by wing walking either, which he later tried. He *had* to get a steady job—and he did not want to go back to the oil fields. He wanted to keep on flying, which presented a problem. Then he heard that F. C. Hall, a millionaire oil tycoon, was interested in aviation and had purchased an airplane.

Wiley had never met the man, but one day he walked into the millionaire's office and presented such a good case for his flying experience that Hall hired him on the spot.

Post was Hall's personal pilot for several years. The Oklahoma oil man soon acquired an affectionate respect for the stocky, dark-browed, Texas-born pilot, who performed his duties with great skill and quiet confidence. After Hall decided to sell the airplane, Post worked for more than a year as chief test pilot at the Lockheed Aircraft Company in Burbank, California. There he fell in love with a Lockheed airplane. It was the sturdy "Vega" high-wing cabin monoplane. He praised the airplane with such enthusiasm to F. C. Hall that the Oklahoma oil man immediately bought a Vega—on the condition that Post would come back to work for him as its pilot.

Post agreed, on his own condition that he could fly it from the Pacific Coast as an entry in the National Air Races' Los Angeles-to-Chicago Air Derby. Hall had no objection.

That was the beginning of worldwide fame for the white monoplane with the purple trimmings. It was also the same beginning for the one-eyed pilot with the trim dark mustache and the thick, almost black curly hair.

All of F. C. Hall's airplanes were christened *Winnie Mae*, in honor of his married daughter, Winnie Mae Fein. On August 23, 1930, the Lockheed Vega *Winnie Mae* touched down lightly on a runway at the Curtis-Reynolds Airport, just north of Chicago. With Post at the controls, it had left Los Angeles nine hours and nine minutes earlier. No other airplanes entered in the Air Derby were yet in sight. And those other airplanes were being flown by many of the most famous racing pilots of the day—including Art Goebel and Roscoe Turner.

Hall was so pleased by the Post victory that he not only gave his personal pilot fifteen thousand dollars of the prize money—but he also gave him the airplane.

Wiley Post decided to fly the *Winnie Mae* around the world. In the summer of 1931, with Australian Harold Gatty as navigator, he made the trip in slightly over eight days, establishing a record for navigation. Two years later he beat his own record and established another first: around the world alone in seven days, eighteen hours, forty-nine minutes.

The flights placed the young flier in aviation's hall of fame, alongside Charles Lindbergh, Howard Hughes, Italian Air Marshall Italo Balbo, Germany's Dr. Hugo Eckener, Spain's Juan de la Cierva, and C. W. A. Scott of the United Kingdom. For these flights, Wiley was awarded the Gold Medal of the Fédération Aéronautique Internationale and the Harmon International Trophy "for outstanding achievements in the arts and/or sciences of aeronautics."

But a fact not generally known is that Wiley Post conceived the idea of a full-pressure stratospheric space suit immediately after his first globe-circling flight (June 23 to July 1, 1931). During this flight he had noted that the higher you fly, the faster is your true air speed.

Two days after he returned to the United States from his second global flight (July 15 to July 22, 1933), he told a reporter for the Oklahoma City *Times*: "The next development for long-distance flying, after blind flying and blind landing, will be high-altitude flying, flying in the stratosphere." At this point he began to work seriously on the design of a stratospheric pressure suit.

Post set up a stiff schedule for himself. He wanted to wear the suit while competing in the England-to-Australia air race the following year. His attitude was: "If I can fly it in the stratosphere, I'll win that race hands down." But it wasn't for the prize money that he was entering the race.

The real reason Post wanted to win the race was that it would demonstrate the validity of his concepts about long-distance flying through the stratosphere. If a pilot could survive for an extended period in the stratosphere he would not only gain considerable speed for his aircraft, but he would also be flying high above the normal weather disturbances of the troposphere.

The troposphere is the level of the atmosphere below the stratosphere. It varies from sea level to between 35,000 and 45,000 feet. The top of the troposphere is a region called the tropopause, where the rapidly lowering temperatures of the troposphere abruptly cease and stay almost constant from there on up through most of the stratosphere. By this time, however, the Fahrenheit temperature has fallen to some 60 to 70-odd degrees below zero.

Wiley Post devised an ingenious way to beat the problem of extreme cold by simultaneously heating and pressurizing his stratospheric suit. His system was elegantly simple. The exhaust pipes of his Pratt & Whitney Wasp engine always became exceedingly hot in flight. He merely wound hollow metal tubing around the pipes and fed one end of the coiled tubing into his engine supercharger and the other end into his pressure suit. As the supercharger pumped

air through the coils, the exhaust gases heated the air before it
entered the suit. Valves permitted him to manually control both the
air pressure and the temperature.

But there was still the problem of finding a reliable fabricator to
build his suit. He approached two fabricating-design experts at the
B. F. Goodrich factory's technical department in Los Angeles,
William R. Hucks and John A. Diehl. Hucks eventually became the
project engineer in building the space suit, with Diehl assisting him.
Post described to them what he had in mind:

"A rubber suit which will enable me to operate and live in an
atmosphere of approximately twelve pounds [per square inch] absolute. I expect to fly through rarefied areas where the pressure is
as low as five pounds absolute. . . . The temperature incident with
high-altitude flying will be taken care of by heating the air from
the supercharger by coiling it around the exhaust manifolds."

Hucks and Diehl were intimately familiar with the use of rubberized fabrics for aviation purposes, since the Goodrich Company
not only manufactured automobile tires but also made boot de-icers
for airplane wings, abrasion shoes for aircraft brakes, and stabilizer
covers. Immediately after talking with Wiley Post, William Hucks
sent an air-mail letter to the Goodrich Company's headquarters at
Akron, Ohio. It was dated April 6, 1934, and requested "about six
yards of parachute silk, rubberized and doubled on the bias to give
light weight, minimum diffusivity and ease of fabrication on the
sewing machines . . . by April 20 at the latest. . . ." Hucks asked for
an appropriation of seventy-five dollars to cover the cost of the suit.
This was granted.

But on June 20, 1934, Hucks again wrote to headquarters that
"a hurried survey of the figure indicates that the cost will be approximately $60 of the total appropriation of $75, as per authoriza-
tion from Mr. W. T. Zink to the writer."

Apart from the fact that Post was falling behind his schedule for
delivery of the suit, the economics involved seem rather naïvely
ludicrous today. In a news release dated August 9, 1967 (a little
over thirty-three years after Hucks' last letter), the U. S. Space
Agency issued the following information about a new contract for
space suits:

*The National Aeronautics and Space Administration has selected the
Radio Corporation of America, Defense Electronics Products Division,
Camden, N. J., for negotiation of a contract for a new dual space-suit
communications system for use on the moon.*

*Estimated value of the cost-plus-fixed-fee contract is less than $5
million. [Underscoring mine]*

The reason was that in the art of tailoring pressure suits, unanticipated quirks were always to be expected.

Post encountered a few quirks right at the beginning. His first rubber suit was slow in taking shape. One hot day in early June, Post became impatient as he sweated and watched the Goodrich engineers measure, seam, and tape away at the rubberized fabric. "Get a tailor!" he yelled. "I'll tell him what I want and he can make a pattern and you can follow it."

So a professional tailor was quickly hired. After being told what was wanted, he measured Post and deftly cut a pattern from canvas. The Goodrich engineers now had something tangible to follow.

An aluminum shroud, or helmet, was simultaneously being cut and riveted together by Lowell Peters, a Los Angeles metalworker. It was to weigh only three and a half pounds and have a curved glass window two and three-quarters inches high and seven and a half inches wide. Since Post had only one eye, the window provided plenty of visibility.

Ordinary rubber boots were cemented and taped to the trousers of the two-piece suit, which itself was cemented and taped along the seams inside and outside. Specially made pigskin gloves were sewed to the sleeves of the rubber jacket. A metal belt of Duralumin was designed to fit tightly around the waist over jacket and pants to keep the suit airtight.

Finally the space outfit was completed and Wiley Post wriggled into it. It was a fine fit—except for one thing. The engineers had not thought of the fact that a pilot has to be able to move his arms forward—if he wants to reach the controls of his airplane. When the suit was inflated, Wiley could neither lift nor stretch his arms. They hung motionless at his sides, imprisoned in stiff rubberized cloth.

After this embarrassing goof was altered, the suit was ready for another ground test. By this time word had leaked to the press about the suit. William Hucks, as technical manager of the project, was spokesman for the Goodrich Company. One reporter asked him about the safety factor in a rubber suit. Wouldn't it burst like a balloon if it were fed too much air pressure?

Hucks' reply was that the rubberized fabric had a bursting point of fifty pounds per square inch of pressure. "In this rubber suit," he said, "receiving air pressure from the plane's supercharger, a pressure of not more than fifteen pounds will be applied. In the stratosphere, pressure falls to approximately five pounds to the square inch in place of the 14.7 pounds to the square inch at sea level. So there will be a ten-pound safety differential [between inside and outside atmospheric pressures]." He added that this would provide a five-to-one safety factor, considering the bursting point of the fabric.

So Wiley Post took the suit all the way across the continent for a critical test in the low-pressure chamber at Wright Field near Dayton, Ohio. On June 21, 1934, technical personnel of the Army Air

Corps gave the suit a tryout. It was first pressure-tested at ground level, became extremely rigid as it was inflated, sprang a leak at the waist—and ruptured with a loud bang and hiss.

That was the end of Suit Number One. It was beyond repair. Post next got together with Russell Colley, an engineer at the Akron headquarters of the Goodrich Company. Colley improved upon the deficient fabricating methods employed on the first suit and came up with a second suit, using the same Duralumin helmet.

Here's how an Air Corps historian described the preliminary test of this second pressure suit:

On an especially hot and humid day late in July 1934, Wiley attempted to try on the revised suit and helmet. It was a tight squeeze and he got stuck. It was strikingly hot and exceedingly uncomfortable for him, immobilized as he was with his arms, shoulders and neck tightly bound by the suit. Understandably, he was very anxious to get out of the garment as quickly as possible. He expressed this feeling loudly and distinctly. . . . They were only able to remove the upper suit by cutting it off.

That was the end of Suit Number Two.

Next came a period of serious study. Russ Colley and Wiley Post agreed that the first two suits had failed because they were made of a single fabric layer. The single layer was forced to perform a double function: it had to keep its shape and yet prevent the pressurizing gas from leaking out through the fabric pores. It did neither.

Both suits had blown up like balloons under pressure. One of them also leaked. The second suit wasn't given a chance to prove whether it would leak or not; chances were that it would have. So a decision was made on the design of a third suit. It would have two distinct layers. Each layer would carry out a separate function: the inner layer would be a rubber container for the gas pressure, and the outer layer would be rubberized cloth planned to keep its shape and mobility at a pressure of seven pounds per square inch. It would be a one-piece suit with a wide neck opening through which Post could step. In this way, he could pull the suit up around him, much as men used to enter red-flannel union suits. There would be no jacket-over-trousers interface to permit leakage of any kind.

The third and final pressure suit was built for a sitting position. The sleeves were formed to assume a stretched-forward attitude when the suit was inflated. In this way, Post could reach the necessary controls of the *Winnie Mae*. There were no limb joints on the suit, but with the addition of extra material to hang loosely over the knees Post would be able to move his legs enough to manipulate the plane's rudder pedals.

Although this suit was built by Russell Colley at the Goodrich plant in Akron, it was financed by the Phillips Petroleum Company

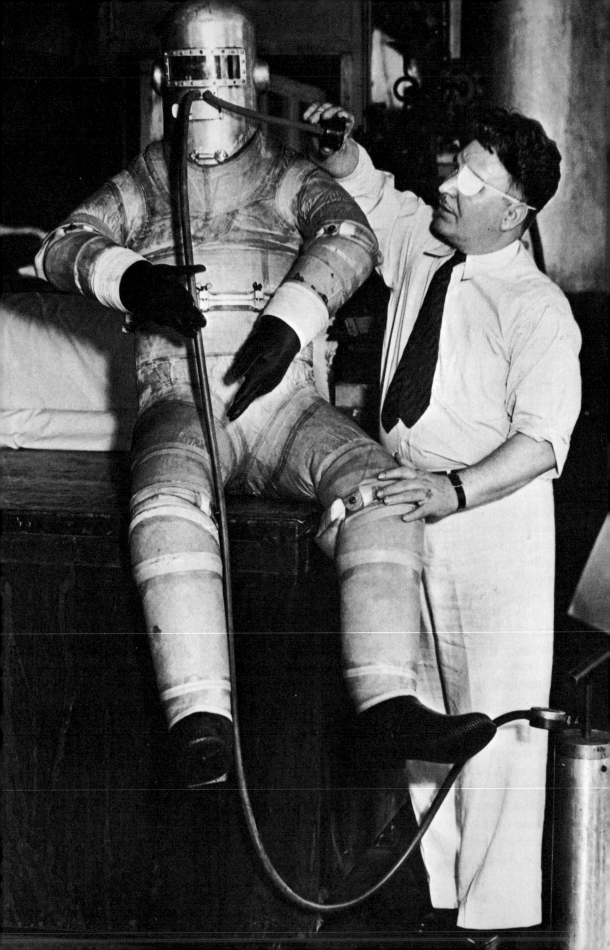

of Bartlesville, Oklahoma. The Aviation Department of Phillips
also financed a series of high-altitude flights with the suit. Altogether, Post took the suit up to altitude eleven times. His initial
flight was a world "first"—the first time that anyone had ever
flown in a space suit, or, if you will, a stratospheric pressure suit.

But before Post made any of his flights, the suit had to be tested
in an altitude chamber. It had to be proved airworthy before it could
safely be taken into the sky.

Following are excerpts from the Goodrich Company's "Experimental Problem #5967," as reported by Russell S. Colley:

*8-19-34: Suit assembled and tested to 5 pounds. Suit ripped open
down seam under arm and Anode [inner] Suit ballooned out but did
not burst.*

8-20-34: Patched outer suit and reenforced seams.

*8-21-34: Second test of assembled suit at 7# [pounds]—outer suit
burst open between legs and ruined it beyond repair.*

*8-25-34: [New] suit completed and reenforcing band added—this
band consisted of three plies of 822 fabric extending from the neck band
in front down between the legs and up the back to the neck band.
The purpose of this band was to take the longitudinal stress on the
body of the suit and keep the helmet in position when suit was inflated.*

*Note—in later tests it was found this was not sufficient and a sling
was made for Mr. Post to sit in and parachute cords were used to tie
the helmet to this sling.*

*8-26-34: Suit . . . brought to Goodrich and assembled with helmet
and given pressure test to 7#.*

Not only was Suit Number Three an entirely new design from
the two preceding suits, but its helmet was also completely new.
This helmet looked like an inverted tin bucket with a round porthole

*This is the second Post stratospheric pressure suit,
which was built at the Goodrich Company's Akron, Ohio, plant.
The same helmet was used, salvaged from the ruins of the first suit.
Also a two-piece suit, this one was bolted together
across the stomach with wing bolts.
Shown here is a technician inside the suit being tested
by Wiley Post, whose thumb is closing off a breathing valve in
a helmet hose. Note the big hand pump in lower right
foreground of picture. It was used by Post
to inflate the suit—and was also carried by motorists
in those days to inflate tires after blowouts on the road.
Post got stuck inside this suit and had to be freed by cutting
its torso open, thus ruining space suit number two.*

Courtesy B. F. Goodrich Company

cut into it. Although heavier than the first helmet, it was larger in volume and stronger. It was pressurized with 100 percent pure oxygen, rather than with air like the earlier helmet. Mr. Colley continues his report:

8-27-34: Went to Wright Field with Wiley and made necessary arrangements to conduct tests in the Altitude Chamber. . . .
At an altitude of 21,000 ft., Mr. Post indicated by a prearranged signal that he wished to descend. . . .
Failure of the oxygen generators to provide sufficient volume [of life-giving gas flow in the suit] had caused him to halt decompression to a higher altitude. Numerous leaks in the oxygen generators had kept the pressure on the liquid oxygen varying—and when it started to drop below 11# on the liquid, Mr. Post realized it would be dangerous to try to go higher and risk the possible loss of all oxygen.

Wiley Post was using liquid oxygen (LOX), a gas compressed into a liquid. As such, its eternal tendency is to become a gas again. It must be kept under constant pressure to maintain the liquid state, since it begins to boil off into a gas at any temperature higher than 297 degrees below zero Fahrenheit. For this reason, the LOX in Post's gas generators—which were designed to convert LOX to GOX, or gaseous oxygen, in a controlled manner—were operating out of control. At altitudes higher than the 21,000 feet where he cut off the chamber test, pressure would have dropped so low that the LOX would have swiftly boiled away into GOX and been dissipated before he could save himself.

Again we return to Russell Colley's report:

8-28-34: Spent most of the day hunting and repairing small leaks in oxygen generator. Later in afternoon another test was made in the Altitude Chamber and raised to an altitude of 23,000 ft. Leaks in the walls of the Chamber itself were making the lowering of the pressure rather a slow process, so Mr. Post signaled to be brought down.

Apparently as gas pressure was increased inside the stratospheric suit, the pressure blew the helmet above Post's head. It had to be strapped down tightly in a position that enabled him to see through the glass porthole. With this unanticipated situation corrected, Post and Colley were ready to make actual flight-tests of the suit at Chicago's Curtis Reynolds Field. The first three days at the airfield were taken up with making repairs on the *Winnie Mae*'s engine and ground-testing the suit in the cockpit of the airplane.

It was five days later before Wiley Post could make the first full-scale flight test of his pressure suit:

9-5-34 (Wednesday): . . . Was in the air two hours and forty-nine minutes and attained an altitude of 42,000 ft. Maximum pressure used in the suit—3# [pounds].

When he returned to the field he expressed the opinion that the suit was much more comfortable than he had ever hoped it could be. He had experienced no discomfort either going up or coming down. And when the suit was removed, I found practically no moisture in the suit. . . .

The suit and all the equipment connected with it were pronounced highly satisfactory and as soon as repairs can be made to the [airplane] engine, I have no doubt that Mr. Post will break the altitude record with ease and without discomfort or danger to his health.

The next item of any consequence was reported by Colley almost three months later:

12-3-34 (Bartlesville, Oklahoma): Wiley Post attempted to break the [world] altitude record, using the Winnie Mae and the Goodrich Altitude Suit inflated with pure oxygen from a liquid oxygen generator. Mr. Post was in the air about two hours and was not satisfied with the results of the flight and, having landed at a field other than the one from which he took off, he did not send in the barographs [altitude-recording instruments] for calibration.

On this flight, the pop-off valve at the outlet line from the suit had been tampered with and had been jammed in a completely closed position, the result of this being that when he inserted the glass face door [the helmet porthole] at about 18,000 ft., the pressure began to build up in the suit—and since there was no relief [of the pressure because of the jammed relief-valve, it] kept on building up. The pressure went to approximately seven pounds in the suit before Mr. Post could reach for and open an emergency relief-valve.

This might have cost Mr. Post his life unless the pressure could be relieved before the suit reached a bursting pressure.

It was a clear case of sabotage, with an implied attempt to murder Wiley Post. The implication became a fact less than three months later. But let Russ Colley tell about it:

2-22-35 (Burbank, California): Mr. Post attempted a transcontinental flight from Burbank, Calif. to New York using the Winnie Mae and the Goodrich Altitude Suit. . . . Due to sabotage, the flight was terminated at Muroc Dry Lake in the Mojave Desert about 125 miles northeast of the starting point. . . . Foreign material had been introduced into the engine through the supercharger, causing the engine to overheat and scoring the cylinder walls, necessitating new pistons and reboring the cylinders. Mr. Post was very fortunate to be able to find such an ideal spot to land on.

After landing, they found six things had been done to the plane, any one of which would have prevented the completion of the flight [and, incidentally, possibly killed Wiley Post]. Mr. Post flew the ship back to Burbank the following day.

There are rumors that a jealous mechanic, who was hired to keep the *Winnie Mae* in good shape, was responsible for the sabotage. For some reason the mechanic intensely resented Post and tried to frustrate the one-eyed flier's attempts at record breaking.

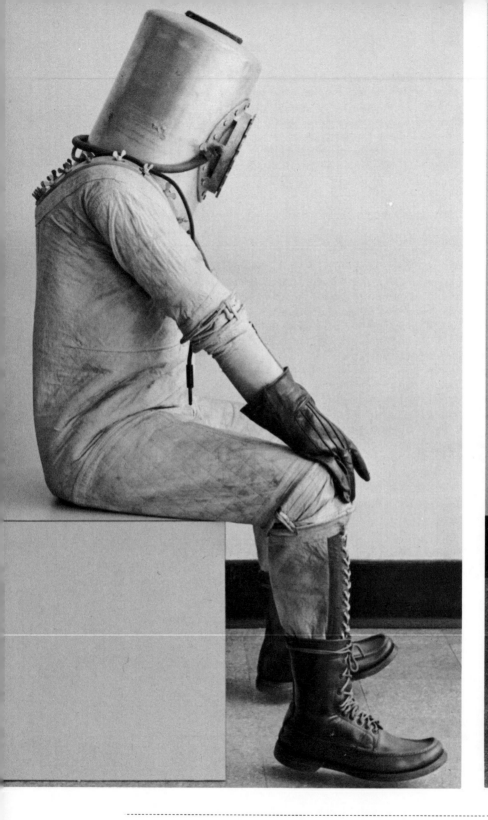

*Wiley Post's third full-pressure suit to explore the stratosphere
is now on display in the National Air Museum
of the Smithsonian Institution at Washington, D.C.
These three close-up views from different positions will give the reader a chance
to study details of the first suit ever to protect a pilot's life*

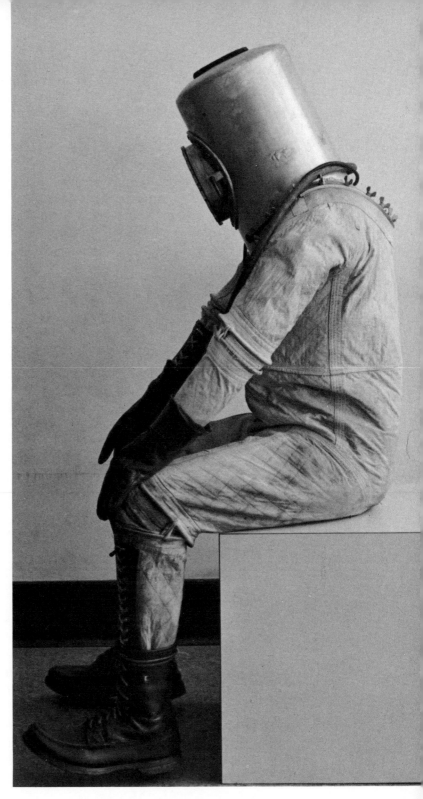

in actual flight to regions of the sky where extremely low atmospheric
pressures are a constant threat to human survival.
Note the wing bolts that fasten the new helmet on the suit as well as
its similarity to a deep-sea diver's outfit.

When Post learned about this, he refused to prosecute the man. But, naturally, the mechanic was fired.

Wiley Post made five attempts to break the transcontinental-flight speed record by flying at high altitudes while wearing the Goodrich Altitude Suit. He failed every time, due to one malfunction or another of his airplane. He did, however, fly at 34,000 feet between Denver, Colorado, and Lincoln, Nebraska, at a constant speed of 380 miles an hour—a high-altitude, high-speed record for that period (March 1935). Anyway, it proved his point that air speed could be much increased at high altitudes. The normal cruising air speed of his *Winnie Mae* at lower altitudes was about 150 mph.

However, during eight trial flights to the top of the troposphere and beyond, Wiley Post did establish an unofficial world altitude record of some 50,000 feet. These flights were made over Bartlesville, Oklahoma, headquarters of the Phillips Petroleum Company. In a private communication, Will D. Parker, manager of the Phillips Aviation Department, had this to say:

In my opinion Wiley broke the world altitude record here at Bartlesville, but this was never confirmed by the NAA [National Aeronautic Association] because two barographs had to be carried and the requirement was that they agree with each other within a small percentage. On one flight, one barograph worked perfectly but the other failed. On [another] five flights both barographs failed.

Later Post made three more high-altitude flights from the old United Air Terminal, now called the Lockheed Air Terminal, at Burbank, California. Again, no official record could be established. But all the altitude flights—including the one to some 40,000 feet over Chicago on September 5, 1934—proved that pressure suits were practical devices which could, with safety, allow men to fly ever higher through the atmosphere and even someday into outer space.

Yet despite his disappointments and lack of official recognition, Wiley Post in his day spent more time in the tropopause and stratosphere than any other airplane pilot. He flew the first Stratosphere Air Mail for Transcontinental and Western Air (now Trans World Airlines, or TWA). On April 14, 1935, he flew through the stratosphere from Burbank to Lafayette, Indiana—a distance of 1,760 miles. Again, on June 15, 1935, he streaked through the stratosphere at more than 300 miles an hour from Burbank to Wichita, Kansas—some 1, 188 miles.

Altogether Post must have spent at least eight full flying hours in the stratosphere. During his officially ignored first record-breaking flight to 50,000 feet, he discovered an unsuspected atmospheric anomaly—the jet stream. The stream is composed of horizontal winds moving from west to east with the earth's rotation at velocities ranging from a hundred to two hundred or more miles an hour. Today, commercial pilots routinely make use of the jet stream to gain speed on eastbound flights at high altitudes.

For reasons not exactly clear to the author, Wiley Post never did enter the MacRobertson Derby—the London-to-Melbourne air race—in October 1934. Maybe he felt that his pressure suit was not yet safe enough to be worn for that long a flight. More probably he reasoned that the *Winnie Mae* was becoming too tired and senile—for he retired her from service the following June. Instead, he made a fateful decision: he would put together a new airplane and make his third flight around the world backward. He would fly against the earth's rotation—traveling from east to west, rather than from west to east, as he had on his first two globe-circling flights.

With the cooperation of the Lockheed Aircraft Company, he constructed a hybrid seaplane. It had the wing of a Lockheed Sirius and the fuselage of a Lockheed Orion. (All Lockheed aircraft were named after stars or constellations.)

The airplane was ready to fly by the summer of 1935. The famous cowboy-comedian-philosopher Will Rogers accompanied Post on that third attempt to break another round-the-world flight record. They both died when the Sirius-Orion crashed just after take-off near Point Barrow, Alaska, on August 15, 1935. It was ironical. The cause of the crash was engine failure. And Wiley Post had always given aircraft engines the best of tender loving care.

Wiley Post was not quite thirty-seven years old when he died, but he had already opened the door to space flight. The Mercury astronauts wore Goodrich space suits that were based in principle on Post's third suit.

It is equally true that Wiley Post wanted more from his pressure suit than he got from it. One of his major aims was to outperform the altitude flight of Commander Renato Donati of Italy. On April 11, 1934, Donati had piloted an airplane to a height of 47,352⅛ feet. He didn't stay up there long—but he broke the world's altitude record *without* a pressure suit and without a pressurized cabin. He simply breathed pure oxygen through a mask—and almost killed himself.

Post wanted to prove that flying in the stratosphere could become routine. Beating Donati's record and staying at an even higher altitude for an extended period would have established that proof. But he was not able to make the record official.

Post did prove his point—to himself. His experimental Altitude Suit also proved a general point to European aviators: it *actually worked* during flights in an airplane. Soon Italy, France, Germany, Spain, and Russia were hotly engaged in a race to perfect their own full-pressure suits.

Chapter 3

OLD WORLD VERSUS NEW WORLD

But it was England—thirteen and a half months after the untimely deaths of Wiley Post and Will Rogers—that finally took the altitude record for aircraft away from Italy. On a gray morning of September 28, 1936, Royal Air Force Squadron Leader F. R. D. Swain reached an altitude of 49,967 feet. His barograph recordings established the flight as an official world record.

Squadron Leader Swain had been wearing a full-pressure suit and helmet. They were a modified version of the suit and helmet worn almost exactly three years earlier by the American Mark Ridge when the Massachusetts daredevil had been locked into a low-pressure chamber by Professor J. S. Haldane and Sir Robert

Davis. Swain's newer pressure outfit had also been designed by Haldane and Davis. As before, it was built by technical experts of the deep-water diving-suit manufacturer Siebe, Gorman & Co., Limited.

The RAF squadron leader flew to altitude in a Bristol 138a, a low-wing monoplane made entirely of wood. Its wing-loading capacity was very light—little more than eight and a half pounds per square foot. The Bristol's closed cockpit was not pressurized, to minimize weight. Swain's life depended entirely upon his pressure suit and helmet.

Preparations for the flight as well as building of the pressure garment were kept secret by the British Air Ministry because of the obvious military advantages in high-altitude fighting and bombing. Therefore, Mark Ridge—who had actually sparked the Air Ministry's interest in developing a protective flight suit by successfully testing one in a low-pressure chamber—was completely unaware of what was going on behind the scenes in England. It was another bitter irony for him when news of the flight leaked out. He had been flatly refused by the Air Ministry when he requested a chance to test the Haldane-Davis suit in actual flight conditions.

Another irony was that Swain's pressure suit was generally made in a manner that almost matched the design of Wiley Post's first suits. It was a two-piece affair, incorporating a rubberized fabric. The trousers were fastened around the waist with a ring of rubber, while the jacket was attached with a waistband of flexible steel.

Only the helmet was different. It was fashioned of the same rubberized fabric as the suit. Its window, or faceplate, was curved out of two layers of a kind of celluloid called Celastoid. The double layer was separated by an air space through which a "drying tube" ran to absorb moisture and thus prevent fogging.

A closed oxygen system pressurized the suit and supplied breathing oxygen in the helmet. The oxygen entered the suit through a flexible tube attached to the right side of the faceplate. Moisture and exhaled carbon dioxide were forced out of the left side of the helmet through another tube that carried these to a chemical cannister which absorbed the moisture and purified the gas. Since carbon dioxide contains molecules of oxygen as well as of carbon, the oxygen was liberated by the chemicals and sent back to the helmet by another route. Fresh breathing oxygen was automatically added as it was needed. This was an ingenious self-replenishing cycle.

The suit was automatically controlled at a maximum pressure of two and a half pounds per square inch. Nevertheless, the RAF pilot complained of "a little discomfort" as his suit began to inflate at higher and higher altitudes. His right arm felt slightly cramped

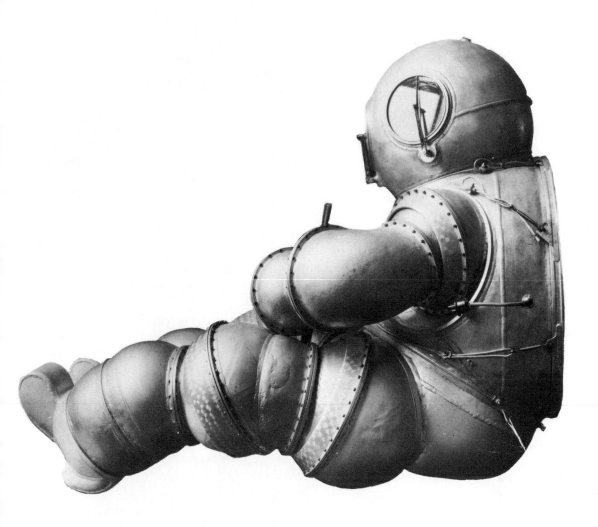

*Looking more like a robot than a space suit, this early Italian
design was apparently based on medieval suits of armor.
It was a torture chamber to don because the wearer had to enter
the suit through an open panel in the back and wriggle
his way into position. He probably swung his feet in first and then
bent over to fit his arms in place while raising
his head into the helmet, like doing a double situp. The suit could
withstand all kinds of pressure, but was too heavy
and immobile to be useful.*

Courtesy Dr. Charles L. Wilson, Lieutenant Colonel, USAF

An early British full-pressure
suit was mobile,
comfortable, and fairly lightweight.
Uninflated it weighed
eighteen pounds. On September 28,
1940, it performed
successfully at 35,000 feet.
Cross-lacing up front from boots to
thighs was probably used for
fitting suit to an individual's size.
Note emergency oxygen bottle
on lower right thigh of wearer.
It is connected to a rather clumsy
gas-regulator valve at end of
helmet's rubber hose.

Courtesy Dr. Charles L. Wilson,
Lieutenant Colonel, USAF

and he found it difficult to move his arms and legs. When he was coming down from his record-breaking height, some frightening problems developed. Here's how they were described by T. W. Walker in the May 1956 issue of *The Project Engineer,* a company magazine published by the the Thermix Corporation of Greenwich, Connecticut:

At 45,000 feet the window of the helmet, as well as the cockpit canopy, hazed over and only the glare of the sun gave any indication of direction. Control of the aircraft was difficult under these circumstances [an epic of understatement], and as the Bristol 138a continued to lose altitude in an "erratic manner," Squadron Leader Swain felt as though he were suffocating.

Fearing that his oxygen supply was depleted, he unsuccessfully endeavored to unfasten the emergency panel [of the helmet] to free his head. Control of the airplane was lost as he struggled, and in desperation he grabbed the knife which was fitted into the left sleeve of the suit and hacked out the celluloid window.

As fresh air rushed into the helmet and visibility was regained, Swain brought the Bristol under control. He was now at 14,000 feet, the nightmare over, and the completion of the flight was made without incident.

As with all experimental test flights, the near disaster provided invaluable technical data to improve future flight equipment. This was apparent nine months later, on June 30, 1937, when the British again took an altitude record away from the Italians. The previous month, Colonel Mario Pezzi of Italy had outclimbed Squadron Leader Swain's record by 1,394 feet. On May 8, 1937, Colonel Pezzi piloted an airplane above Montecello ("Sky Mountain") to a height of 51,361 feet. He was wearing a space suit designed by a Captain Cavallotti, which closely resembled the armor worn by medieval knights in battle. In fact, the suit was built by an Italian manufacturer of armor. This spurred the British Air Ministry to attempt another flight into the stratosphere, using a still further modification of the Haldane-Davis pressure suit.

Flight-Lieutenant M. J. Adam of the Royal Air Force took off in a Bristol 138a from Farnborough, England, as had Swain before him. Not only the pressure suit but the airplane as well had been much improved. Without any trouble, Lieutenant Adam flew to an altitude of 53,937 feet—thereby beating Colonel Pezzi's record by 2,576 feet—and returned safely to earth.

That was the last attempt on the part of the British to establish altitude records for heavier-than-air aircraft until after the end of World War II. This may seem remarkable, considering the fact that the following year Colonel Pezzi shattered Adam's record and gave Italy a return to altitude supremacy by climbing into the

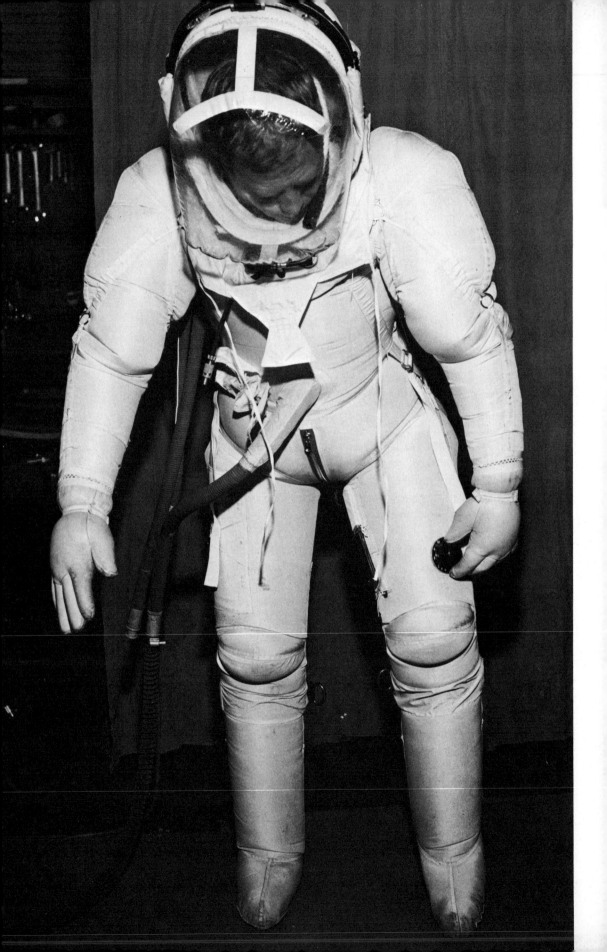

Front and rear views
of a much later British
full-pressure suit,
which was sent to the Aerospace
Medical Research Laboratory
at Wright Field in the
autumn of 1962 for evaluation.
Designated the British
Mechanical Engineering Type B
Suit, it is shown here
pressurized to 2.25 pounds
per square inch.
At this pressure level,
which is too low to sustain life
in a near vacuum, the
suit lost much of its mobility.
Other objections to
the suit that came out of the
evaluation tests were
poor optics, hampering visibility
of helmet, and the
two-piece clamshell arrangement
of the helmet.
One good aspect of the suit
was its light weight.
Its zippered entry for donning—
from front of the crotch
downward to rear and
up the back—was similar to the
entry designed into the later
Project Apollo
space suits, including the ones
used to walk on the moon.

Courtesy Don Bowen, Group Leader/Pressure
Suits, 6570th Aerospace Medical
Research Laboratory, USAF

stratosphere an unprecedented distance of 56,046 feet. The flight was made on October 22, 1938—less than a year before the outbreak of World War II in Europe. But the British Air Ministry was undoubtedly much too busy with preparations for war to take time off for another altitude attempt.

Otherwise, a space-suit race was on. Wiley Post's successful, if unofficial, record flights into the stratosphere with his third Altitude Suit interested the Russians. They were planning to build a stratospheric fleet of bombers and fighters to achieve air superiority over the Free World. They were also worried about Nazi Germany.

And indeed Germany was not idle in the space-suit business. The war only intensified their earlier efforts, which had begun earnestly in the autumn of 1935. During March of that same year, Dr. Philip Klanke, a pilot and meteorologist, built a pressure suit for scientific exploration of the atmosphere. The suit was unsuccessful—like the earlier suits of Wiley Post, it inflated into a billowing balloon and was too restrictive—but it led the way toward further experiments by the German Air Ministry.

Even as the British, the German government worked with a fabricator of diving suits. Not so experienced a firm as Siebe-Gorman, the Drägerwerke, located at Lübeck, Germany, encountered serious problems from the beginning. They started with a new concept for the material: laminated layers of rubber and silk. When the suit was formed it was strengthened externally with a fish-net outer layer of silk cord. The helmet, made of the same material, was incorporated as an extension of the suit: it was an integral, rather than a separate, part to ensure added strength. With a man inside, the whole thing resembled a weird monster, almost as horrifying as the one created by Frankenstein.

Despite its strength, this pressure suit stretched into a grotesque-looking "animal" when it was inflated. It blew up to such a size that even the integrated helmet was bloated to the point where no one inside the suit could see through the faceplate, which was generously large.

The next attempt by Drägerwerke engineers was to replace the silk-cord netting with steel wire. This held the shape better, but it frustrated pilots by hooking onto anything that was sticking out of the instrument panel and controls in the cockpit of an airplane.

Finally the German engineers took a hint from their Italian counterparts. They covered a fabric suit with a "coat of mail" like that worn in the days when knighthood flowered. The engineers felt that the metallic outer suit would prevent ballooning during pressurization of the garment. It did. But it led to other, more serious, problems. It was the problem of making limb joints that moved with ease and still were airtight enough to keep an altitude

suit pressurized which defeated the Drägerwerke engineers. They
continued to experiment for a while after their defeat, but finally
gave up—until Nazi Germany had been at war for more than a year.

At that time they went back to the coat-of-mail concept. They
felt that this was still the answer to the problem of stretching and
ballooning in a pressure suit. After careful analysis of how a pilot
maneuvers in his cockpit during flight, they decided that such a
closed-in space did not require him to move his upper arms while
controlling an aircraft. He had only to move his forearms forward
or backward and this could be accomplished by a simple movement
of the upper arms *in one plane*.

Airtight ball-bearing sockets to accomplish the elementary movement were built into the suit at the shoulders. Other bearing sockets,
also airtight, were placed over the biceps and between the elbows
and wrists. This reduced everything to a single type of joint—a
kind of cylinder shaped to fit over the elbows and knees. The thighs
and ankles were fitted with the same airtight socket-and-bearing
unit as the shoulders, upper arms, and forearms. Although it may
sound complicated, this system *was* a gross simplification of the
German engineers' earlier models. Besides, it worked—while the
earlier models did not.

There was only one drawback: the coat-of-mail suit was so heavy
and awkward that it proved to be more of a successful experimental
oddity than a practical, operational pressure suit. So it, too, was
dropped.

Officers of the German Air Ministry were becoming impatient,
so in October 1941 they ordered the people at the Drägerwerke to
design and build an *emergency* pressure suit. This was to be a lightweight garment that could be worn in the *pressurized cabins* of aircraft with comfort, so long as it was not inflated. It was to be a
back-up suit that would inflate automatically and save the lives of
crewmen in case the cabins were punctured by enemy gunfire.
As it turned out, this suit was not automatic: it was pressurized
by air from an aircraft engine-operated compressor. The compressed
air was fed through an oil filter into a two-way suit valve that was
activated by hand.

The helmet was actually a pressure vessel to keep the suit pressure
intact. It did not supply breathing oxygen, which came to the
crewman by way of an ordinary oxygen regulator that fed the life-
supporting gas into a standard mask. Pressure in the mask was
controlled by pressure in the suit: the suit-pressurizing air was tied
into the diaphragms of the oxygen-regulator system so that there was
always the same amount of pressure acting on the regulator. Otherwise, as altitude increased and atmospheric pressure decreased,
there would not be sufficient external presure on the regulator to

keep it operating. The diaphragms would lock in a closed position and the aircraft crewman would strangle, unable to inhale.

To explain: the diaphragms of a standard oxygen-mask regulator open as the mask wearer inhales, permitting just enough oxygen to enter his lungs. When he exhales, the diaphragms close so carbon dioxide can bleed off through a vent in the mask. The regulator automatically adjusts the oxygen flow to match the external atmospheric pressure. But after a certain altitude is reached, that outside pressure is too small to activate the regulator. In this case, the problem was resolved by using the suit pressure to supply the outside pressure. Of itself, it was a very clever idea. But it would have been unnecessary if the German engineers had been able to devise a full-pressure helmet.

Even the simple helmet first used to enclose the oxygen mask proved to be troublesome. Every time a crewman turned his head, the mask would scrape against the inside of the plastic helmet or otherwise restrict his head movements and thus his visibility. The restriction of motion was caused by antifogging tubes and structural supports inside the the helmet.

Finally, the Drägerwerke people hit upon a solution to this annoying problem. They eliminated all structural supports and tubes and cast the main portion of the helmet as a cylinder of clear plexiglass. On top of the cylinder they cemented a dome, also of plexiglass.

Ultimately, the emergency pressure suit transcended its initial design concept and was worn as a full-time suit in unpressurized cabins of aircraft flying above 40,000 feet.

Another kind of backup suit was substituted for fliers in pressurized-cabin aircraft. This suit was an elementary version of the full-pressure suit just described. It was not formed as closely to follow the shape of the wearer's body and it had no movable limb joints. Its one purpose was to keep its wearer alive at high altitudes

---

*The first German space suit resembled a strange monster
out of a science-fiction novel.
It was made of laminated silk and rubber, reinforced
with an outer net of silk cord.
Nevertheless, it stretched so drastically when it was inflated
that its helmet ballooned above the wearer's head
and he could not see out of the faceplate.
The suit as an engineering concept had to be abandoned.*

Courtesy Dr. Charles L. Wilson, Lieutenant Colonel, USAF

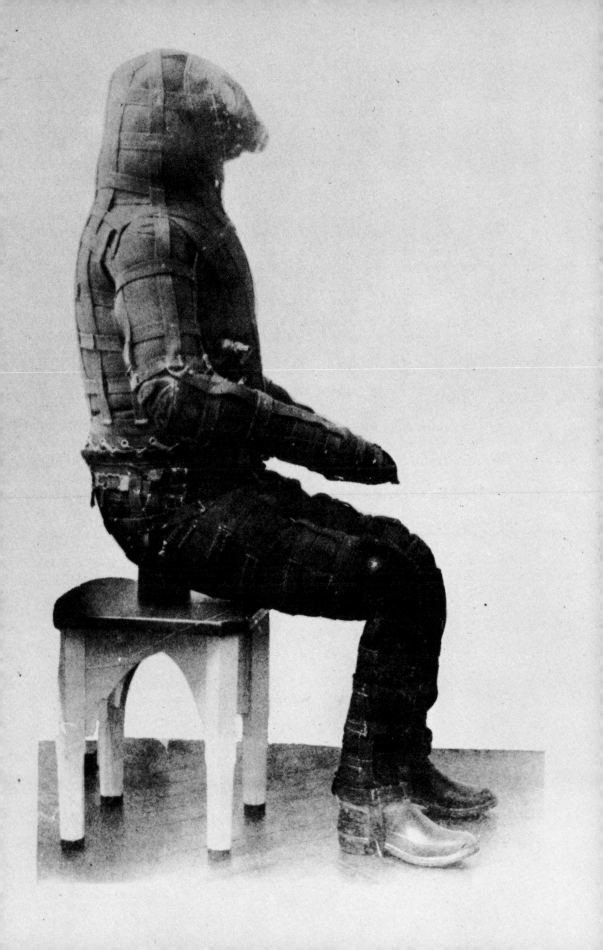

An echo of those years when knighthood was in flower was this 1942 all-metal pressure suit next built by the Germans. It was fairly mobile and could withstand pressures as high as 11 pounds per square inch. But despite its advantages and the choice of lightweight metal for its construction, it was just too heavy for practical use.

—if cabin pressure was lost for one reason or another—until he could dive to a lower, life-supporting level of the atmosphere. Nothing about this "escape suit" was automatic. The helmet had to be closed and the oxygen supply turned on by hand. Such manual operation would have to be accomplished swiftly when an aircraft cabin was explosively decompressed by a bullet or shrapnel puncture. But airmen of the Luftwaffe never had to go through this ordeal. For without restraining joint bearings and limb rings, the escape suit inflated into a big balloon that thoroughly hampered its wearer's movements. World War II was over before the Drägerwerke engineers could overcome such a serious limitation.

Before World War II, the French had also experimented with full-pressure suits for high-altitude flying. In June 1935, a team of two scientists—Drs. Garsaux and Rosenstiel—convinced the Potex Airplane Company to back them in their efforts to develop a kind of space suit. When it was built, it looked like something out of a novel by Jules Verne—or a costume for celebrating Halloween. It had a pumpkin-shaped Duralumin helmet with two rectangular "eyes" cut into it. The eyes were, of course, windows. They were each made of two layers of glass with a ⅜-inch air space between the layers. The air space was evacuated and the glass coated with a special chemical to prevent fogging. Fine-gauge wires were imbedded in the glass and heated with an electrical current further to minimize fogging as well as to eliminate icing.

The suit itself was fabricated of linen enclosed within an outer garment that insulated it. This combination proved to be unsatisfactory, so other versions of the suit were made of carefully laminated silk and rubber. The fabric was then doped with a kind of acetone to ensure that it would be both airtight and watertight. The shoulders of the suit could have been copied from costumes of players in an Elizabethan drama. They soared outward like big wings of cloth. Actually they were joints to allow arm movement.

Basic design of the suit was accomplished by Dr. Rosenstiel, a surgeon in the French Navy. Cooperating with him in its development was Dr. Garsaux, a member of the French Air Ministry. One unique feature of their pressure suit was gloves that were spring-loaded into a closed-fist attitude.

On August 14, 1936, Georges Detre took off from Villacoublay and piloted his airplane to a height of 48,697 feet—thus establishing a world altitude record with aircraft for France. But the record was short-lived: one month and two weeks later, it was broken by British Squadron Leader F. R. D. Swain.

Detre must have been wearing some kind of protective flight clothing on his flight, or else his cabin was pressurized. At any rate, I could find no record to suggest that the French flier was wearing the Rosenstiel-Garsaux suit.

That suit was plagued with the "normal" problems inherent in the space-suit designs of the period. Yet despite ballooning, icing of oxygen-flow valves, and leakage at the joints, Rosenstiel and Garsaux continued for several years to experiment with their suit, adding modifications along the way. Their experiments were abruptly halted when the Nazi Panzer Divisions overran France.

But until the war began in earnest, Italy continued to give England and France a race for their money. The last official high-altitude record for airplanes before the start of World War II was accomplished by the Italians. Wearing the Cavallotti space suit, Colonel Mario Pezzi, on October 22, 1938, climbed his aircraft higher than any man before him. He penetrated into the stratosphere a distance of 56,046 feet above sea level.

Prior to World War II, Spain was also in the space-suit race. But they were more interested in balloon-altitude records than in aircraft records. They tried to develop a pressure suit for use in open-gondola balloons. Their only suit that I know of employed rigid metal coils wound externally around the fabric. The coils gave the suit an odd appearance, somewhat faintly resembling the famous advertising symbol of the Firestone Tire Company—the little man dressed from head to toe in rings of rubber tires.

Other countries that experimented with pressure-suit design included China, Poland, Sweden, Norway, and Czechoslovakia. Most of these experiments were made during 1943, at the height of the war, and were unsuccessful.

The Russians, on the other hand, began their space-suit research in late 1934—some months after Wiley Post proved that a full-pressure suit was practical. Dr. Charles L. Wilson of the U. S. Air Force, an authority on the Soviet space-suit program, reports:

It had become apparent [to the Russians] that there would be a need and a means [new aircraft] to fly large forces of men at ambient altitudes in excess of 15 kilometers [49,212 feet]. Provisions for adequate crew life-support equipment was identified as a major obstacle confronting military planners. In 1936 a task force of All-Union aviation medical talent was mobilized to attack and solve this problem. . . .

. . . By late 1936 . . . the Society for Aeronautics and Chemistry organized an All-Union prize-winning contest encouraging development of stratosphere suits. Participating organizations [in the contest] were the Central Institute for Aerodynamics and Hydrodynamics; Air Force of the Red Army Workers and Peasants; USSR Army Artillery Transportation; and the People's Commissariat for Heavy Machinery.

All of the suit designs submitted were built and tested in a laboratory altitude chamber. Some of them were then tested in actual flight. The contest was won by E. E. Chertovskoy of the Air Force of the Red Army Workers and Peasants. His suit was successfully tested in a temperature-controlled chamber at about 50,000 feet of altitude and roughly 60 degrees below zero Fahrenheit. The suit was later tested in an airplane at a height of 29,568 feet.

Certain features of the Chertovskoy suit were patterned after those in Wiley Post's third suit. Russian newspapers had featured photos of the latter suit. It is not unusual for Soviet engineers to copy the work of other countries. Dr. Wilson writes:

Apparently they [the Soviets] had not considered the advantages of pressure breathing until it was introduced by [Colonel] Pharo Gagge in 1941. Unable to conduct extensive research on any aeromedical problems during World War II, the Soviets used the United States A-14 [oxygen] regulator and instructions.

They were not then concerned with physiological effects of rapid decompression, since most of their aircraft were not pressurized until after World War II. This is in contrast to great interest and research by the Western Allies and the Germans in rapid decompression effects.

An explanation of rapid decompression is in order: when an aircraft cabin is pressurized, say, to the equivalent of 20,000 feet of altitude while it is actually flying at 50,000 feet, a rapid decompression occurs if the cabin is punctured. Pressure in the cabin swiftly leaks out through the opening, no matter how small. In a matter of seconds those in the cabin are snapped upward 30,000 feet so far as atmospheric pressure is concerned. There is a great suction effect through the punctured area, as internal high pressure tends to equalize with the external, much lower, pressure.

In a vacuum, such as is found in outer space, the decompression would be explosive.

Dr. Wilson continues:

Later, when pressurized cabins entered the inventory of research and operational Soviet aircraft, they began to design some pressure-suit helmets and gloves for quick donning after decompression. This may have been an unwise choice. It required the crewmember first to diagnose the decompression event which, in fact, is often thought to be an explosion and fire—due to the [attendant] fog, the thud and flying debris.

Then the crewman must don and secure the helmet and gloves within a total of six to seven seconds. Pressure suits should work automatically.

Soviet engineers neglected to conduct a thorough study of ways of applying pressure to the body. In addition to full-pressure suits and pressurized cabins, they might have included bladder, rigid metal, fabric and closed-cell sponge suits—and at least a theoretical consideration of the feasibility of artificial gravity, liquids and high-energy electrical fields for retention of gas-pressure on the body.

It is surprising that they chose a closed-circuit life-support system instead of the simpler, less expensive, lighter and more reliable ventilation system, using liquid oxygen. Open-circuit ventilated pressure suits are nearly the rule in world aviation today.

Despite their shortsighted limitations, the Soviets have accomplished a fine job in space-suit research, thinks Dr. Wilson:

From 1934 to 1943 and from 1946 to 1955, the USSR had an excellent high-altitude pressure suit program. The effort was staffed with excellent-quality technical personnel and adequate support-facilities were used. From 1934 to 1940 the Soviet program at least equalled and probably exceeded in scope and excellence the combined efforts of all other nations in this technical area. Soviet aerospace life-scientists in general have been serious and vigorous in their efforts to protect their aircrew members.

This still does not eliminate the fact that Soviet engineers are great copiers and get most of their good ideas from the West. In May 1960, the Russians acquired an excellent full-pressure helmet, along with an emergency partial-pressure suit that had automatically proved its airworthiness a number of times when cabin pressurization was lost at extremely high altitudes. The helmet was the MA-2 and the suit the MC-3A—both products of research by the U. S. Air Force. They were worn by the CIA pilot Francis Gary Powers when his U-2 espionage airplane was shot down over the Urals. The same suit and helmet, with a Red Air Force designation, are today used by Soviet bomber crews and fighter pilots while flying in the stratosphere.

At the annual Congress of the International Astronautical Federation in 1967, held at Belgrade, Yugoslavia, the Russians for the first time publicly revealed their cosmonaut space suit. According to an editor of *Astronautics & Aeronautics,* an official journal of the prestigious American Institute of Aeronautics and Astronautics:

This photo was made in the autumn of 1958, approximately a year after the Russians launched Sputnik I, the world's first man-made satellite.
It purports to be an example of a "space suit for people going up into superhigh altitudes." The suit was fabricated of rubberized cloth and used heavy metal lacing for frontal entry and to keep the suit airtight after it was put on.
Full-pressure helmet is of the fishbowl type.
Note that man inside the suit is also wearing an old-fashioned aviator's leather helmet with equally old-fashioned built-in headphones.
Microphone is obscured by reflections on outer helmet, but it, too, can vaguely be seen in outline as a large clumsy early type.

Courtesy U.S.S.R. Academy of Sciences

American bioastronautical specialists at the meeting commented that both the space suit and the food and equipment were very similar to their American counterparts. [Underscoring mine.]

Astronautics & Aeronautics has been only one of many technical and trade journals in the United States to release data on the engineering-design aspects of American civilian space suits. Russian engineers and scientists read every issue of such journals with extreme care. They even study the advertisements of aerospace manufacturers, which often contain clues on equipment-design features.

This is just part of the worldwide race to design and build better pressure suits. As advances in aviation led man into a new era, no one doubted that the space suit was an absolute necessity.

Chapter 4

WHO NEEDS A SPACE SUIT?

The question here is not academic. It can be answered only by other questions. Who needs a seat belt in his car? Who needs a lifeboat? Why do firefighters need oxygen masks? Is there any need for first-aid kits? Who needs a heavy topcoat in a blizzard?

Obviously, a space suit is necessary to protect and maintain human life against known and unknown hazards.

Everyone must know the hazards of automobile traffic, boating, fighting fires, and snowstorms. The real hazards of space flight are not so well known.

They were first recognized more than a hundred years ago by a man whose profession was literature rather than science—although he managed to combine the two disciplines effectively. In 1866, Jules Verne published a novel called *De la Terre à la Lune* (*From*

Earth to the Moon). In it he clearly described the purpose and functions of an EVA (extravehicular activity) space suit. This went way beyond the concept of a standard space suit that for nearly three decades—from the early 1930's through the mid-1950's—confounded the best bio-engineering talent on three continents. With his closed-circuit EVA suit, Jules Verne anticipated the space-walking astronauts of the American Gemini Program and the moon-walking astronauts of Project Apollo in the 1960's.

Within nine years after Verne described his specialized pressure suit, the great Russian physical chemist D. I. Mendeleyev proposed a gas-tight gondola for stratospheric balloon flights. Professor Mendeleyev—best remembered for his invention of the periodic table of the elements—proposed a hermetically sealed big rubber bag inflated with oxygen and reinforced on the outside with an interlaced network of strong cords or cables. Mendeleyev felt that his gondola would keep a man safe and alive to any altitude that a balloon was able to soar.

Fifty-two years after Jules Verne wrote about a manned voyage to the moon—which, incidentally, was launched from a huge cannon in central Florida, somewhere near where the Kennedy Space Center now stands!—a patent for a space suit was awarded to an American, Fred M. Sample. It was U. S. Patent Number 1,272,537, the first patented space suit in history. Application for the patent was made on March 20, 1917, and it was granted on July 16, 1918. The suit included a full-head helmet into which oxygen was pumped.

The Fred Sample "Suit for Aviators" was never tested in high-altitude flight. An impractical piece of space clothing, it remains solely as a monument to the vision of its inventor. Nevertheless, it was prophetic.

There are a number of very good reasons why a space suit is needed.

When man flies into outer space he is quite actually a "fish out of water." He is threatened on all sides by invisible and lethal forces. Some deep-sea fish explode when they are brought to the surface: a man's intestines would most likely do this in space, if he were not adequately protected. We have already described how his blood would burst into a boil and how his whole body would swell up like a balloon because of the rapid expansion of internal gases and water vapor (also a gas).

The fact is, above an altitude of 13,000 feet man is already out of his normal element. At 52,000 feet and beyond, the conditions of the atmosphere begin to duplicate exactly the state of threat to his body that he will encounter in space. Today, man routinely flies above 13,000 feet—and far above that level—in commercial, private, and military aircraft.

Yet Dr. Hubertus Strughold, a pioneer in the field of aerospace
medicine, former chief of the Air Force Department of Space
Medicine and presently on the staff of the School of Aerospace
Medicine at Brooks Air Force Base in Texas, has this to say:

*Above the thirteen-thousand-foot level, decrease of oxygen pressure
has such strong psychophysiological effects that we can speak of the
Hypoxic zone. A critical point, characterized by loss of consciousness,
is reached within this zone. . . .*

*If a subject is brought abruptly from normal oxygen pressure to that
found at twenty-six thousand feet, the first psychophysiological disturbances can be observed after a period of about two minutes; after
another minute, the subject becomes entirely helpless, falling into unconsciousness.*

In other words, at 26,000 feet a man has just about three minutes
in which to repair or replace a defective oxygen-supply system.

But at 46,000 feet, continues Dr. Strughold, "the time of useful
consciousness reaches a minimum value of eleven to twenty seconds
and in experiments performed on animals it was found that at
fifty-two thousand feet respiration ceases, on the average, within
seventeen-point-eight seconds."

He calls this last-mentioned altitude *"the physiological oxygen
dividing line between atmosphere and space*—the borderline zone
of complete anoxia" because "oxygen can no longer enter the lungs,
even if it still can be found in the surrounding air." Such a situation
results because the low atmospheric pressure at this altitude allows
the waste products of the respiratory system—carbon dioxide and
water vapor—to settle in and completely fill up the lungs, thus
preventing the intake of air or even of pure oxygen under pressure.

According to the doctor: "It is not going too far if one makes
the amazing statement that a man, suddenly exposed to the physical
environment in the upper atmosphere or space, is in danger of suffocation by drowning in his own water vapor."

During the early 1940's it was discovered that if a person had
oxygen forced into his lungs *before* he reached the critical altitude
border, and continued to pressure-breathe in this manner, the lungs
would remain reasonably clear. The terms *hypoxia* and *anoxia* used
by Dr. Strughold should be defined. Hypoxia is a condition wherein
lack of a normal supply of oxygen causes first blackout and then
full unconsciousness. But the victim can be revived if treated in
time. Anoxia is another matter: here a serious lack of oxygen pre-
vails, causing certain death.

There are other space-equivalent conditions within the atmosphere beyond the borderline zone of 52,000 feet. Each of them is
a new threat until, by the time 460,000 feet of altitude is reached,
the total threats to life not only amount to five, but also—insofar

F. M. SAMPLE.
SUIT FOR AVIATORS.
APPLICATION FILED MAR 20, 1917.

1,272,537.

Patented July 16, 1918.
2 SHEETS- SHEET 1.

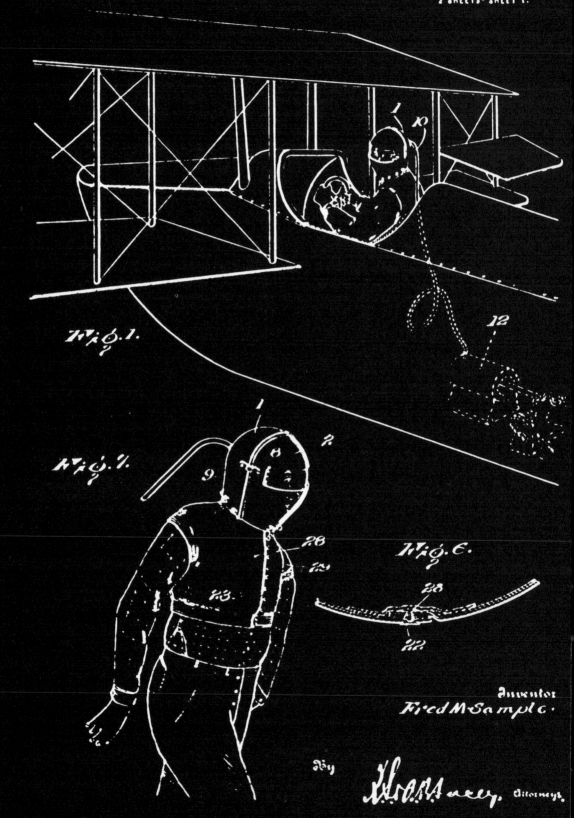

Fig.1.

Fig.7.

Fig.6.

Inventor
Fred M Sample

By
Attorneys.

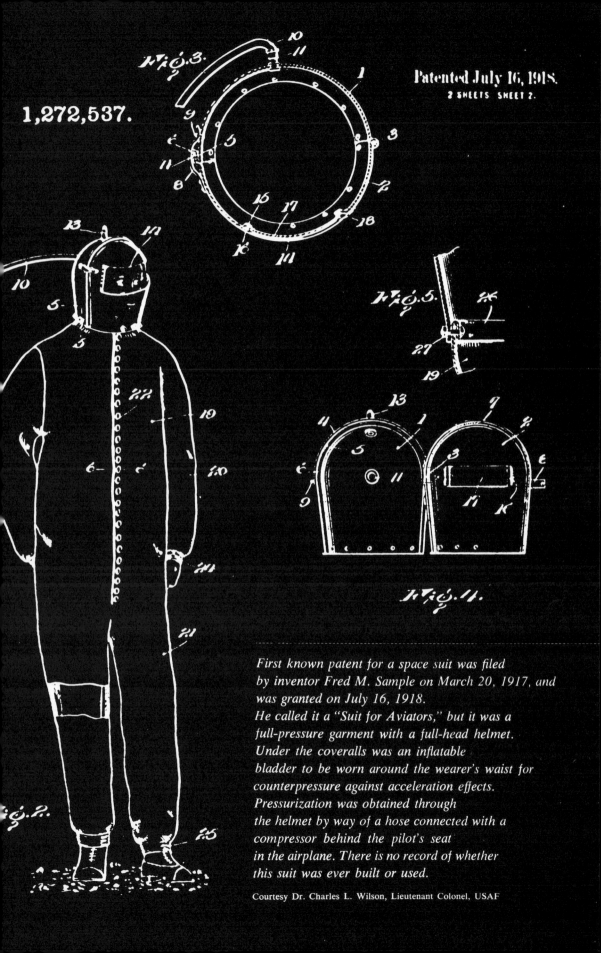

First known patent for a space suit was filed
by inventor Fred M. Sample on March 20, 1917, and
was granted on July 16, 1918.
He called it a "Suit for Aviators," but it was a
full-pressure garment with a full-head helmet.
Under the coveralls was an inflatable
bladder to be worn around the wearer's waist for
counterpressure against acceleration effects.
Pressurization was obtained through
the helmet by way of a hose connected with a
compressor behind the pilot's seat
in the airplane. There is no record of whether
this suit was ever built or used.

as the human body is concerned—completely approximate the full quota of dangers in interplanetary space.

Let's summarize the five space-equivalent conditions that exist within our own atmosphere:

CONDITION 1: At 52,000 feet, as was mentioned, the unprotected lungs can no longer take in air or oxygen.

CONDITION 2: At 63,000 feet, also mentioned previously, the surrounding air pressure is so low that liquids boil at 98 degrees Fahrenheit, which is just about the average normal body temperature—thus the body's inherent warmth will cause all body fluids, including the blood, to explode into a frothy boil and vaporize.

CONDITION 3: Between 65,000 and 98,000 feet the use of pressurized aircraft cabins is impossible for any length of time—usually, such cabins derive their pressure by sucking in and compressing the surrounding air, yet at these altitudes the air is mixed with ozone or triatomic oxygen (O_3), which would poison the body if compressed into the cabin and hence an hermetically sealed cabin containing its own self-cycling atmosphere would be necessary, exactly as in a space ship.

CONDITION 4: At 131,000 feet the ozone layer ends, but since the layer absorbs the most intense portion of ultraviolet radiation from the sun, and thereby shields animal life on earth, the space voyager within the atmosphere at this altitude would be exposed to the full radiation intensity of solar ultraviolet light —severe skin burns and possibly blindness would result— while long before this level is reached (upward from 70,000 feet) he would be exposed to the unhindered force of the heavy primary particles of mysterious cosmic radiation.

CONDITION 5: Beyond 460,000 feet there would be a fairly constant threat of a meteoric strike—below this altitude most meteors and micrometeoroids are vaporized by heat from friction with the atmosphere, but here they would shower about the aircraft or spacecraft with unhindered force: if one punctured a sealed cabin, explosive decompression would result.

Such are the physical and physiological hazards of both high-altitude and space flight. All of them have been faced and conquered by space-suit scientists, engineers and technicians. These men have been their own guinea pigs, facing at the time of their experiments many unpredictable and lethal dangers.

An example of the courage and dedication of space-suit researchers is Dr. Edwin G. Vail, who was project officer on pressure-suit development for many years at the Air Forces' Wright Aero Medical

Laboratory, now renamed the Aerospace Medical Research Laboratories. In those days Dr. Vail, who holds a Ph.D. degree in physiology, was an Air Force captain and senior pilot. One morning Captain Vail was sitting in an altitude chamber at the Wright Field Laboratory, running a test on the then new K-1 full-pressure helmet. He was also dressed in the T-1 partial-pressure suit, a version of which was later worn by the U-2 meteorological and espionage pilots on flights to 70,000 feet. That was exactly the atmospheric pressure equivalent in Vail's altitude chamber during his test—when something unforseen happened. Here's how he described the incident to me:

The face-plate on my K-1 helmet popped off. It just blew right off, because of the inside helmet-pressure. Luckily one of the chamber operator-observers—Kent Gillespie, who is still at Wright Field—saw the thing go. I don't remember what happened myself. The next thing I knew was that Dan Folger [another chamber operator-observer] was in there with me, shaking me and yelling, "Hey! Ed!"

They brought me down real fast. The decompression record showed that I was recompressed at some thirty-eight thousand feet—in something like eight milliseconds. I had rather sore ear-drums after that for a couple of weeks.

All I can actually remember about the accident is hearing a sound, like zzzzzzzzzzit! And that's the last thing I do remember—until I was brought back to consciousness.

So you see, the time-of-consciousness at altitudes around seventy thousand feet is pretty brief. For people who aren't canned in suits—or whose suits decompress—can expect no more than seven to nine seconds of consciousness, depending on how fast the decompression happens.

What it all boils down to is this: the length of time it takes your blood to circulate from the lungs through the heart to the brain. As soon as you decompress, all of the gas is cleaned out of the blood going through your lungs. This oxygen-poor blood then circulates through the heart and reaches the central nervous system. Then you're out. Your time-of-consciousness is the blood-circulation time from the lungs to the brain. This is the case from roughly fifty thousand feet on up.

I have been tested in altitude chambers to 47,000 feet at least five times. I can assure the reader that gases in an unprotected body expand swiftly and painfully. Since I was pressure-breathing pure oxygen, however, the blood in my lungs retained its oxygen. The tests included a quick plunge down to 26,000 feet, where I was asked to take off my oxygen mask to check my tolerance against hypoxia. The tolerance varied from test to test, depending upon the amount of 100 percent oxygen I had been breathing at ground level before the ascent to altitude, On one test, I remained conscious for almost three minutes. On another, I began to black out after two minutes. On still another, I felt woozy after a minute and a half.

Military jet pilots are routinely tested today in altitude chambers at least once a year. The purpose is to keep them familiar with their personal symptoms of hypoxia. Such symptoms vary from year to year. For instance, I at one time experienced a tingling sensation in my toes just before blackout. Two years later, the symptom had changed to an icy feeling in my fingertips. These are signs that warn high-flying pilots something has gone wrong with their oxygen-supply system—built-in physiological alarm clocks to tell them either to dive immediately and steeply to a lower altitude or to reconnect a disconnected oxygen hose.

(For the record, I am not a military jet pilot—only a very curious scientific researcher.)

Let's return to the question, Who needs a space suit? From a military viewpoint alone, pressure suits are a must if our national defense is not to deteriorate into a meaningless posture. This point is concisely emphasized in a formerly secret document, which recounts the preparation of still another document that originally had an even higher security classification:

And because of bends, chokes, gas pains, and some still undefined physiological stresses imposed on individuals at extreme altitudes, the Aero Medical Laboratory doubted that the partial pressure suit principle would ever provide "extremely long-term capability of 100% of the crew members."

When the needed breakthrough had not been made by late 1955, the Air Research and Development Command prepared a technical program-planning document entitled "Airborne Environmental Protection and Maintenance of Personnel," which subsequently was released to prospective contractors. The document very adequately summarized the current state of the art of high-altitude suit development and listed the current shortcomings in equipment.

The document was in reality an explanation of a new technical requirement which assumed that by 1960 airmen would need protection at 75,000 feet for 12 hours in temperatures ranging from minus 40 degrees Fahrenheit to the highest cockpit temperatures that would be encountered in aircraft flying at a true airspeed of 1,200 knots [about 1,300 miles per hour]. By 1965, that requirement would encompass nine hours of flight at 86,000 feet and airspeeds of 1,600 knots [approximately 1,841 mph]. The 1970 estimates were 100,000 feet for seven hours at true airspeeds as high as 2,200 knots [roughly more than 2,500 mph]. . . .

The maximum altitude performance of manned United States Air Force airplanes between 1918 and 1954 showed "approximately a 3% per year increase, compounded annually," and "although performance at times has dipped below this line, eventually an abrupt increase brought performance up to the line at a later date." Thus no long-term change has been introduced by depressions, by wars, or by jet engines.

This Air Force forecast on the need for mobile, long-term, and super-high-altitude pressure suits was further stimulated by the introduction of the giant B-36 Peacemaker jet-and-piston-powered bomber as well as by the B-52 eight-jet Strato-Fortress. The latter was programmed to play a vital role in Operation Castle, a top secret experiment to test miniaturized versions of the thermonuclear (H-bomb) device. The hydrogen-bomb test models were to be dropped over Bikini Atoll in the Pacific Ocean from the edge of the stratosphere during March to May 1953.

The B-36 is now, of course, obsolete. But it was the ultragiant, ultralong-range bomber of the day. Its many crew members would have to survive in the stratosphere for extremely extended periods without having their efficiency reduced. So a comfortable light-weight emergency pressure suit and helmet were urgent require-ments. For these reasons, the program to develop a B-36 pressure suit was called "Project Featherweight." Once the protective strato-spheric clothing was perfected, it would also be available to B-52 crewmen.

As a point of interest, the first emergency partial-pressure suits and full-pressure helmets were ready to wear before either the B-36 or the B-52 became fully operational. The earlier styles were not the most comfortable kinds of flight clothing that stratospheric-flying crews would desire, but they were lightweight and they worked.

The urgencies of national defense in the United States dominated and accelerated the development of both the partial- and full-pressure suit. Out of the latter came the first space suits worn by the Mercury astronauts. Thus the civilian, peaceful manned exploration of space was made possible by experience and knowledge gained through military needs.

America's program to send men on exploratory voyages into space began during early October 1958. Without the space-suit technology already available from the military at that time, it might easily have taken an extra eighteen to twenty years before American astronauts could be sent to the moon and returned safely to their home planet.

Yet how important is it for men to explore the moon—and, later, other planets of the solar system? The importance cannot be gauged by dollars. It cannot be measured alone in terms of earthly wants. Nor can it be scaled against any previous scientific endeavor of mankind. For out there in space among enigmatic worlds lie the answers to many mysteries—mysteries that are not even now antici-pated, answers that will transform the character of civilization for the better.

One or more of those answers could well explain how life, intel-ligent and otherwise, was created.

Lesser, but vitally important, things will be learned to make life more bearable upon the earth. In fact, space-suit research has al-

These three early space suits, vintage 1943,
show interesting variations in attempt to achieve
mobility of the joints while still
keeping the suits airtight.
Suit at left employs accordionlike bellows
held between metal rings and
"stovepipe" sections. Arm and elbow joints
of middle suit look almost exactly
like those used in medieval suits of armor—curved
metal leaves that telescope in a manner
similar to the collapsible aluminum drinking cups
of the day. This suit also features
sturdy metal ring bearings at shoulders,
knees, and ankles to provide rotational mobility.
Its two-piece fabric garment is held
together by a strong, wide metal belt
to prevent leakage of pressure.
Helmet is the fishbowl type.
Third suit, at right, appears to be made entirely
of rubber, which would cause it to balloon
stiffly out of shape when inflated.
Its helmet is also of rubber,
except for the viewing window.

Courtesy Dr. Edwin G. Vail, Hamilton Standard Division, United Aircraft Corporation

ready provided medical science with many new insights into the human body and revolutionary instruments to analyze and treat a variety of diseases.

Who needs a space suit?

The astronauts, of course. Specialists in the life sciences, naturally. The physicists, so they can gain fresh information about the physical universe. Cosmogonists and cosmologists, so they can verify or invalidate their theories about the birth and evolution of the total universe. The surgeons and general practitioners, who benefit from the engineering and scientific by-products of space research. Farmers and engineers, shoemakers and dentists, all will retrieve something of value from space exploration.

Without space suits, or similar protective capsules, there can be no manned exploration of space. It took many dedicated men many years to evolve a suit of clothing that would allow other men to walk safely upon the moon. In the process, the experimenters tortured their own bodies to analyze and conquer the dangers of living in a vacuum, in a condition without gravity, and in a state where the forces of gravity slammed against their vital systems from all directions.

They felt that a space suit was needed and that their self-torture was a small price to pay for it.

Chapter 5

THE LATEST STYLES IN TORTURE

Most men like their working conditions to be as pleasant and comfortable as possible. But the men who develop and wear space suits willingly expose themselves to conditions that would make the average man wince just to think about them. The custodian of a medieval torture chamber would have rubbed his hands together with glee if he could have seen some of the modern devices and instruments that are required to develop pressure suits and train men in their use.

Apart from the altitude chambers, there are the human centrifuges, escape-ejection simulators, crash-landing simulators, zero-gravity simulators, tilt tables, rocket-powered sleds to produce high gravity forces against a human subject, heat chambers and cold chambers in which human subjects are parbroiled and frozen, noise chambers, shake chairs for vibration tests, sealed revolving tanks that abruptly change their direction of rotation while a subject sits inside in utter darkness, and the Coriolis chair. This last is a more refined "torture" device. I should know: I have ridden in one at the Aerospace Medical School on Brooks Air Force Base in Texas.

The Coriolis chair is casually referred to as a "biaxial stimulator" and tests a pilot's or astronaut's response to stresses caused by changes of attitude in a high-performance airplane or spacecraft. A medical technician straps you into the chair and temporarily blinds you by fastening a pair of big rubber goggles over your eyes. Inside the goggles are electrodes, not lenses. The electrodes provide electrical contact between your eye areas and a recording instrument. A pair of rubber-cushioned headphones is plugged into your ears, so you can hear questions from the chair operator. You are supposed to answer him verbally and tell him where you *think* you are. You're usually in a much different position than you think.

Action of the chair is simple: it rotates on one plane and at the same time slants over on another axis. The combination of effects, however, is not so simple. You can be whirling around to the right while the chair abruptly tilts to the left. Then, almost without a pause, before you know what's happening, the movements are reversed: you're turning swiftly to the left, as the chair tips over to the right. Then you're twirling right again and the chair is going with you, then against you, then the rotational direction reverses and rereverses as you spin around and the tilt angle changes like the movement of a pendulum, only faster, until you begin to feel like a rat in a maze on a merry-go-round. All this time you have been unable to see a thing, but the electrical contacts over your eyes have been sending messages about your eye movements to a recorder.

By studying your eye movements in compensation for the contradictory chair motions, aerospace medical specialists can accurately determine your sensitivity to change of body attitude and the quickness of your recovery from deluding situations. They can also detect any insidious abnormalities that may exist in the balancing mechanism of your ears.

It's difficult to imagine more refined torture than the Coriolis chair. Yet the developer of the first successful emergency partial-pressure suit, Dr. James P. Henry, had the imagination to combine a series of refined tortures, one upon another. He not only conceived these tortures but performed them on himself. Air Force authorities have repeatedly honored Dr. Henry for his unshakable determination and courage in subjecting himself to tests for the development of pressure-suit equipment. He has proved himself to be a true pioneer in this field.

The first successful partial-pressure suit, for example, has made it possible for pilots to fly in the stratosphere for long periods without fear of sudden decompression of their aircraft. To develop it, Dr. Henry had to sit many times in airtight chambers while the air was gradually withdrawn to simulate tremendous altitudes.

Then there are the centrifuges, Dr. Henry's special province during the period that he was Chief of the Acceleration Section at the Wright Aero Medical Laboratory. A centrifuge is as wicked a mechanical device as any that man ever dreamed up to torture himself into an understanding of the effects of violent motion on the human body. But Dr. Henry managed to add a few refinements, as we shall see later.

The human subject in a centrifuge can be compared to a heavy object tied to the end of a rope which is being whirled with feverish intensity overhead in a horizontal plane. An example of the tremendous centrifugal force exerted upon the object can be obtained by abruptly releasing the rope as it spins: it will shoot madly away, carried by the object, which has the speed of a projectile. In biblical times the same principle was used in warfare, to release stone pellets from a sling. Even today, in the mountains of Spain and on the pampas of Argentina, the principle operates in the bola, a deadly hunting weapon that can kill large game with its smashing force.

Sitting in the cab or strapped down to the platform of one of these whirling machines, the centrifuge men routinely allow themselves to be accelerated to the point of blackout or unconsciousness. Their purpose is to gather accurate information about the effects of increased gravity force on the pressure and distribution of blood in the lungs, heart, brain, and legs.

When you ask Dr. Henry how he knew at what point it was time to stop the machine, he answers simply: "In negative acceleration, the end point is where the little blood vessels by your eye whites begin to burst. Now that sounds very formidable, but we were quite pleased to find this safe end point. The tricky part was to be sure that the blood vessels of the brain weren't breaking at the same time, since this would result in paralysis and a few other disastrous things."

The man who engaged in these hazardous scientific investigations was born in 1910 in Leipzig, Germany, of an American father and English mother. Jim grew up in England and took his M.D. degree at Cambridge University. He and his bride moved to Canada, where he worked in pediatrics at Vancouver and Montreal. But Dr. Henry's true interest had always been scientific research. He began to work on the mechanism of a simple blood test that could be used to diagnose obscure infections. This led to a fellowship at McGill University, in Montreal, where he was able to spend full time as a researcher in the field of blood substitutes. He was next offered a fellowship at the California Institute of Technology, Pasadena, to continue his research.

At Cal Tech, he modestly claims, the work in blood substitutes produced very little of value. But his experience with blood action led to another research assignment at the University of Southern California, Los Angeles. It was here that his wide scientific interests, energy, enthusiasm, and impatience with obstacles paid off. World War II was already in full swing. There were many kinds of physiological investigations in progress at the university's Aero Medical Laboratory. Dr. Henry willingly became a jack-of-all-research. The senior scientists were so involved with the pressing problem of getting their new human centrifuge built that they turned over to young Henry—he was not yet thirty—most of the loose ends and half-started experiments. These were connected with a big government-sponsored program of physiological investigation into the respiratory problems of high-altitude flight. The supervising agency was the Army Air Corps's Aero Medical Laboratory at Wright Field in Ohio. The experiments required, among other things, certain physical risks.

Aircraft were then flying operationally above 30,000 feet, with the pilots and crews on pressure-breathing, and there was little doubt that turbojets on the engineers' drawing boards would soon be built to exceed 40,000 feet. The problem was not mechanical: it was human. What would happen to the human circulatory and respiratory systems if a future pressurized cabin failed at an extreme altitude where the pressure of air and its lowered oxygen content became less than the minimum needed to sustain life?

Most of the basic facts had already been established by scientists at the School of Aviation Medicine in Texas and elsewhere. It was known then, for example, that somewhere above 38,000 feet the ordinary oxygen mask, which supplied the gas on demand (as the lungs of a flier required it and drew it in), was useless. A new concept of breathing was called for. Pharo Gagge, who was a Lieuten-

*Astronaut Scott Carpenter's face shows the pain
he feels while being subjected to an increased force of gravity
under high acceleration in a human centrifuge.
His body is instrumented with sensors that record his rate of
heartbeat, his brain functions, and his respiratory rate.
It's all a routine part of astronaut training.*

Courtesy NASA

ant Colonel when he took over the Aero Medical Laboratory of the Air Corps, solved the problem by introducing pressure-breathing. The standard mask was again inadequate, except at nominal altitudes above the 38,000-foot level, since oxygen pumped into it under certain pressures would push it away from the wearer's face. A sealed helmet had to be devised; this provided sufficient additional pressure around the entire head of a flier to push pure oxygen into his lungs. He then had to exhale by force—the reverse of normal breathing. The amount of extra pressure that could be added was limited, since the muscular power of the lungs—try blowing up a toy balloon, for instance—is quite small. However, it did increase the pressure in the lungs enough to prevent the collection of water vapor and carbon dioxide there and thus made breathing possible. There was no counterpressure against the rest of the body in the preliminary days of pressure-breathing.

Although the early pressure helmets were naturally crude, in time more efficient and more comfortable helmets would be developed. So the respiratory problem was on its way toward solution, at least up to an altitude of 50,000 feet

There remained the closely associated circulatory problem. Pressurized aircraft cabins were one solution, but there was no way of protecting pilot and crewmen if a cabin were to be punctured by enemy fire, as might easily happen in warfare, or if it sprang a leak due to structural failure. The full-pressure suits, which were in a primitive experimental stage during that period, were impossibly clumsy. Anyone strapped into a strait jacket would have had more freedom of motion. Therefore, flexible emergency life-saving equipment was an absolute necessity.

For example, a rapid lowering of air pressure to about one-fourth its initial value—as in an aircraft pressurized for an internal cabin atmosphere equivalent to 8,000 feet, if it lost its pressure at 34,000 feet—would cause the blood of crew members to expand and develop nitrogen bubbles. Excruciating pain would result, destroying their ability to control the aircraft, and they would be likely to crash before they could recover. At 50,000 feet or higher, their pressurized helmets would soon fail them because the oxygen pressure inside their lungs would fall below the vital minimum even when it was applied by force. Within a few seconds, the reserve oxygen in cells and tissues would be devoured and death would be the swift and inevitable result. This grim situation could be avoided only if there were some way to provide the flier with a personal atmosphere inside a special suit or capsule set at a sufficient pressure to keep him alive until he could get down to the denser air below.

There seemed to be no other escape from the situation, unless some emergency means was found to support the chest and trunk mechanically during the use of high breathing pressures. The Committee on Aviation Medicine of the nation's wartime Office of Scientific Research and Development was well aware of these problems and had asked a number of scientists to look into them. One of the problems to be tackled at the University of Southern California was that raised by Colonel Gagge when he introduced the idea of gaining altitude for aircraft crewmen by having them breathe against high added oxygen pressures. Dr. James P. Henry automatically stepped into the role previously reserved for the test animals with which he had up to then been working. He became a pioneering human guinea pig.

Dr. Henry learned that Dr. Henry Bazett, the great physiologist at the University of Pennsylvania, had proposed the use of a counterpressure vest together with inflatable trousers for high-pressure breathing. Jim Henry finally put together a makeshift outfit which combined the ideas of Bazett, Dr. D. R. Drury, professor of physiology at the University of Southern California, and a number of other workers in the field. The resulting hodgepodge was submitted to trial first in breathing tests at ground level, then in an altitude chamber.

Dr. Henry was understandably terrified the first time he stepped into an altitude chamber. Mainly, his "protective" clothing consisted of a pair of modified canvas puttees, laced tightly about the calves of his legs; light nylon-web tights, form-fitted and extending from his waist to his knees, also laced tightly against his flesh; a suit of antigravity coveralls—fitted from the waist down to his ankles with a bladder that could be inflated for additional pressure —which was worn over the other units; an inflatable pressure vest developed by the Royal Canadian Air Force, worn on top of the coveralls; and finally, a sealed pressure-breathing helmet.

The outfit, when inflated at altitude, was quaint: it made Dr. Henry look like a huge lopsided balloon. But it worked with a fair amount of efficiency and set the pressure-suit research program moving in the right direction. This pleased Dr. Henry, but it didn't make him any happier about continuing to be locked inside an altitude chamber.

Essentially, such chambers are big airtight tanks with windows that allow the control operators to observe the subject or subjects, as the case may be. Observation of the chamber interior is exceptionally important. If anything should go wrong with the subject's breathing or safety equipment at "altitude," an operator must immediately bring him "down" to a life-sustaining pressure level. This is done by rapidly dumping air back into the chamber through a big, specially designed quick-acting valve. Air can be withdrawn from a chamber at varying rates to simulate an ascent to altitude.

Nowadays, altitude chambers are used matter-of-factly as training tools for astronauts and pilots. But when Jim Henry first stepped inside a chamber, he wasn't at all sure of what was going to happen.

The then unproved theory of Dr. Bazett was that counterpressure against strategic parts of the body would be the corrective for high-high-altitude emergency decompression situations. A series of experiments by Dr. Henry with rats, cats, and dogs seemed to bear out the theory. He had found through these animal experiments that the lungs could take any amount of internal pressure so long as the chest was tightly bandaged.

Gradually, Dr. Henry accustomed himself to higher and higher altitudes. His makeshift counterpressure suit seemed to be working reasonably well. He finally reached 50,000 feet without any disturbance of his physical well-being. About this time, the Lockheed Aircraft Company was preparing to produce a new turbojet airplane. The engineers wanted to know if a pilot in a counterpressure suit could survive at 55,000 feet. They asked Dr. Henry to try such an experiment.

At 7:15 on the evening of November 16, 1944, Dr. James P. Henry sat down in a low-pressure chamber for an hour of preoxygenation before his unprecedented flight. Preoxygenation may be an impressive-sounding word, but all it means, really, is saturating your blood cells and tissues with 100 percent oxygen. This is accomplished at ground level and at lower altitudes, so your blood and tissues will be holding much more than their normal amount of oxygen by the time you reach a critical altitude, where that higher blood and tissue oxygen content considerably increases your tolerance to the oxygen-rare air. Dr. Henry was intending to better the request of the Lockheed people by going to 58,000 feet, an altitude dangerously near that where his blood could boil from the warmth of his own body. So he was very careful about the length of the preoxygenation period. He had found previously that an hour was long enough to allow the pure oxygen to rid his tissues of their store of nitrogen—a gas that causes the painful, sometimes lethal, bends.

He patiently sat in the chamber, absorbing pure oxygen at sea level, then at 10,000 feet, at 15,000 feet, 20,000 feet, and progressively higher. By 7:55 P.M. the pressure inside his suit was equivalent to that at 40,000 feet. By 8:15 he was ready for the "ascent" to top altitude. About twenty-five minutes later he reached the peak and began to feel ill. It was not incapacitating, however. By now he was used to operating in the fuzzy restricted world of acute oxygen lack.

According to Wright Air Development Center's Technical Report 393, now declassified, "the chamber altitude was then kept constant at 58,000 feet. The subject was somewhat anoxic but he was able to carry out routine tasks such as taking his pulse and adjusting mask and suit pressures and he responded satisfactorily to the observers' requests for information. His condition did not differ materially from that he usually exhibited when at 43–44,000 feet, breathing oxygen at ambient pressure."

Nine minutes later, however, the situation changed dramatically.

Dr. Henry had been alternately sitting and standing, swinging his arms and writing on a note pad to demonstrate the flexible freedom of movement allowed by his pressure suit, when he noticed the observers at the chamber windows gesturing wildly. They were pointing toward his right hand. He glanced down quickly. It was swelling like a balloon before his eyes. He felt no pain, but the spectacle was alarming. Even as he watched, his left hand also began to expand in size. Steadily and swiftly the hands, seemingly no longer his own, blew up until they were nearly twice their normal dimensions.

After almost a half-minute of watching the strange phenomenon, the observers brought up the chamber pressure, taking him down to 40,000 feet in less than fifteen seconds. During this descent, his hands "deflated" with increased atmospheric pressure until they assumed their natural size and shape.

"It is doubtful whether a fluid swelling could develop so rapidly," Dr. Henry later said, "and it is even more dubious that it would vanish in a matter of a few seconds. . . . Moreover, when the evidence obtained by H. G. Armstrong [later Surgeon General of the Air Force] with living rabbits at 58,000 feet is considered, it becomes probable that the swelling was gaseous."

The obvious suggestion was that heat of the hands had caused the expansion of water vapor and the vestiges of nitrogen in the tissue fluid because the chamber's extremely low pressure was not sufficiently dense to resist such expansion. Since only the doctor's head, trunk, and legs were counterpressured—his arms and hands were unprotected—it followed that a method was demanded for pressurizing the body more completely.

A series of experiments with anesthetized cats and rabbits was begun. The animals' chests and abdomens were counterpressurized with miniature pressure vests, but all the limbs were left unprotected. Their heads were bandaged firmly to apply pressure. All the animals were taken up to 55,000 feet at least and kept at altitude for a half-hour. In every case, swelling of the limbs occurred due to expansion of gases in the tissues beneath the skin. The swelling always disappeared when the altitude was reduced to 40,000 feet and there were no harmful aftereffects to the muscles. Most important of all, there were no hemorrhages. The vest, applying counterpressure against the chest and abdomen, seemed to keep the blood within bounds. Thus Dr. Henry discovered that the swelling could be simply controlled by the use of tight-fitting gloves and sleeves of a nonstretchable material.

There remained, however, the problem of blood action at higher altitudes. No one had ever analyzed blood at extremes of altitude. Knowledge of the blood's ability to absorb oxygen in relationship

to its carbon-dioxide content at various atmospheric pressures had to be made available. It was generally accepted in the medical profession that 80 percent oxygen saturation of the red corpuscles was an absolute minimum for a normal person if he was to operate with any efficiency. So Dr. Henry, with one assistant, set about making the necessary analysis.

First, they developed a miniature modification of a new instru-

Training in zero gravity
is another chore that astronauts must bear.
They have to learn how to
maneuver their bodies and perform useful work
while in a gravity-free, or
weightless, condition—where everything
not tied down, including
themselves, floats uncontrollably.

Courtesy Wright Aerospace Medical Research Laboratories, USAF

ment that, superficially, at least, compared nicely with some of the more refined medieval torture devices. It was a long hollow spinal needle within which was fitted a finer hollow needle. The points of both needles were ground to match perfectly. A third, much thinner needle, called a stilette, was designed to fit neatly within the outer needle also.

Here's how the instrument worked: the first two telescoped needles were inserted into the radial artery of the wrist. The inside needle was then pushed in slightly farther, "to insure that the outer needle is also within the arterial wall." This was then determined by partially withdrawing the inner needle: if blood flowed easily through it, everything was fine. The bigger needle had to be inside the artery also. Next, the inner hollow needle was completely removed and the third needle, of solid steel wire, was slid into the first needle to act as a kind of plunger, plugging the flow of blood into the big needle. With the plunger in place, the instrument was then eased along inside the artery for a distance of one-half to a full inch and strapped down to the wrist with adhesive tape. Operation of the device was simple: at various intervals and altitudes, during a period of an hour or two in the chamber, the plunger was removed and a hypodermic inserted into the big outer needle to take a blood sample from the subject.

The subject, naturally, was Dr. James P. Henry or his co-worker in the chamber flights, a man named Eli Movitt. It got to the point, says Dr. Henry, where each of them could take his own blood samples without assistance.

Actually, the instrument proved to be extremely useful. Prior to it there was no easy way to analyze the condition of blood at a specific moment of altitude. It eliminated the necessity of inserting a series of blood-sampling needles into an artery at various intervals throughout a chamber flight—an especially difficult procedure at the very high altitudes, where the two experimenters were woozy from oxygen lack. With the careful use of novocain, claims Dr. Henry, the three-needle system becomes painless.

Out of the experiments Dr. Henry was able to draw up a chart showing the relationships among mask pressure, suit pressure, oxygen absorption by the blood, and altitude. By varying mask and suit pressures to keep the blood's oxygen saturation point above the 80 percent minimum at any altitude, a man could prevent fatal anoxia and remain efficiently conscious long enough to save himself in an emergency by descending to a denser part of the atmosphere.

As a result of these experiments, Dr. Henry was able to confirm that an earlier theoretical table giving the "proper" helmet pressures necessary for any selected chamber pressure (or external atmospheric pressure) would in fact accurately predict the amount

of oxygen that would be held in the blood each time. Hence the
physical condition of a subject—in terms of the ratio between
altitude pressure and helmet pressure—could be determined in advance.

The pressure differentials were now worked out. This left a single
question: how to design a suit that would be adjustable quickly
enough to meet the changing pressure-ratio requirements? For best
results, the suit should be self-activating. This presented an apparently formidable problem. But Dr. Henry was well on his way to
success.

His problem was solved when the doctor learned about an idea
being worked on by a Yale professor who was attempting to improve the bladder-type antigravity-force suits, or g-suits, as they
are commonly known to fliers. The professor, Dr. Harold Lamport,
was experimenting with inflatable tubes that were bound closely to
the suit's fabric by horizontal strips of nylon. When oxygen was
pumped through the flexible tubes they expanded against the nylon
strips, which were pushed away from the suit, stretching its fabric
and creating a surface tension across the body of the wearer. By
interlacing the nylon strips—like fitting the fingers of your hands
together and bending them over each other—along the whole length
of the tube, a strong even tension on the suit fabric was achieved
in all directions.

When lengths of tubing were fastened in this way around the
outer edges of a suit—from the ankles to the shoulders and along
the sleeves—the tension was effectively applied to the entire body,
including the arms. If the interlocking nylon strips were arranged
with a slight looseness, a variety of tensions was available as pressures within the tubes increased or decreased.

After much trial and error, the Aero Medical Laboratory of the
Army Air Corps, which took over the suit, developed a simple,
foolproof pressure-valving system, making the altitude-emergency
suit fully automatic. As external pressures lowered to a certain
point, the valves would open, inflating the tubes with just enough
oxygen to create a compensating tension, or protective counterpressure, against the body.

During 1945 and the first half of 1946, at the request of Colonel
Pharo Gagge, Dr. Henry practically commuted between Los Angeles
and Wright Field, near Dayton, Ohio. Each new improvement of
the suit that he accomplished in the laboratory at the University of
Southern California had to be demonstrated to the technical people
at the Wright Aero Medical Laboratory. Everybody was anxious to
have the emergency suit in a practical shape as soon as possible. The
rocket-powered Bell XS-1 airplane was already being given preliminary flight tests, and it promised to reach altitudes as well as

speeds hitherto only dreamed about. The Air Corps needed the suit as a protection for the XS-1 pilots.

Dr. Henry finally satisfied even the most skeptical engineers one day by sitting down in the stratosphere chamber at Wright Field after telling the control operator to take it up to its limit. The suit functioned perfectly at 95,000 feet.

The program was completed. Using special skin-tight gloves to prevent swelling of his hands, a high-flying pilot could now maneuver his aircraft to safety after loss of cabin pressure. He not only could move around and reach controls with ease while the suit was inflated, but he could also lift an arm high enough to touch the back of his head when at 50,000 feet. While pressurized, it wasn't the most comfortable kind of flight clothing available, but in terms of its purpose it was a satisfactory temporary solution to the serious problem of pressurized cabin failure. The Army Air Corps gave the suit the designation "S-1 Partial Pressure Suit."

Regardless of his successful work with altitude chambers, Dr. James Henry has no affection for them. "Familiarity might breed contempt," he once told me, "but if it's a choice between two poisons, I'll take the centrifuge anytime."

The fact is that centrifuges are more in his line than low-pressure chambers anyway. Although he didn't accomplish much in the acceleration field at the university, he became permanently attached to the Aero Medical Laboratory shortly after World War II and began to work with the centrifuge. Dr. Otto Gauer, world-famous German authority on the nature of blood and a pioneer in centrifuge investigations, had just come to the laboratory as scientist-in-residence for an extended period. Dr. Henry would be working with him.

A program of basic research had already been started at the laboratory by Dr. Gauer to investigate the distribution of blood in the veins and arteries of animals under extreme gravity pressures. In collaboration with Dr. Henry and five assistants, the program finally solved important riddles of negative and positive acceleration, leading directly to the development of equipment that today extends the endurance of man to these g-forces by roughly twice his normal capabilities.

When Henry and Gauer first collaborated, the general opinion of acceleration experts was that negative-gravity forces, or minus g's could not be endured beyond fractions of a second because they produced hemorrhages of the brain, with insanity or death resulting. Therefore, said the experts, there was no way of combating this kind of acceleration. In experiments dogs, rabbits, and monkeys appeared to hemorrhage, as the experimenters had predicted. Thus, no pilot would dare expose himself to negative g's. Aircraft then

were not even designed to maneuver in a way that would cause
negative-*g* loading. This obviously hampered a flier in the military
as well as in the experimental sense: he couldn't outmaneuver an
enemy in battle and he could neither make an outside turn nor
level off sharply at the end of a steep climb in a subsonic or
supersonic airplane. (The so-called sound barrier had just been
conquered, and already rocket-powered interceptor aircraft—which
normally would climb steeply and level off sharply—were being
considered.)

This conclusion about negative *g*'s was based on circumstantial
evidence, of course, for almost nothing was known then about the
behavior of the human heart, blood, or brain when they were subjected to high negative-*g* pressures.

Both negative and positive *g*'s are identical in nature. They are
distinguished only by the direction of their action upon a mammal
or upon a mechanical structure. Since structural stresses can easily
be compensated for in any direction by engineers, it's the human or
animal system that finally defines *g* action. A man leaping straight
up from a standing position is being subjected to positive *g*'s because gravity is pulling against him in a natural footward direction
—the force exerted is from the foot or away from the head. If the
same man's feet were lassoed and he were swung around in a circle,
head tilted toward the ground, he would be fighting negative *g*'s—
since centrifugal force would be pulling outwardly against gravity
and acting on him from the head, or away from the foot, a reverse
of the norm. A pilot is, of course, subject to positive and negative *g*'s.
Regardless of his angle or its direction—with two notable exceptions
—either positive or negative *g*'s will act upon him with a varying intensity that depends upon the rate of acceleration of his airplane or
spacecraft.

One of the exceptions is the effect caused by being whirled
around while the subject is lying stretched out flat on his back or
belly. The effect here is called a transverse *g*: the gravity pull is
from chest to back or from back to chest. The second exception is
the nullifying gravity effect of a Keplerian trajectory, or ballistic
curve—a flight path that curves over the top of a climb and downward in a free fall, caused by the uncontrolled inertial weight of
an airplane or spacecraft, just like a bullet or an artillery shell
falling over the top of a trajectory onto a target. The result is
zero *g* or weightlessness during the fall.

The ultimate difference between positive and negative *g*'s is the
difference between a man standing on his feet and on his head. In
the former case, his blood and all his organs are pulled toward his
feet. In the latter case, they are drawn toward his head.

Before the work of Gauer, Henry, and their associates at the

Aero Medical Laboratory, positive-*g* forces had been somewhat successfully coped with by the use of pressure tights. When blood is pulled away from the brain, blackout or unconsciousness results. By pressurizing the abdomen and legs sufficiently, blood is forced to remain above the diaphragm and enough of it stays in the chest to feed the heart the proper amount needed for the maintenance of consciousness, as the heart keeps pumping it into the brain. No similar method, however crude, had been developed to stop the blood from slamming into the brain from the lower part of the body, as happens with negative *g*'s. Nor was it known in precise detail why the pressure tights and various self-protective pilot maneuvers were effective aids against positive *g*'s.

Several years of imaginative hard work with two centrifuges gave Drs. Henry and Gauer the answers to many mysteries. What they came up with, finally, amazed even them: the human body had hidden its secrets well from previous physiologists—it acted, under the pressures of motion and gravity, in a manner almost exactly opposite to that which had been assumed.

Dr. Henry's description of riding a centrifuge is simple, brief, and very graphic:

It feels as if you're lying under a couple of elephants. When you're subjected to extremely high g's while lying flat, there is a dull ache in your chest. You can't breathe properly. Almost exactly, I suspect, the feeling of a heart attack. With negative g's instead of pain in the chest, your sinuses and eyes ache terribly. When you get a good positive g, everything starts to go. You feel yourself fainting, because of the rapid drop in blood pressure. The signal lights in front of you fade out and in again, as you momentarily lose your vision and consciousness blurs.

But if you go up to a certain g-level, where the lights just black out, and if you are willing to wait without signaling the operator to slow you down, then the lights may come on again and stay quite clear. You've become adjusted to that g. The operator, after a few seconds, will ask through your headphones whether he should step things up a bit. You say, Okay. And he tries another half-g. And so it goes.

The early g-runs we made were all under fifteen seconds duration, because the acceleration produced by airplanes of that period lasted for a short time only. Now we take it more gradually and for longer periods, to correspond with the longer turns that must be made by the newest jet and rocket aircraft. The longer tests are more rigorous and continue for two or three minutes, until the subject is unconscious.

Among the subjects tested through four years of concentrated experimentation were fifty human volunteers and twenty-three goats and dogs. The entire second half of the program was devoted to the development of devices for protection against negative acceleration. This was more or less routine work. It was the first two years that were difficult. As Dr. Henry was previously quoted: "The

tricky part was to be sure that the blood vessels of the brain weren't
breaking at the same time" as the eyes were hemorrhaging. Nobody
knew, when the program was started, just how many negative g's
it would take to rupture the blood vessels of a human brain. It was
soon discovered that at two and a half minus-g's the blood vessels
of the eyes began to burst. At minus three g's these hemorrhages
were extreme. Other symptoms were a considerable slowing of the
pulse rate, indicating retarded heart action, puffiness of the face,
mental confusion, and intense headaches that lasted anywhere from
a half-day to two days. All of these effects increased in violence
with an increase of exposure time to the same negative-gravity
forces.

Until more specific data were gathered, Drs. Henry and Gauer
felt that two and a half negative g's endured for five seconds or less
must be considered the maximum of human tolerance. In order not
to risk the lives of their volunteer subjects, they carried on their
experiments from here with animals. Goats were used at first because in physical size they approximated a man. Dogs were later
used, since their respiratory system was similar to man's. All
animals were anesthetized before centrifuge runs to prevent pain
and for ease of instrumentation.

Early in the series of tests an important discovery was made:
animals subjected to high negative g's for long periods were dying
from asphyxia: their sinuses and lungs were being blocked by a
gross swelling of the mucous membrane, epiglottis, and tongue.
Those that did not die remained in a stuporous state for one to two
days, recovering from the anesthetic with extreme slowness. Therefore a breathing tube was attached surgically to an animal's wind-
pipe, and the animal was subjected to fifteen negative g's for thirty
seconds. Not only did it survive the run, but it showed neither
hemorrhages nor major ill effects. The swelling of its tissues returned
to normal. This information contradicted the earlier theory that
negative g's caused brain hemorrhage.

But there were other equally terrifying aspects to negative acceleration. Although Drs. Gauer and Henry had determined finally
that the boxlike skull containing the brain supplied enough counterpressure to prevent hemorrhaging, they had not yet been able to
solve the enigma of blood pressure itself. Swelling of the veins and
arteries caused by negative g's was a seriously dangerous condition.
It was responsible for violent pain in the eyes and sinuses, which
would incapacitate a pilot. It also led to an erratic action of the
heart. In some instances, the heart would not only skip beats and
slow down, but would stop entirely for a moment until a new surge
of blood through it would start it up again. Obviously, such a condition, if extended over a long interval, could be fatal.

Furthermore, it must be emphasized that the blood pressure increases with the duration: exactly the same g-force causes a steady mounting of pressure in the head veins the longer it is sustained. You cannot tell that damage is being done before some damage has occurred.

This made things difficult for Gauer, Henry, and their associates. They started to search for a negative-g yardstick. The logical first step was to determine the nature of the circulatory system. Borrowing a page from the textbooks of hydraulic engineering, the circulation of human blood can be compared to a closed hydraulic system. Their premise for a yardstick automatically followed. It was what the engineers called a "hydrostatic column."

This theory of hydrostatic columns had been assumed by all research workers in the field of gravity forces. They felt that the longer the column, the greater would be the pressure developed at its bottom end. It is a known fact that the veins in the feet and calves swell into a firm bulge when a person stands upright for any length of time in warm weather. And the taller the person, the greater is the swelling. The hydrostatic column from foot to heart, through which the blood must rise to return for recirculation, is so long that the pressure in the foot veins must be over two pounds per square inch to send the blood upward.

The same thing holds true for both positive and negative g's. If the person is stood on his head, his face will become red and swollen: he'll feel mighty uncomfortable. The column from heart to head is about one foot long, yet this is a sufficient length to make the veins in the eyes, eyelids, and sinuses swell annoyingly, even at one negative g.

If the hydrostatic-column theory of the blood vessels was valid, as all workers in the field had believed it to be, then by simply varying his posture a person's tolerance to gravity forces should increase or decrease by a predictable amount. If a person were placed on his back or his belly, the pull of gravity would be at right angles to the hydrostatic blood column. The negative or positive g's would be transformed into a transverse g-force and pressure would be uniformly distributed along the system, between the heart and the head or between the heart and the feet, thus permitting freer circulation.

Dr. Gauer had shown much earlier that either a full prone or full supine position of the body would triple human tolerance to positive g's. He and Dr. Henry now studied a long-held theory: that as the body was tilted backward through an arc its tolerance would progressively increase. Their assumption was that a 60-degree tilt would exactly double human tolerance to negative gravity— since the effective hydrostatic blood-column length should be reduced by one-half. Since they had set the safe limit for human endurance of negative *g*'s at five seconds of two and a half *g*'s, a 60-degree backward tilt should increase tolerance to five negative *g*'s for five seconds.

The only way to measure blood pressure under negative-*g* conditions was directly in the vein itself. Three men, including Drs. Henry and Gauer, volunteered as guinea pigs. Their test instruments were essentially simple: an aluminum chair with a movable back and seat and a miniature manometer invented by Dr. Otto Gauer. The chair was bolted to the platform floor of a centrifuge. The manometer, connected to one end of a tiny glass chamber with a hypodermic needle at its other end, was inserted into the supra-orbital vein of the forehead. As the hypodermic needle punctured the forehead vein, the glass chamber filled with blood at normal pressure. Then as gravity pressure increased on the vein, an additional flow of blood entered the chamber and compressed the blood already there. This change in pressure was recorded by an electrical signal from the manometer. Fluctuations of the chamber-blood compression were analogous to negative-gravity force fluctuations in the supraorbital vein.

It was the first successful device of its kind. Previously, with only the standard large blood-pressure gauges available, the direct measurement of venous pressure at the exact spot desired had been impossible. No anesthesia was used on the human subjects in this centrifuge experiment. Their reactions to pain from negative-gravity weights were a valuable aspect of the investigation.

There are undoubtedly many more pleasant ways to spend one's time than whirling madly on a centrifuge with a needle stuck into one's forehead; yet Dr. Henry, Dr. Gauer, and an associate sweated it out through a series of runs in a variety of body positions. Their exposure to acceleration was for fifteen seconds in every case. Each time, the number of negative gravity forces was increased by one-half *g*, ranging from zero to three *g*'s.

What they learned was very discouraging.

Dr. Henry sums it up quietly: "The results were unexpected. . . . Tilting [the chair] gave no clear advantage, even when the backward inclination was sixty degrees. The subjective sensations confirm this for the discomfort was as severe when tilted at any particular acceleration as when seated upright."

Jim Henry and Otto Gauer rigged up a new device. The aluminum chair was attached to a motor-driven gun turret, which was then anchored to the centrifuge platform. In this way, the subject could be revolved in his chair while the centrifuge was spinning. A whole range of blood pressures could be recorded as he was turning over slowly from front to back and through all the angles in between.

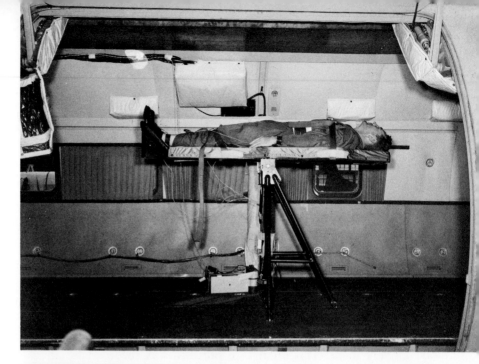

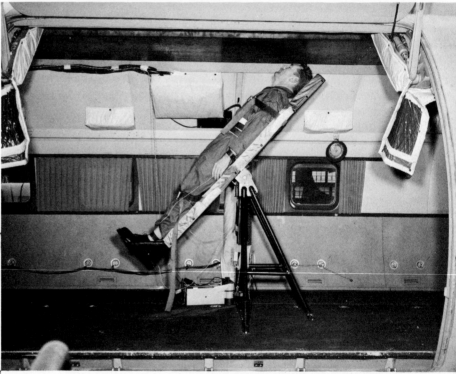

The tilt table, shown here in four of its basic positions,
is another device of refined torture.
It is used to obtain cardiovascular research data from subjects
undergoing motion stresses while in states
of both zero gravity and high acceleration of gravity forces.
The subject, fully instrumented,
is strapped to the table, which is bolted to the deck of an aircraft.

*As the airplane goes through zero-g dives
and highly accelerated pullups or turns, the table
is tilted through a 180-degree arc.
The process can be reversed,
or stopped at will by the operator.*

Courtesy Don Bowen, Group Leader/Pressure Suits, 6570th
Aerospace Medical Research Laboratory, USAF

An essential requirement was, again, the poking of a long instrumented needle into a big forehead vein.

With this machine a continuous record could be obtained of every shifting gravity effect on the brain. Earlier, using the chair alone, the records had been spasmodic: each run on the centrifuge had to be accomplished at a fixed, if different, body angle. The new runs produced some interesting phenomena. When the subject began his rotation from a position on his back with legs in the air, his forehead blood pressure reached a higher peak as he was turned through an upright sitting posture than it did when he started rotation on his belly with legs hanging down.

Drs. Gauer and Henry knew now that the lower part of the body had to be involved; the answer was definitely in the legs.

A subject lying on his back or belly experienced less negative-g discomfort in his head than when he was sitting up, as the two doctors had already guessed. What they had not guessed at was the far-reaching effect of negative gravity. When a person was subjected to negative-g weights with his legs in line with his trunk, blood flowed steadily into his trunk, until the vessels of his legs were practically empty and the increased volume of blood in his trunk then added more pressure to his heart. This in turn caused an increase of pressure to the brain as he sat upright. But if he was bent double at the hips so that the blood remained trapped in the venous reservoir of his legs, its addition to the total blood column could be temporarily prevented and thus the pressure at head level would be lessened.

The hydrostatic blood-column theory had not been wrong, as this discovery proved. In their original theory, the doctors simply had not extended the blood column to its proper length—the entire body, rather than just the distance between heart and head.

They demanded absolute proof that their discovery was correct. So they bound a subject's legs tightly with tourniquets as high up the thighs as possible, to hold back venous blood flow from the extremities to the heart, and rotated him on the gun-turret merry-go-round. The needle in his forehead vein now registered the same pressure for the posture with the legs bent double as for the legs-stretched-out position. More importantly, vascular pressure in the head was generally reduced. By isolating the venous blood of the legs from the rest of the pressure column under the impact of negative g's, human tolerance could be increased.

Following this proof, an intense effort was made to tie up the loose ends of the experiment. By analyzing the complex relationships between blood volume and arterial and venous pressure in terms of the effective length of the hydrostatic blood column, Drs. Gauer and Henry were able to lay the foundation for swift development of protective anti-g devices and clothing.

Their original discovery that negative gravity forces produce death by suffocation, or oxygen starvation, rather than by cerebral hemorrhage, meshed perfectly with Dr. Henry's earlier high-altitude experiments. It was found that an ordinary pressurized helmet would more than double a man's tolerance to negative *g*'s. Using such a helmet, a pilot in an upright sitting position can now endure five negative *g*'s for ten seconds with no ill effects—not even the minor effect of tiny blood vessels bursting in the eyes. The latter effect, for unprotected persons, occurs after five seconds of two and a half negative *g*'s.

By using inflatable pressure cuffs on his thighs, a pilot can increase the five-negative-*g* limit somewhat farther. As for positive-*g* endurance, the safe limit is quite a bit higher. Thanks to the pioneering work of men like Drs. Gauer and Henry, the modern *g*-suit is designed with all counterpressure points carefully located for most effective protection. A pilot today can easily withstand six or seven positive-*g* weights without blacking out. This is equivalent to the gravity forces that an astronaut must absorb for any length of time in accelerating away from the earth's gravity pull.

In fact, it was the discoveries of Drs. Henry and Gauer that led directly to the design of form-fitting astronaut couches. These couches are built to hold astronauts in the most effective body position to endure the impact of *g*-forces after rocket-booster lift-off and acceleration to orbital or escape velocity.

Another aerospace medical pioneer, who contributed much to the design of restraining belts for astronauts strapped into their couches, was Colonel John Paul Stapp. When most medical scientists were not even faintly concerned with the gravity problems of sending men into orbit around the world, Colonel Stapp was already pondering the question of how best to launch men entirely away from the earth's gravity pull and send them safely on their way to the moon and planets. Here's how he summarized his work before a group of eminent engineers and scientists:

Tolerance to high g applied in the transverse axis to the human body for several seconds, and of lower g for several minutes, must be determined in order to find configurations of propulsion that are feasible for rocket flight to escape velocity out of the earth's atmosphere.

On December 10, 1954, three months after he made that revolutionary statement, Colonel Stapp performed an experiment designed to provide at least some of the required data. At Holloman Air Force Base in New Mexico, where he was Chief of the Aero Medical Field Laboratory, Stapp rode a rocket sled down 3,500 feet of track at 632 miles an hour—and was braked to a stop in less than one and a half seconds. This was like stopping on a dime after accelerating to nine-tenths the speed of sound.

Colonel Stapp had begun his rocket-sled experiments eight years before at Muroc in the Mojave Desert of California. There he had a 2,000-foot track for the sled. His first run was slow— ninety miles an hour—with a slow stop at the end. He experienced no ill effects, only a few stiff muscles. By the time he had gotten up to 150 miles per hour with a quick stop in 19 feet, he'd experienced several minor brain concussions, twice within a year fractured his right wrist, fractured a rib, acquired one splitting headache that lasted three days, and suffered a hemorrhage of his right retina which left a small blind spot in his field of vision for a number of days.

Before he ever rode on a rocket sled himself, however, Colonel Stapp made some ninety experiments with chimpanzees and hogs. Since the rocket-powered sled at Muroc was the first of its kind in the world, a series of animal tests was necessary to check out the system—and also to determine the best kinds of protection.

Properly strapped in, to prevent collision with solid objects, the animals held up very well. According to Colonel Stapp: "The maximum deceleration sustained by a chimpanzee was from 169 miles per hour to a stop in 18 feet in the supine head-first position. It is many times what would be encountered in any automobile collision or plane crash, short of complete demolition of the vehicle."

Following the chimp tests, and in order to evaluate the death-dealing qualities of impact, a series of tests was conducted with anesthetized hogs. "Uninjured survival of anesthetized hogs," says Stapp, "occurred in all experiments up to 80 g's in the backward-facing seated position and up to 125 g's in the forward-facing seated position."

Then the animals were tested using only a partial harness or none whatever. "The same gravity forces," continues the colonel, "that could easily be sustained without injury while the subject was restrained with webbing, now produced fatality when the subject was impinged (or thrown) against solid test objects."

The conclusion appeared to be firm: an efficient system of safety belts could save lives under extreme crash conditions. It seemed to Colonel Stapp that "crash survival, or the survival of a highly accelerated take-off, does not depend upon the human body's ability to withstand the force applied, but upon its ability to withstand the mangling effects of the device which is housing it as that device is destroyed by these same forces."

This discovery of John Paul Stapp in a California desert led straight to the development of automobile safety belts and the improvement of then existing seat belts for airplanes. It also led directly to the safety harnesses now worn by military jet pilots and astronauts.

According to Stapp, in terms of the development of new crash-proof seats, safety belts, and ejection devices, his research has saved the government "from fifty to a hundred million dollars in the cost of redesigning aircraft alone." In the past, many high-speed aircraft have had to be partially rebuilt to accommodate new safety devices. The colonel had obtained enough data on all kinds of acceleration-deceleration forces so that such devices can now be incorporated in every new airplane design from the beginning. Today this is equally true of the design of manned spacecraft.

The man who discovered Colonel Stapp while he was an Air Force captain was Colonel Henry M. Sweeney, better known to his Air Force medical colleagues as Mike. Colonel Sweeney, another great pioneer in aerospace medicine, initiated a tradition which is now standard operating procedure: that it is obligatory for every project engineer or scientist in the Air Force medical research field to be his own test leader. He must be the first human to try out any new developments in his own project, regardless of how hazardous or painful these might be. Mike Sweeney's theory was that such an approach would tremendously build morale. A project leader would have no trouble getting volunteers for an experiment if he showed everybody that he wasn't afraid to take the first chance himself. The theory proved to be correct.

In this way, he inspired volunteers to ride the ejection towers and also to make live tests of a prototype ejection seat. A practical ejection seat had become an urgent requirement if flyers were to escape safely from a damaged aircraft. The speeds of military airplanes were becoming so great that it was impossible for an airman to bail out in the ordinary sense of stepping over the side, falling, and pulling the ripcord of his parachute. So Colonel Sweeney pushed hard for a foolproof ejection seat that could be exploded out of and away from a crippled aircraft. The idea was that the man riding in the seat could then kick it away from him and open his parachute to descend safely to the ground.

Actually, things were not as simple as all that. The one factor that had kept everybody from shooting a man out of a near-supersonic (and later, supersonic) airplane was a stubborn quirk of gravity. No mystery attended this stalemating quirk of gravity: its mechanism was all too clear. On earth, gravity is acceleration at the rate of thirty-two feet per second *per second*. This means that its action upon any object, regardless of weight, increases in multiple stages with the time required to draw that object to the earth's surface.

During the first second, gravity pulls an object downward thirty-

two feet. During the next second, the pull is sixty-four feet (in addition to the first thirty-two feet). At the third second, it is ninety-six feet. The fourth second increases the downward velocity to 128 feet (plus the total of all previous distances of drop). And so on.

Of course there are minor hindrances to gravity's accelerating pull on a falling body, such as atmospheric density, which resists an object's fall, and centrifugal rotation, which sets up counterforces. But gravity is always a tough opponent.

All animal life on earth, including the human, has adapted itself physiologically to one g, or the accelerating force of earth's gravity. Therefore, the movement of arms and legs is no problem, because of the balance between muscular power and the power that draws against it at a steady thirty-two feet per second per second. Only when one g is exceeded—as it can be with the application of additional power, such as that supplied by an automobile, airplane, or rocket engine—do problems arise. These problems increase many-fold with an increase in speed. The faster an object is accelerated away from the pull of gravity, the greater is the multiplication of gravity forces against that object.

In the case of the ejection seat, things were even more complicated: there was the acceleration of the airplane as well as the acceleration of gravity to overcome. By using a sufficiently powerful explosive charge, the seat could easily be ejected fast enough to overcome all obstacles. The only trouble was that a human being sitting in the seat might not be able to survive the terrific g forces that would be generated. There was the important matter of "jolt," a unit that has since been renamed "stapp," in honor of Colonel Stapp's great contributions toward an understanding of the nature

This later version of the X-15 full-pressure helmet
was tested with the suit on a dummy during a high-speed rocket-sled run
at Edwards Air Force Base in the Mojave Desert of California.
Acceleration and wind
blast didn't bother the helmet,
but right arm of the suit was badly ripped, causing it to lose
pressurization. Luckily a dummy was riding the sled:
note also that its hand ripped through glove and its forearm was torn
through suit sleeve, both twisted at right angles to its shoulder.
From tests like this the weak points of personal equipment
for fliers and spacemen can be noted and design changes made to
overcome the defects and increase the safety factors.
The test shown here was made just a year before the first manned
flight of the rocket-powered X-15.

Courtesy Don Bowen, Group Leader/Pressure Suits, 6570th
Aerospace Medical Research Laboratory, USAF

*The subject in this test may look bored, but he's not:
he's trying to concentrate on communicating
through his helmet microphone with experimenters outside
his anechoic chamber while being blasted
with noise from the cluster of loudspeakers in front of him.
Since chamber is echoless, the full blast
of 135 decibels strikes him directly.
Purpose was to test the soundproof qualities
of the newest X-20 helmet.*

Courtesy Don Bowen, Group Leader/Pressure Suits, 6570th Aerospace
Medical Research Laboratory, USAF

of acceleration and deceleration. This unit measures the rate of
change of acceleration in terms of time. For instance, accelerating
to ten g's within a half-second would be twice as severe as reaching
ten g's within one second.

Mike Sweeney's big puzzler lay in finding a method by which to
extend the time of acceleration without reducing the speed required
to fire a man out of a hurtling aircraft before the tail assembly
caught up with him and struck him. The acceleration required to
reach the needed speed was sixty-five feet per second per second.
Sweeney was hoping to achieve this on a minimum number of g's
at a jolt rate of two hundred to three hundred stapps per second.

Everybody on the project, especially First Sergeant Lawrence
Lambert, the man who was going to be ejected from an airplane in
the first experimental seat, knew the odds against him—but they
all worked like mad ants. Finally they came up with a light-enough
seat and an explosive charge they felt would do the trick. The day
before the first live ejection test, Mike Sweeney demonstrated the
seat in a ride on the upward acceleration tower at Wright Field.
He wanted to show Sergeant Lambert that there was nothing to
worry about—a man who is relaxed and confident has a much better
chance for survival than one who is doubtful and hesitant. The fact
is that something did go wrong, but because of Sweeney's stoicism
and courage the sergeant never knew that anything was amiss.

Sweeney sat down in the tower seat, not noticing that a valve
had been activated in the inflatable seat cushion, and strapped himself in. He gave the ready signal and the seat shot like a missile to
the top of the tower. Before he knew what was happening, he was
struck with thirty-three g's at nearly eighteen thousand stapps per
second.

"I felt that I had to yell, it was so painful. I even felt justified in
yelling. But I didn't. If I could help it, I wasn't going to give any
emotional hint that something was wrong—there were too many
volunteers, as well as the project man who was going to ride the seat,
down there watching me. So I put my thumb and forefinger together
in a circle, the Okay symbol, and waved my hand to indicate that
everything was just fine. I came on down gritting my teeth.

"That inflated cushion put me high enough above the seat-pan—
which was designed at that time for a flat, thin cushion—so that
I was left pretty far behind the seat at the start of the ejection. The
seat just came up, already accelerating at a good rate, while I
was literally sitting still. By the time it had squashed me down
into the cushion, I was forced to take a considerably higher jolt
than was planned by the explosive charge, in order to catch up
with it."

The error was corrected immediately, and Sergeant Lambert

made a calm and successful ejection the next day. Mike Sweeney spent at least ten days recuperating from severe internal injuries.

During the following few years, ejection-seat cartridges and catapults were so well refined that their jolt factor averaged only from 150 to 200 stapps per second—a fraction of the maximum jolts originally encountered. In fact, three years after the first live ejection (made in August 1946), an assistant of Mike Sweeney's, Captain Vince Mazza, proposed a program of ejection-seat tests at very high altitudes in order to study the tumbling characteristics of the then current seats. What he learned has contributed much to the success of escape systems used in present-day stratospheric aircraft and cemented the foundation of the escape systems now employed on manned spacecraft.

The styles of self-inflicted torture may vary with the project in aerospace medical research, but they have one thing common among them: a payoff of safety and survival for high-flying aircrews and space-flying astronauts.

Chapter 6

FROM BRAS TO BRITCHES

If the history of space-suit development could be inscribed on a coin, it would be the most lopsided coin ever minted. Heavy with trial and torture on one side, its other side would be light with a curious humor. For the builders (and often the designers) of early pressure suits were companies that manufactured ladies' corsets and girdles. A few of the companies were noted for the production of baby-formula bottle nipples, teething rings, and other rubber products such as automobile and airplane tires. At least one of the companies learned how to engineer high-quality brassieres from experience acquired in building g-suits and pressure suits. This was a unique switch.

The pressure-suit-turned-bra-manufacturer was the David Clark

Company of Worcester, Massachusetts. Mr. Clark himself, now retired, put it this way to me:

We began making bras in 1947, after we had been in the g-suit and pressure-suit business for some eight years. Designing bras was fairly easy. It's another g problem, a weight-supporting problem, that's all. . . .

"In the early days, an anti-g 'suit' was only an inflatable rubber vest to pressurize the chest or a pair of dungaree britches with bladders to protect the thighs and legs. Sort of like the *bandeaux* that women used to wear underneath their breasts.

After the war was well underway, I found out that Berger Brothers, which was the Spencer Corset Company, was making anti-g suits for the Navy. They were the real pioneers in the g-suit field. . . . The Berger Brothers' anti-g suit really worked—but it was heavy, weighed something like thirty pounds. All the David Clark Company did was come along with a three-pound suit. We merely took out the complexities that were in the Berger Brothers' suit. They had a lot of rubber hot-water-bottle-type bladders tied together with tubes for inflation. We got around this by making our bladders of vinyl-coated parachute nylon and shaping them in an odd configuration that fitted the body of the wearer. The suit itself we made of ordinary nylon. . . .

"The Berger Brothers' suit was replaced by the Clark suit. And they got very, *very* tired of the whole rat race. They got to make some suits on military contract, but they had to make our kind of suit, to our specifications—after having been the real pioneers in the field. It kind of took the heart out of them, I think."

The whole business of developing and making anti-g suits and high-altitude pressure suits was a heartbreaking business during the decade-plus between 1939 and 1950. At least one suit experimenter was killed in the line of duty within the decade—although the cause of his death was not a defective suit, but a malfunctioning aircraft as he was returning from live tests of a full-pressure suit. Yet that decade was—for the United States, at least—the keystone in the development of protective clothing for both stratospheric airplane pilots and future space-going astronauts.

This was evident from an official report—"Case History of Pressure Suits"—first classified restricted and then upgraded to confidential:

The [Army] Air Forces began to develop high altitude pressure suits as early as 1939. . . . Three companies—the B. F. Goodrich Company, the Goodyear Tire and Rubber Company, and the United States Rubber Company—were working on these suits and on anti-g suits.

As early as 1939 the plan was to combine both suits into one if the suits proved practicable. Dr. [Vannevar] Bush [later the Chief Scientist of the United States] suggested appropriate action to promote a pressure-suit development program and offered the cooperation of NACA [National Advisory Committee for Aeronautics]. During the latter part of 1940 the Matériel Command [of the U. S. Army Air Forces], Wright Field, executed two contracts: one with the B. F. Goodrich Company, Akron, Ohio, for one experimental high-altitude pressure suit; and one with the United States Rubber Company, Mishawaka, Indiana, for two experimental pressure suits.

The B. F. Goodrich Company was, because of the foresight and inventiveness of Wiley Post, the American pioneer in building high-altitude pressure suits. Basically, the United States Rubber Company and the Goodyear Tire and Rubber Company were newcomers in a field that was then so new that it was open to all comers. Among the prominent companies of the decade who tried to win that race were the already mentioned corset and brassiere manufacturers plus a producer of women's girdles and babies' milk bottles, the Playtex Division of International Latex, and the Arrowhead Rubber Products Company, a subsidiary of the Federal Mobile Bearings Company, at Long Beach, California.

That was the essential line-up in America for the 1940's. But working behind all of them, conceiving basic requirements and ideas, was the Aero Medical Laboratory of the Army Air Forces' Matériel Command at Wright Field near Dayton, Ohio. The laboratory's earliest approach to the problem of high-altitude flying, apart from the simple concept of pressurized breathing of pure oxygen —where the oxygen was pumped into the lungs under pressure and had to be exhaled forcibly, the opposite of normal breathing—was the full-pressure suit. In essence, this is the space suit of today— taken to a much more sophisticated level in its engineering design. But in those days, there were apparently insurmountable problems.

Again quoting from the confidential "Case History of Pressure Suits":

Until World War II, according to Air Forces Technical Report Number 5769, the design of full-pressure suits had almost completely sacrificed mobility in order to deliver oxygen under pressure sufficient to maintain life at very high altitudes. The Report stated that "basically, all attempts to develop equipment around the principle of full pressurization for survival at altitude [had] failed because of the inability to resolve the fundamental paradox of adequate mobility at high pressure." The Report further stated that "it would be extremely unwise and most unfair to state categorically that the fully inflated suit [might] never be used at high pressures for long periods of time (4–6 hours)."

Meanwhile, the Aero Medical Laboratory continued to set up design goals and award contracts for the development of experimental high-altitude full-pressure suits. Code name of the project

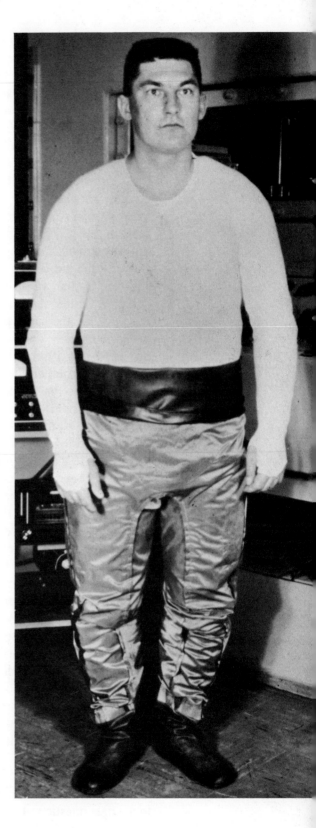

*Designed and built by the
David Clark Company, a brassiere
manufacturer at the time,
this odd-looking full-pressure suit
protected a rocket pilot
on a flight to what was then called
the edge of space.
Lieutenant Colonel Marion E. Carl
of the U. S. Marine Corps
wore the suit while he climbed
to 83,235 feet above
California's Mojave Desert in the
D-558-II, commonly known
as the Douglas Skyrocket, on August
21, 1953. The fabric and
seams of the suit's restraint layer show
a brassiere-making influence.*

Courtesy Don Bowen, Group Leader/Pressure Suits,
6570th Aerospace Medical Research Laboratory, USAF

*The word BRITCHES in
the title of this chapter was suggested
by the antigravity clothing
that was developed to protect pilots
in high-performance aircraft
who had to endure high changing rates
of gravity acceleration.
Subject here is modeling an anti-g
bladder for his belly and the
outer covering over bladders to keep
blood from pooling in his
thighs and legs. Later, similar bladders
were incorporated in high-altitude
pressure suits to provide
counterpressure against the low
atmospheric pressure of great heights.*

Courtesy Don Bowen, Group Leader/Pressure Suits,
6570th Aerospace Medical Research Laboratory, USAF

was MX-117. Suit designations were all preceded by an X, for "experimental." The project officer was Captain, later Major, John Kearby—an intense and dedicated person.

An indication of Kearby's high motivation in his job was given by Colonel A. Pharo Gagge, who was successively Acting Chief of the Aero Medical Laboratory and Chief of the Medical Research Division in the Office of the Air Surgeon General. During an informal interview at Washington, D.C., Colonel Gagge said: "In early December 1941, Captain Kearby came to me and asked my opinion on what effect 'supercharging' the air to the lungs would have on man's performance at altitude. Captain Kearby was interested in this procedure as an emergency one in case his full-pressure suit was damaged during flight at high altitude. . . .

"With the aid of Captain Kearby, the Goodrich Company made a rubber bladder to place around the chest wall. Around the bladder a rigid outer vest was placed and sealed by a zipper. Essentially this vest had the same principle as the [Professor John D.] Ackerman Vest which was used at the Mayo Clinic in the fall of 1942 and spring of 1943. This pressure vest was used with the blower unit of the compensated-metabolism apparatus and the pressure-breathing was made possible by a loaded exhalation valve on the vest. This system was used [successfully] at 50,000 feet for the first time around March 1942. . . .

"In the spring of 1943, Dr. [Henry] Bazett, of Toronto, and Captain A. R. Behnke, of Navy-Bethesda, visited Wright Field for the first Joint Services Pressure-Breathing Conference. At the time, considerable disbelief had been expressed by leading authorities in the field of respiration that pressure-breathing did any good at all, especially at the relatively low levels we were using. In reality our levels were much higher than that used by Dr. Alvin Barach, of Columbia [University], for [physical] therapy purposes. Dr. Barach was at this particular meeting.

"Demonstrations of pressure breathing under conditions of severe exercise at 48,000 feet were made by Captain Norman Molomut, of my staff, before the assembled group. The doubting Thomases still remained, as several [present] even questioned the accuracy of our [altitude-chamber] altimeters and even the [readings of our] mercury barometers. All calibrations later proved to be accurate."

Here was a classic example of a classic syndrome: the retardation of scientific progress by recognized authorities, who have clamped their bulldog minds shut around the "facts" that made their reputations.

At any rate, pressure-breathing was an interim emergency measure in the long climb upward among a mountain of evasive answers to a single question: How do you protect the lives of men who have

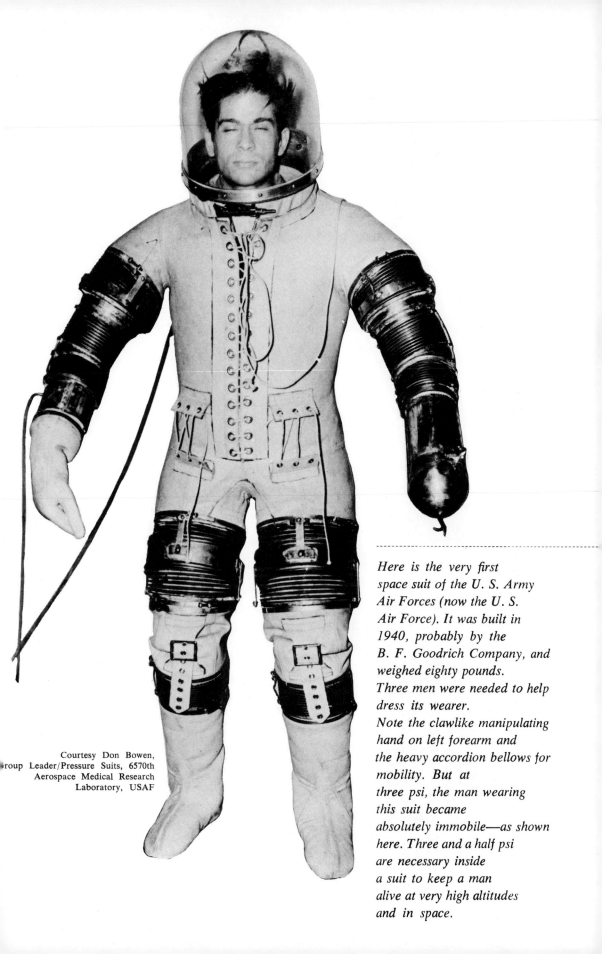

*Here is the very first
space suit of the U. S. Army
Air Forces (now the U. S.
Air Force). It was built in
1940, probably by the
B. F. Goodrich Company, and
weighed eighty pounds.
Three men were needed to help
dress its wearer.
Note the clawlike manipulating
hand on left forearm and
the heavy accordion bellows for
mobility. But at
three psi, the man wearing
this suit became
absolutely immobile—as shown
here. Three and a half psi
are necessary inside
a suit to keep a man
alive at very high altitudes
and in space.*

*The XH-1 full-pressure stratosphere suit
was first of a series of XH types
developed under Project MX-117 for the
U. S. Army Air Forces. Delivery
of seven suits costing $750 each was made by
the Goodyear Tire & Rubber Company
in November 1942. Major John Kearby, the
Pressure-Suit Project Engineer at
Wright Aero Medical Laboratory,
is pictured here wearing the XH-1. It
was designed for crew protection
in the unpressurized B-17 Flying Fortress.
Among its shortcomings were a lack
of ventilation, poor mobility,
and excessive bulkiness when inflated.
However, along with the XH-3 suit,
it became a serious contender
for operational use. The "X" stands
for "experimental" and the "H"
for "high altitude."*

Courtesy Don Bowen,
Group Leader/Pressure Suits, 6570th
Aerospace Medical Research
Laboratory, USAF

an urge to fly where the stars are brighter than they appear to be
from the earth?

For continuity, we must go back a few years in time. Toward the
close of 1941, two aircraft companies joined the ranks of the corset
and rubber-products manufacturers by expressing an active interest
in the development of full-pressure suits. Both approached the Matériel Division at Wright Field with their proposals.

The Boeing Aircraft Corporation (now simply called The Boeing
Company) had been working with Professor John Ackerman of the
University of Minnesota on the development of a high-altitude suit
that would protect the lives of air crews well beyond the region
where an oxygen mask—even with forced pressure-breathing—
could be effective. Professor Ackerman had designed, built, and
tested three such suits. The Ackerman pressure suits were successfully tested in 1942 and were given official approval by authorities
from Wright Field, the University of Minnesota, and the Mayo
Clinic. Yet so far as I could discover, nothing concrete ever came
of the Boeing suit as such. But some of its features were later incorporated into a combined high-altitude/anti-*g* suit. This resulted
from a standard approach of the Aero Medical Laboratory at Wright
Field. Their procedure was always to sift out the best qualities of any
design and put these together to achieve a higher-quality total product. Often these good-design qualities were patched in from the
experimental pressure suits of several companies.

The second airplane company to get into the space-suit business
was the Bell Aircraft Corporation (today called Bell Aerospace
Systems). Bell had been working on the development of the Air
Corps' P-39D fighter, a turbo-supercharged-engine airplane. They
proposed the concurrent development of a full-pressure suit so that
the fighter airplane could be piloted at extremely high (for that time)
altitudes. As their price to fabricate one prototype suit, they submitted to the Matériel Division a quotation of $12,695 (later volun-
tarily reduced to $7,051.76). Wiley Post's first pressure suit had
cost sixty-odd dollars.

Actually, the Ackerman-Boeing suit was funded for less than
the final cost of the Bell Aircraft suit. Boeing received five thousand
dollars from the Air Corps for their suit-development program, with
the stipulation that later "production" suits would be priced at only
a thousand dollars apiece. (That word "production" is set off in
quotes because until very recently every single full-pressure suit
produced had to be both handmade and hand-fitted.)

During 1942 and 1943 the dollar cost of experimental full-pressure suits ranged into six figures. Goodyear and Goodrich were
producing suits in the XH and X6 series of designations. All of these
were flight-tested by Major John Kearby and air crews in a B-17
Flying Fortress and other types of combat aircraft at the Air Prov-

A late model of the XH-2
somewhat resembled the XH-1,
but on close inspection
the many differences of its
features become obvious.
Examples: its boots are an
integral part of the suit
as are its gloves; knee and
shoulder joints are
less complicated, following
more closely the wearer's natural
form; and there is no
restraining bar across the chest
to resist ballooning: the
corrugations, or indentations,
in the rubber fabric
alongside the chest and the twin
cables extending up from the
crotch, across the chest,
and around the back of the head
do the job better with less
added weight. These three views
of the improved XH-2 illustrate both
its mobility when inflated
and its comfort to the wearer
when uninflated. But it still had
poor ventilation and was not
combatworthy in the B-17.

Courtesy Don Bowen,
Group Leader/Pressure Suits, 6570th
Aerospace Medical Research
Laboratory, USAF

ing Ground Command over Eglin Field on the west coast of Florida near Fort Walton Beach.

A classified report stamped "confidential" made the following comments on the efficacy of the XH-1, XH-2, XH-3, XH-3A, XH-3B, XH-5, and X-6B suits:

> *The officials conducting [all of] the tests concluded that not one suit was sufficiently mobile to warrant quantity production. At a meeting which followed the completion of these tests, the following opinions were expressed: (1) the Matériel Command believed it was time either to buy the suits as they were—or to close the project, and that the development [of the suits] had gone as far as possible at that time; (2) Goodrich was at least a year ahead of all other companies on pressure-suit development, having made one hundred and fifty models, none of which worked perfectly; (3) the Navy, though interested generally, had [then] no need for high-altitude suits; (4) the suit was not comfortable; (5) one suit should be kept for determining fatigue and metabolism characteristics and for characterizing movements [mobility] physiologically.*

Seventeen days later, the MX-117 (full-pressure suit) Project was canceled completely. The date was October 29, 1943.

Although the Army Air Forces (née Army Air Corps) had dropped all research and development work on high-altitude full-pressure suits, the U. S. Navy had actually much more than a "general" interest in perfecting this kind of protective clothing. The Navy started out actively in the field by working with the "Big Three" rubber companies: United States Rubber, Goodrich, and Goodyear. As early as September 1941, the Navy's Bureau of Aeronautics had asked the National Bureau of Standards to evaluate a kind of space suit produced by United States Rubber. The director of NBS, Dr. Lyman J. Briggs, submitted a single-spaced typewritten report of nine pages to the Bureau of Aeronautics, with the following summary of recommendations:

> *It was found that the mobility decreased rapidly with suit pressures in excess of 2 psi [pounds per square inch].*
> *Fire hazard was reduced and oxygen economy obtained by maintaining suit pressure and ventilation with air while the pilot is supplied with oxygen as needed through an extended two-stage demand system.*
> *Helmet fogging at low temperatures is avoided with adequate air supply to the helmet, provided that an oxygen mask which exhausts well into the suit is worn.*
> *The inlet and relief valves should be redesigned to have better flow characteristics.*

The suit was rather grotesque in appearance, but it led to a continuing series of improved Navy stratospheric suits that ultimately evolved into an actual, practical, lightweight space suit.

After a hiatus of nearly seven months, the Army Air Forces got back into the pressure-suit business—but with an entirely different

The XH-3 full-pressure suit was
fabricated by the U. S. Rubber Company
and was preferred by project
engineer Major Kearby and others who wore
this suit during flights in a B-17E
from Eglin Field, Florida.
Of all the different suits tested on
these flights, the XH-3 was the lightest
in weight and the easiest to put on
and take off. In fact, the
Navy was impressed enough with the XH-3
to request a loan of one in October
1942 for comparison testing with its own
suits at the Naval Aircraft Factory.

Courtesy Don Bowen,
Group Leader/Pressure Suits, 6570th
Aerospace Medical Research
Laboratory, USAF

Major John G. Kearby is shown here about to take off in a fighter
aircraft to evaluate a suit that appears to be a modification
of the XH-3, known as the XH-3A. The flight was made in the closing
months of 1942 at Eglin Field, from where he made many of his
flight tests. Major Kearby was never seriously hurt because
of a malfunctioning pressure suit, although he risked his life many
times in both altitude chambers and actual flight.
Ironically, he was killed in an airplane crash on August 2, 1943,
while returning from Eglin to Wright Field, his home base
in Ohio. He was posthumously awarded the Legion of Merit by the Army
Air Forces for his valuable work on the full-pressure suit.

Courtesy Don Bowen, Group Leader/Pressure Suits, 6570th Aerospace Medical Research Laboratory, USAF

approach. Resumption of work on pressure suits at the Aero Medical Laboratory, Wright Field, came about at the request of headquarters in Washington. The Requirements Division in the Office of the Assistant Chief of the Air Staff saw the handwriting on the wall and, in April 1944, called for the development "of a pressure suit which could be used satisfactorily" at altitudes of 55,000 to 60,000 feet. The handwriting was contained actually in a bound series of fourteen volumes that carried the general title *Toward New Horizons*. All fourteen of these reports would not be completed until the following year, but the first volume alone was enough to start things rolling again at high speed. It was called *Science: The Key to Air Supremacy*.

The volumes were written by an imposing list of leading scientists that had been gathered together as members of the newly founded Scientific Advisory Board to the Air Forces to "investigate all possibilities and desirabilities for postwar and future war's development as respects the AAF." For its day, *Science: The Key to Air Supremacy* read more like fiction than science. In it were proposed missiles that could travel accurately from one continent to another, infrared detection devices, over-the-hill radar, rocket-powered airplanes, and supersonic jet combat aircraft. All of these then far-out ideas have since been realized.

The first volume was only in manuscript form when the Army Air Forces took a second look at pressure suits. The *need* for such suits was now glaringly obvious. A new scientific approach was mandatory, since the old full-pressure-suit approach had failed. The war was still in violent progress when the men at the Aero Medical Laboratory remembered a study contract that had been awarded to the University of Southern California a year and two months earlier. The university was provided $54,100 "to conduct studies and experimental investigation in connection with (i) the development of methods to prevent blackout and (ii) the selection and indoctrination of pilots to withstand acceleration effects."

Because of the shortcomings of the full-pressure suit, the University of Southern California's scientists were investigating, on their own, another kind of pressure suit. Dr. James P. Henry was the principal investigator in this field. Luckily he had the suit ready in a workable, if crude, form when it was urgently needed. It was the partial-pressure emergency high-altitude suit. The story of Jim Henry and the suit's development was told in the previous chapter.

By the fall of 1945, the partial-pressure emergency suit had been much refined by Dr. Henry, and the Aero Medical Laboratory at Wright Field asked for a price quotation on one completed suit. The price was $2,500.

A few months later, on February 19, 1946, the David Clark Company of Worcester, Massachusetts, offered to furnish almost

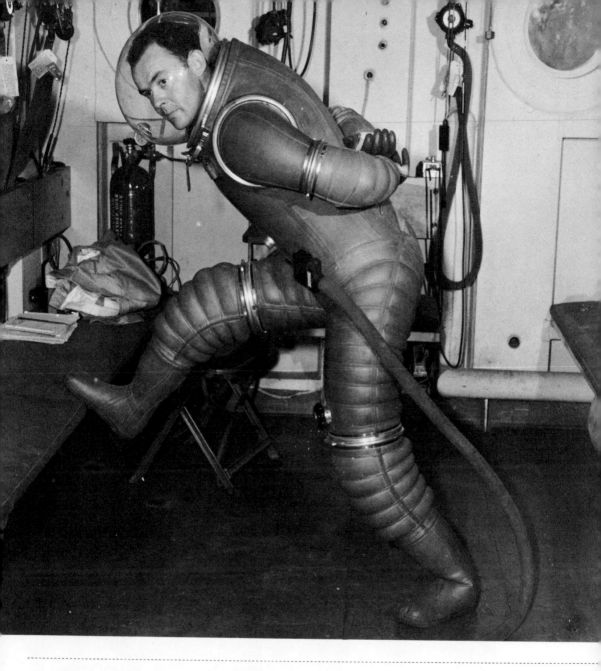

Russell Colley designed and built the XH-5, which looks more like
a true space suit than anything before it. He got the idea
for its improved mobility by watching a big fat tomato worm moving in
his garden one day in the spring of 1943. The XH-5 was then
designed with big bellows resembling the segments of a tomato worm's
body and thus received the nickname of "tomato-worm suit."
It weighed twenty pounds, had detachable arms and legs, could be donned
in four minutes without assistance, and could take pressures
up to three psi. A prototype XH-5 was ordered from B. F. Goodrich by
the Army Air Forces on April 10, 1943, at a cost of $3,000
for the suit plus $350 for a neck-ring junction. The three views of
the tomato-worm suit here show it inflated, uninflated, and
inflated during a mobility test in an altitude chamber at Wright Field.

Courtesy Don Bowen, Group Leader/Pressure Suits, 6570th Aerospace Medical Research Laboratory, USAF

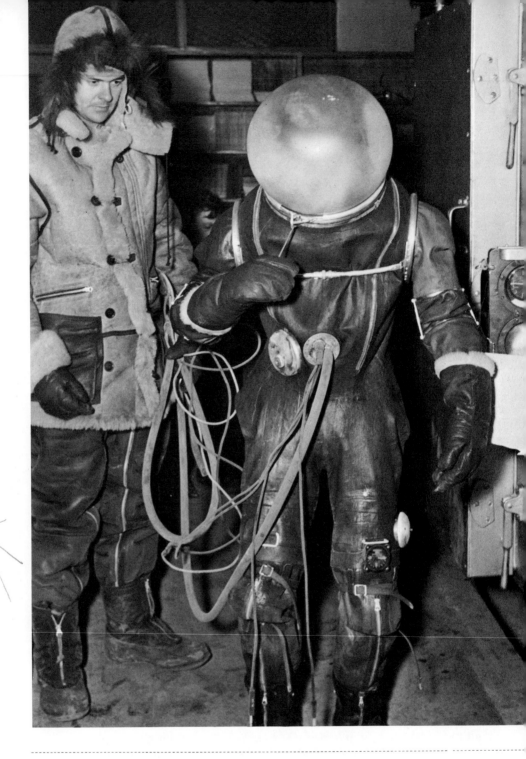

The X6-B full-pressure suit is shown here just after experimental
subject wearing it stepped out of a cold chamber. Inside of fishbowl
helmet was still thoroughly frosted from moisture exhaled by the
subject as well as from poor suit ventilation. Note the heavy fur-lined
gloves on subject. The X6-B was fairly easy to don and was tested
in actual flight at Eglin Field, but when inflated it proved
to be unworthy for combat use in the Flying Fortress.

Courtesy Don Bowen, Group Leader/Pressure Suits,
6570th Aerospace Medical Research Laboratory, USAF

the identical suit for $1,500, with delivery promised within sixty days. It took only nine days for the Wright Aero Medical Laboratory to issue a purchase order for the David Clark Company.

This action was unusually swift, as was the purchase of the Henry suit from the University of Southern California. It had been received at the laboratory a month earlier "as a model for pilot acceptance." But it was not accepted by the pilot chosen to test it. He was Jack Woolams, an experimental test pilot for the Bell Aircraft Company. According to the laboratory's report: "The suit was not acceptable because of intense pain on the ears by high-pressure breathing." Dr. Henry's helmet was made entirely of cloth. People at the Aero Medical Laboratory then developed "a practical pressure-breathing helmet that pressurized both sides of the ear drum. This helmet was [successfully] tested by Dr. Henry at simulated [chamber] altitudes up to 90,000 feet," the laboratory's report stated.

Another report, this one from the Historical Division of the Air Forces' Matériel Command, stated:

The introduction of the emergency partial-pressure suit and the use of the capstan principle by Dr. James P. Henry and other scientists at the University [of Southern California] in 1946 brought about the removal of many obstacles.

"The capstan principle" was an ingenious combination of inflatable tubes along the sides of the arms, chest, thighs, and legs that pulled the suit's fabric tightly against its wearer's body to apply mechanical counterpressure against the internal expansion of gases and water vapor in the blood vessels and tissues.

Although Jim Henry was the actual inventor of the partial-pressure high-altitude emergency suit, Dave Clark played a very helpful role in its development. He provided Dr. Henry with equipment and personnel for the experimental work on the suit. The David Clark Company then undertook to manufacture partial-pressure capstan suits for the Army Air Forces and later the United States Air Force.

A year after the David Clark Company began manufacturing the emergency partial-pressure capstan suit (S-1), it was used in an altitude chamber at the Wright Aero Medical Laboratory to establish an unprecedented record "flight" for Captain H. H. Jacobs to a height of 106,000 feet. Three years later, during developmental tests of an improved capstan suit, Major D. I. Mahoney and Mr. Charles C. Lutz, both of the Aero Medical Laboratory, reached the same altitude without ill effects.

One year later, during the summer of 1951, a Douglas Aircraft

Dr. James Henry, its inventor, models the world's first partial-pressure suit. Designated the S-1 suit by the U. S. Army Air Forces, it was handmade and tested at the University of Southern California in 1945. Purpose of the S-1 and all follow-on partial-pressure capstan suits was to keep an airman alive until he could get down to lower altitudes if his cabin pressure failed at a high altitude.

Company test pilot, William Bridgeman, wore the improved emergency suit (T-1) on three flights in a rocket-powered airplane—flights that were considered epic at the time. The airplane was the Navy's D-558-II, known more popularly as the "Douglas Skyrocket." On June 11 of that year, Bridgeman piloted the Skyrocket to a combined world speed and altitude record: 1,200 miles an hour to a height of about 70,000 feet. On August 7, he added 38 miles an hour to his former record. Eight days later, he climbed higher than any human being had ever before ventured in an airplane—79,494 feet. On all three flights he was adequately protected by the T-1 emergency partial-pressure suit.

A third capstan-type partial-pressure suit was the MC-1, designed by the Aero Medical Laboratory people specifically for use by crews of the giant B-36 Peacemaker bomber.

All three of the improved partial-pressure suits were direct descendants of the original S-1 suit developed by Dr. Jim Henry.

A fourth emergency suit, called the MB-1, was never accepted for operational use. Designed for the Air Defense Command, it, too, contained a chest-and-abdominal bladder—but no capstan tubes. The MB-1 was limited in both altitude and time of usefulness—a maximum height of 55,000 feet and a "get-me-down" time of six minutes. It pressurized the legs, belly, and chest but not the arms of its wearer.

The T-1 capstan suit was manufactured in twelve sizes by the David Clark Company. By manipulation of the laces in front of the legs and knees as well as along the thighs and sides, the suit could be made to fit men through a range of thirty-six sizes. This meant it could be fitted on 92 percent of all Air Force flying personnel. Four percent of the flying crewmen were too small and 4 percent were too large for the suit. As a result, the Aero Medical Laboratory contracted with Berger Brothers—the Spencer Corset Company—for the production of T-1 suits that were fitted individually to the 8 percent of flying personnel who could not get into the standardized suits.

A K-1 full-pressure helmet was designed and developed at the Aero Medical Laboratory to be worn with the partial-pressure suits. A more advanced version of the K-1 helmet was the K-2, which sported a one-piece outer shell of fiber glass.

Both helmets were rugged and moderately comfortable. Proof of their ruggedness was unwittingly experienced by Herman "Fish" Salmon, a well-known engineering test pilot for the Lockheed Aircraft Corporation. On April 19, 1955, Fish Salmon was piloting an XF-104 Lockheed Starfighter at 47,500 feet. He was wearing a T-1 suit with K-1 helmet and strap-fastened boots. One purpose of his flight test was to prove out the armament on the Starfighter. A

The K-1 full-pressure helmet and the T-1 partial-pressure suit were a vast improvement over the early S-2 suit and its helmet. Actually the T-1 was a later, improved S-2 with the addition of an inflatable bladder across the belly and thighs to protect its wearer against high gravity forces. As can be seen from photo, the K-1 helmet had a two-piece split outer hard shell and a window, or faceplate, with considerably better visibility. The plastic half-shells were fitted over the rubber bag and nylon full-head covering of the basic helmet, and were fastened together with a curved metal fairing.

Courtesy Don Bowen,
Group Leader/Pressure Suits, 6570th Aerospace
Medical Research Laboratory, USAF

An advance over the S-1 was this early S-2 partial-pressure suit. It had a full-head sealed helmet, eliminating the need for an oxygen mask. Compare with the S-1 helmet. Also, the capstan tubes for counterpressurization along the arms and sides of the body were larger on the S-2. The S-2 suit eliminated the anti-g bladder, and was therefore much lighter, so that it could be worn in comfort for longer periods. Note oxygen bottle strapped to wearer's thigh for emergency bailouts at high altitudes. Chuck Yeager, then a captain, wore the S-2 suit and helmet when he became the first person to break through the sound barrier in level flight, as he piloted the rocket-powered Bell XS-1 on October 14, 1947.

Courtesy Don Bowen, Group Leader/Pressure Suits,
6570th Aerospace Medical Research Laboratory, USAF

report from Wright Field, originally classified secret, describes what happened:

As he triggered his guns for a second burst of fire, the gun gave way and the airplane cabin decompressed very quickly, The [T-1] suit inflated immediately, while fog and water formed on the [K-1] helmet and aircraft canopy. The pilot [Salmon] made repeated attempts to air-start the [jet engine of the] XF-104, but failed. He finally left the doomed XF-104 at 15,000 feet. Mr. Salmon later told the pressure-suit project officer:
"I landed in a field of rocks ranging from one foot to five feet in diameter. My right arm was injured and my head struck on a rock. The K-1 helmet hard-shell was cracked but there was no injury to my head. It took me ten to fifteen minutes to get out of the suit with my injured arm. Rescue was effected by helicopter approximately two hours after escape [from the airplane]."

At the time, the pressure-suit project officer was Dr. Edwin Vail, now chief space-suit scientist at the Hamilton Standard Division of the United Aircraft Corporation. According to the formerly secret document, Fish Salmon reported to Dr. Vail

that the K-1 helmet was excellent for "rugged parachute landing" and his only complaint was that "the visor may impair vision at extreme altitudes. A great variation in light-intensity between sky and [airplane] cockpit interior makes it difficult to read instruments. With the sun on the fore-quarter, the condition was worst. The visor seems to glow. An exact discription is difficult.

Apart from this restrictive defect of the K-1 (and also the K-2) helmet, there was another rather serious shortcoming of the helmet: mobility of the wearer's head was severely hampered and this greatly reduced his field of vision. So Dr. Vail set about designing improvements to correct these failings of both the K-1 and K-2 helmets. The result was an MA-1 full-pressure helmet that could be worn with both partial-pressure and full-pressure suits.

The MA-1 helmet ultimately proved to be unsuitable for combat use because of its weight, oxygen leaks, and an instability of its general sealing system that showed up when dummies were used in wind-blast tests to simulate ejection-seat bail-outs. Although the helmet was not blown off the head of a dummy, there was internal failure which caused its neck-sealing bladder to balloon and rupture with increased air pressure. But the MA-1 was a successful innovation that broke ground for a series of ever more efficient helmet concepts. These led eventually to bonafide practical space-suit helmets.

Because of the great success of the emergency partial-pressure suits with capstan tubes, the Army Air Forces in 1947 drew up

An advance over the T-1 was the T-1A partial-pressure suit, here shown being modeled by Air Force Master Sergeant Earl Sayre, a pioneer in the testing and development of partial-pressure suits and full-pressure helmets. The T-1A suit was styled with larger capstan tubes and an improved anti-g bladder. Capstan bleed valve to equalize gas pressure in tubes is fountain-pen-like object on Sergeant Sayre's crossed forearm. The helmet on his lap is the MA-1, a revolutionary advance at the time, designed and built by the Bill Jack Scientific Company of Los Angeles. Five versions of this helmet were built, each an advance over the other. The entire MA-1 helmet assembly moved as an integral part of the wearer's head, vastly broadening his field of vision to match his normal field.

Courtesy Don Bowen, Group Leader/Pressure Suits, 6570th Aerospace Medical Research Laboratory, USAF

The K-2 helmet pictured here was a modification of the K-1: its outer hard shell was a one-piece affair of glass fibers imbedded in plastic. Both the K-1 and K-2 doubled as crash helmets along with their high-altitude protective qualities. The suit shown is a Navy version of the Air Force T-1.
Missile alongside the suited F9F-8 jet fighter pilot is the Navy's Sidewinder, an infrared-seeking weapon that was being evaluated in the spring of 1956 at the U. S. Naval Ordnance Test Station, China Lake, California.

Courtesy U. S. Navy

an informal agreement with the U. S. Navy on the development of suits for use at high altitudes. The two military services mutually agreed that the Navy should concentrate on developing a full-pressure suit, while the Air Forces would dedicate their development efforts to improvement of the partial-pressure suit. The agreement worked fine through the years. Each service informed the other of its progress through liaison offices. Both of them benefitted scientifically from the interchange of technical data on pressure suits. An example from the Navy side was the testing of the Douglas Skyrocket, which was immeasurably helped by the use of the Air Forces' partial-pressure suit. On the other side, the Air Forces were building up a backlog of experimental information related to full-pressure clothing—to be used when and if they needed it, despite the fact that the Navy's requirement for a pressure suit differed distinctly from Air Forces' requirements.

However, in July of the same year of the suit-development agreement, 1947, the Army Air Forces became a separate military department by presidential decree and was henceforward to be known as the U. S. Air Force, or USAF. At first this radical change in the military services provided no complications to the pressure-suit programs of either the Navy or the USAF. The Wright Aero Medical Laboratory operated as usual. It was not until the USAF established the Air Research and Development Command in April 1951 that things became a little sticky. The new command correlated all scientific research and development programs throughout the Air Force by placing them under the direction of one headquarters. Previously, the Air Matériel Command had been responsible for most of this direction.

More than two and a half years later, in December 1953, the Research and Development Command set up a requirement for the protection of B-52 Stratofortress crews. It was an unprecedented requirement for pressure suits, in terms of useful time and comfort. But it was also wholly reasonable if the Stratofortress was to meet its design goal as an effective weapon system. The B-52 was an eight-jet global bomber, which meant that its crews would have to travel through the stratosphere for long periods of time. The time-altitude requirement for crew-protection clothing was eleven hours above 46,500 feet, plus at least three hours above 50,000 feet.

Meanwhile, the world's first supersonic bomber was already in the works at the Air Research and Development Command. This was the B-58 Hustler, a delta-winged airplane designed to zip through the stratosphere at twice the speed of sound. The pressure-suit time-altitude requirement for the Hustler was even more complex than that of the Stratofortress: at least one hour between

*A 1956 photo of the new MC-1 partial-pressure suit shows it with
capstan tubes inflated to stretch suit fabric tightly across the body
of its wearer. Helmet is the MA-1. Note addition of pressurized
gloves as components of this suit, which was designed originally for
use by crewmen of the giant B-36 Peacemaker bomber. It contained
a rubberized inflatable bladder across the chest and abdomen to relieve
muscle strain and reduce fatigue of airmen on long flights.
No anti-g protection was needed, since the huge bomber could not
perform tight fast turns or other maneuvers that would
excessively increase gravity forces. These capstan tubes, smaller than
those on the T-1 and S-2 suits, provided comfort for long periods
with the suit inflated.*

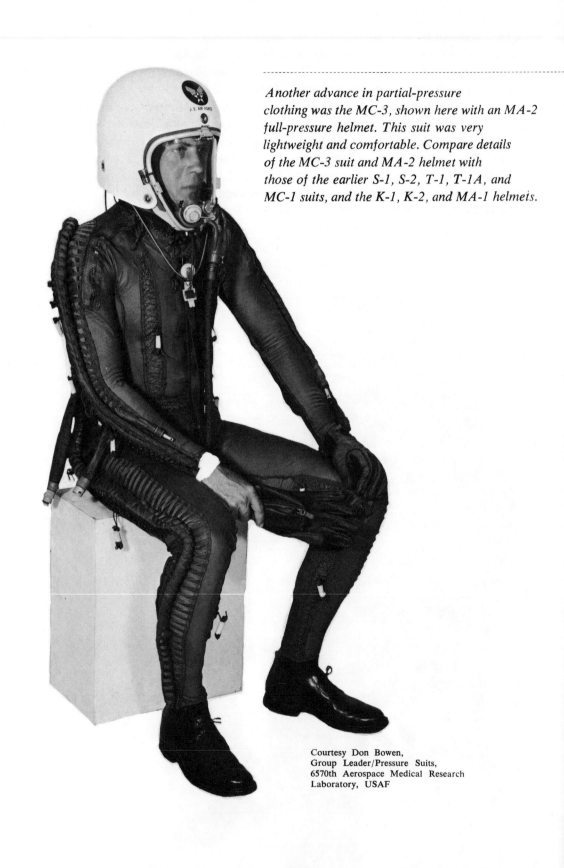

Another advance in partial-pressure clothing was the MC-3, shown here with an MA-2 full-pressure helmet. This suit was very lightweight and comfortable. Compare details of the MC-3 suit and MA-2 helmet with those of the earlier S-1, S-2, T-1, T-1A, and MC-1 suits, and the K-1, K-2, and MA-1 helmets.

Courtesy Don Bowen,
Group Leader/Pressure Suits,
6570th Aerospace Medical Research
Laboratory, USAF

54,000 and 70,000 feet on a bomb run over a distant target, with a total of eight hours at 52,000 feet or above on the B-58's return-to-home-base flight.

Obviously, the T-1 and S-2 capstan partial-pressure suits could not meet these requirements. They were designed for short-term emergency use. People at the Aero Medical Laboratory, now directly under supervision by the Air Research and Development Command, began to look at the MC-1 partial-pressure suit as a possibility for B-52 and B-58 crewmen. They felt that with modifications it might do the job. Speed of development was essential, since the new suits had to be ready and crews trained to wear them at the same time that the Stratofortress and the Hustler became operational. The MC-1 capstan suit with its combined chest and belly bladder stubbornly refused to be modified in a way that would make it serviceable for crews of the new global bombers.

Designers turned to an experimental suit devised by Captain Terence F. McGuire. It had no name originally and was being used specifically in studies of the physiological stresses endured by men who wear pressure suits. Captain McGuire had asked the Clothing Branch people at the Aero Medical Laboratory to build the suit as a strictly experimental tool.

Anonymous though it was, the experimental suit incorporated certain features of the T-1 and MC-1 suits. It retained the capstan tubes and bladders. But the big difference was in the bladder. The T-1 and MC-1 had bladders that merely protected the chests and bellies of their wearers. The nameless suit had a bladder that wrapped around the whole trunk of the body, from the groins to the shoulders. When its wearer inhaled oxygen, the torso bladder automatically deflated, allowing room for chest expansion. The reverse occurred automatically when its wearer exhaled: the bladder inflated, pressurizing his torso.

During the frenzy of searching for a new suit design to be worn by air crews of the Stratofortress and Hustler, the experimental suit without a name was demonstrated to specialists. Later, on February 7, 1956, a Personal Equipment Conference was held at headquarters. Three-star general Thomas S. Power, then Commander of the Air Research and Development Command, announced at the conference that a new high-altitude suit "which was developed for a special application has proved to be so successful that its replacement for the MC-1 was mandatory." General Power called the new item of protective clothing a "partial-full-pressure suit." It was finally designated as the MC-3. An MC-4 version was equipped with anti-g protection bladders in addition to the high-altitude-protection torso bladder.

A budget of $7,400,000 was established for the purchase of

Pictured here is the evolution of anti-g protective clothing for the years from 1941 to 1957. From left to right are the earliest arrangements to the latest. First outfit applied counterpressure by brute force, with a tight corset and tightly laced puttees. The second garment looks like a farmer's sleeveless overalls with laced puttees around the legs, but actually it introduced the use of inflatable bladders under the "overalls." From then on toward the right are various modifications of the bladder-counterpressure

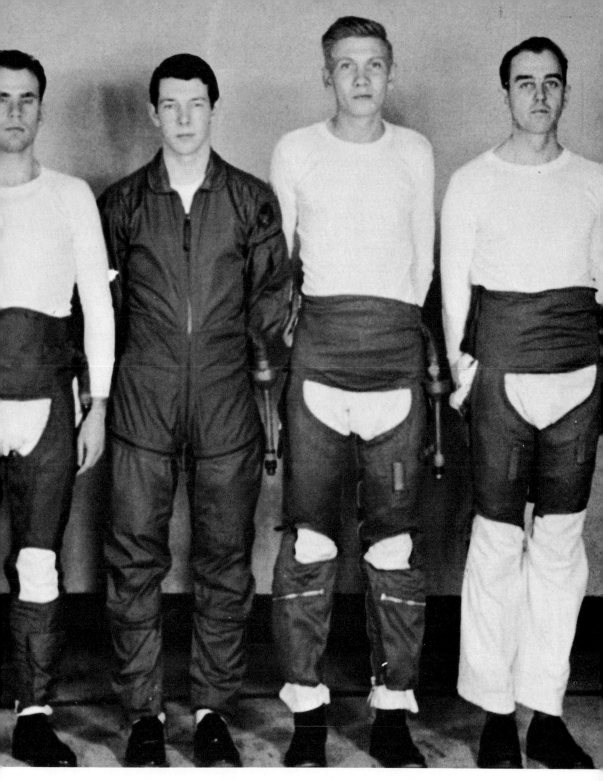

idea. The only man who seems to be fully dressed is actually wearing a flight suit of the day, with the inflatable rubberized bladders underneath the suit. All of these antigravity devices were either worn beneath or over standard flying clothing. The anti-g bladders for stratospheric fliers were built into their altitude pressure suits.

Courtesy Don Bowen, Group Leader/Pressure Suits, 6570th Aerospace Medical Research Laboratory, USAF

MC-3 partial-full-pressure suits. The suits were to be used not only by Strategic Air Command crews but also by air crews of the Tactical Air Command and the Air Defense Command in their light bombers, fighter bombers, fighters, and interceptors—new supersonic and subsonic turbojet-powered aircraft.

All existing contracts were canceled on the previous emergency partial-pressure suits. These included the S-2, the T-1, the T-1A (an improved version of the T-1), and the MC-1.

In the meantime, for the same reasons that caused the Air Force to scrap all short-term emergency suits in favor of the MC-3 and MC-4, a program had been re-established to develop a full-pressure, or space-suit, type of garment for fliers. No work had been done on full-pressure suits by the Aero Medical Laboratory since October 1943. The situation was also snarled somewhat because of that agreement with the Navy some seven years earlier, wherein full-pressure-suit development became proprietary with the Navy. The problem was finally solved without rancor on either side.

The Wright Air Development Center people met with personnel of the Navy's Bureau of Aeronautics in January 1954 to plan for expanding or accelerating the full-pressure-suit program. Air Force Headquarters transferred $130,000 to the Navy for five experimental full-pressure suits to be delivered "not later than 1 June 1954."

According to a secret report by the Historical Division at Wright Field:

Through the following months the Air Force evaluated several versions of the Navy's full-pressure suit. As a part of the test program, in April 1954 a Navy-developed full-pressure suit was evaluated in a mock-up of the XB-58 [experimental prototype of the Hustler], but its lack of mobility (even in this relatively clean cockpit), low-comfort factor, restricted vision, inadequate ventilation, poor land-survival qualities [in case of emergency bailout by the wearer], and the extreme difficulty of getting it on and off the pilot, made it unacceptable for that aircraft.

Furthermore, in September 1954, in spite of several improvements resulting from Air Force efforts, it appeared impossible for the Navy suit to meet the requirements of the swiftly developing B-52.

The reader may be wondering why the Air Force was so frantically trying to perfect a full-pressure suit at this time. There were two reasons: the MC-3 partial-full-pressure suit had not yet come on the scene in 1954 and the MC-1, with its serious limitations for use by air crews of the stratospheric global bombers, was just becoming operational. Even after the MC-3 suit was introduced in 1956 and was placed on a whirlwind production schedule, it was still considered to be an interim compromise. Yet the MC-3 suit also had its limitations. Although it provided much longer periods

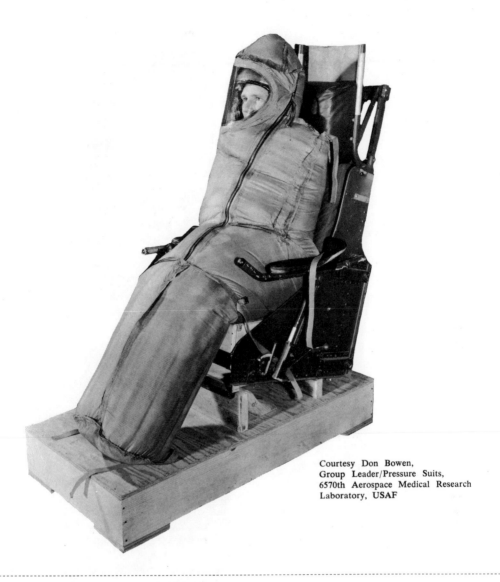

Courtesy Don Bowen,
Group Leader/Pressure Suits,
6570th Aerospace Medical Research
Laboratory, USAF

*During 1951–52, experimenters of the Aero Medical Laboratory at
Wright Field concentrated on the development of aircrew emergency
pressure cells. Since an operational full-pressure suit still seemed
to be far off in the future, and since aircraft were proposed that
would fly so high that an emergency partial-pressure suit would be
inadequate in terms of time to get a crewman down to a life-sustaining
level of the lower atmosphere if cabin pressurization failed in the
high stratosphere, it was necessary to find a method for survival
of the crewmen. Individual pressurized cells appeared to be an answer.
Shown here is a mockup of the idea, built by people at the
laboratory to provide the designers employed by prospective civilian
contractors with the basic mechanics of the concept.*

A contractor tried to get around the
limitations of the pressure cells by adding
a robot arm and hand to the cell.
A crewman could now get in the cell and
zipper it closed himself—maybe. At the very
least he might be able to control an
airplane in a limited way. But the word
limited *is significant*, for he could use only
one hand—and no feet. The contractor
in this case was the Berger Brothers Company,
which owned the Spencer Corset Company.

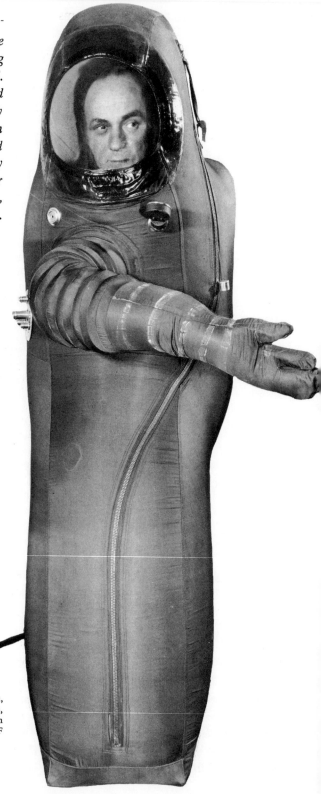

Courtesy Don Bowen,
Group Leader/Pressure Suits,
6570th Aerospace Medical Research
Laboratory, USAF

of protection at higher altitudes than any of the earlier capstan suits, it was beset by three problems that were difficult to resolve: mobility, wearer comfort, and ventilation. The third problem seemed to be almost insurmountable. Because of the bladder wrapped around his entire torso, the MC-3 held in the wearer's body heat and restricted the normal breathing of his skin pores.

From the beginning of the B-52/B-58 bomber programs, scientists at the Aero Medical Laboratory had felt strongly that the fundamental answer to be question of air-crew safety was a true full-pressure suit of light weight, maximum mobility, and natural comfort. So even after the MC-3 was released by the laboratory for operational use by the new bomber crews, the search continued intensively for ways to develop an ideal full-pressure suit. In this respect, the formerly secret report continues:

Because of the failure of the Navy [full-pressure] suit to meet the Air Force requirements, the Air Research and Development Command on 3 February 1955 served notice that the Aero Medical Laboratory was developing a full-pressure suit of independent design to fill Air Force requirements. . . .

Acting quickly, the Aero Medical Laboratory asked thirty companies to bid on a competitive design-study of a full-pressure suit. From this group, the [Laboratory's] project office intended to select at least six to eight firms to conduct [the actual] design-studies. These studies would become the basis for a composite suit-design incorporating the best engineering features of the lot. Finally, interested manufacturers would be invited to bid on the construction of the suit.

The closing date for design-study bids was 16 May 1955. By that time, the Laboratory had received ten proposals. Four of these covered complete suit systems, five were for component developments and one represented a human-engineering evaluator system. One contract was negotiated with the International Latex Corporation, for a full-pressure suit. Several other proposals had merit, but additional funds were needed before contracts could be considered.

International Latex was, of course, the manufacturer of women's bras and girdles with the famous trademark Playtex. The company was no stranger to the Aero Medical Laboratory: during February 1949 the Air Matériel Command awarded it a contract to develop a prototype full-pressure oxygen helmet, along with nine additional such helmets to be modified from the prototype.

For almost exactly five years after its venture into the building of full-pressure helmets, the well-known manufacturer of bras, girdles, and teething rings concentrated its main energies on Playtex and more closely related products. Then it got back into the space business with that contract award from the Aero Medical Laboratory for a full-pressure suit. It was a prophetic award, for two years after International Latex delivered its first full-pressure suits to the

Courtesy U.S. Navy

Courtesy Don Bowen,
Group Leader/Pressure Suits,
6570th Aerospace Medical Research
Laboratory, USAF

*Two views showing modifications of the Navy's 1953 prototype
stratospheric suit. Note here that fishbowl helmet is used mainly as a
container to hold in total suit pressure, while actual breathing
of oxygen is accomplished through a mask attached to a standard
naval aviator's crash helmet. Also changed are the hose connections for
the entry and exit of gases to pressurize and cool the suit. One of
these is now located just above the crotch. Circular plate in center of
chest is a regulator to supply the mask with an oxygen-and-air
mixture on demand or pure oxygen under pressure. Other modifications
are the position change of the cross-hatch restraints against
ballooning built into the torso and the addition of a cross-shaped
restraint in the crotch area.*

A 1954 advance over the 1953
stratospheric full-pressure suits is
this Navy garment-and-helmet that
is obviously more mobile, since
it combines a soft rubberized cloth
(probably nylon) with the hard and heavy
rubber sheeting. Gloves are also a
mixture of cloth and rubber, although
they still retain the tire shapes
in thumbs and fingers. Boots, too, are
less clumsy and contain more cloth
than rubber. Helmet is of full-pressure
style, with no need for an oxygen
mask. Although it is a Navy suit-and-
helmet combination, the outfit
here was used in April 1954 by the
U. S. Air Force to evaluate its
effectiveness for crew-station wear in
the delta-winged twice-the-speed-of-sound
B-58 Hustler bomber. This photo
was classified secret for many years.

Courtesy Don Bowen,
Group Leader/Pressure Suits,
6570th Aerospace Medical
Research Laboratory, USAF

Laboratory at Wright Field, in July 1956, the United States established a national program for the exploration of outer space.

Within another three years, President John F. Kennedy announced that "this nation should commit itself to achieving the goal, before this decade is out, of landing a man on the moon and returning him safely to earth." That announcement was made on May 25, 1961. It was the beginning of a great future for the manufacturer of those very earthly Playtex products. International Latex's proposal for a "moon suit" got it a contract from the National Aeronautics and Space Administration to develop the space suits that are now worn by the Apollo astronauts as they explore the lunar surface.

Evolving a space suit with ideal qualities, including great reliability, was no easy task—as the following chapter will illustrate.

Chapter 7

CLOTHES MAKE THE ASTRONAUT

The 1950's could truly be called the decade of the space suit. For from its middle to its close, that decade saw the U. S. Air Force building a reservoir of advanced technical knowledge about full-pressure clothing that later had to be tapped if men were to fly safely through space in the 1960's. The design-and-development suit projects of the Aero Medical Laboratory at Wright Field, with a single exception, provided the basis for the construction of all the types of protective clothing that were to be worn by astronauts in the civilian program to land men on the moon.

Project Mercury was the exception. This was the first in a series of three carefully planned step-by-step programs initiated by the National Aeronautics and Space Administration (NASA) to train astronauts for the ultimate achievement of exploring the lunar surface before the 1960's faded into history. The Mercury

By 1956, the Navy, working with Russell Colley at
the B. F. Goodrich Company, had made phenomenal progress
toward a true space suit.
Shown here are front and back views of the Mark II suit.
Its helmet was obviously a great advance
over previous naval pressurized headgear, both in
terms of visibility and comfort.
The Mark II, a soft suit of lightweight rubberized fabric,
led directly to the Mark IV, the space garment
that a few years later was chosen as the basis for the suits
to be worn in earth orbit by the Project Mercury astronauts.
Note that the gloves of this suit protect only the fingers,
palms, and wrists: the thumbs are left free
for added mobility. The Mark II
was over-all more mobile than any previous Navy full-pressure suit.

Courtesy Don Bowen, Group Leader/Pressure Suits,
6570th Aerospace Medical Research Laboratory, USAF

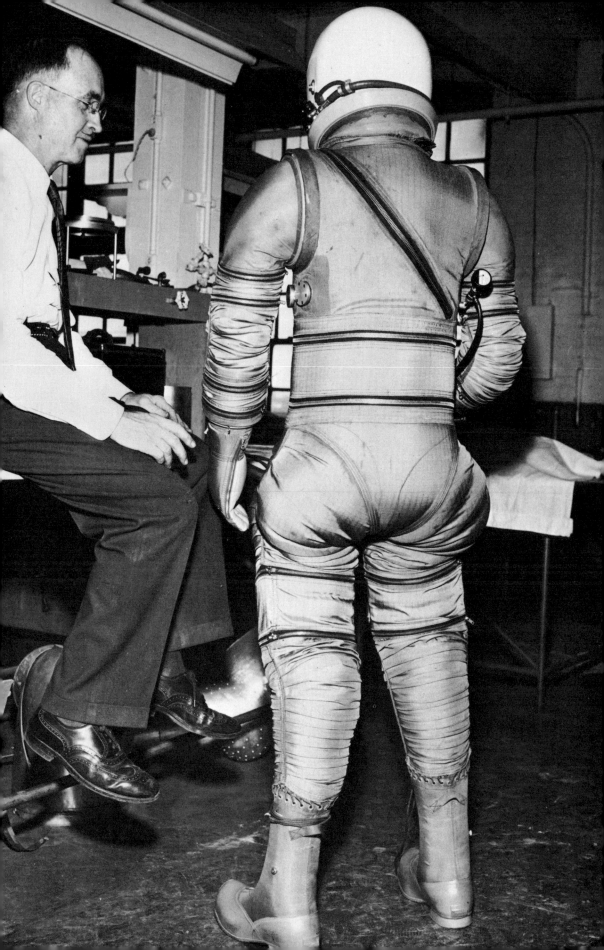

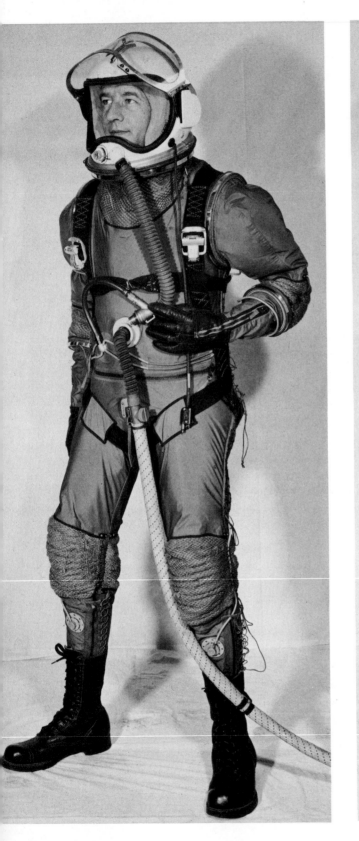

astronauts rode into space alone, aboard one-man spacecraft. The
suits they wore for protection against the hazards of space were
derived from a full-pressure garment finally perfected by the U. S.
Navy and the B. F. Goodrich Company. But even the Mercury
space suit, as it was modified from Navy to NASA use, became
somewhat dependent on data tapped from the Air Force storage
basin of technical knowledge.

The space clothing worn successively by flight crews in the two-
man Gemini and three-man Apollo spacecraft projects came
straight out of that Air Force reservoir.

The Air Force reservoir of knowledge at the Aero Medical
Laboratory was known only by initials and a number: XMC-2.
Other initials were tagged on to it for identification of specific
contractors who were developing full-pressure suits for the Air
Force. Examples were the International Latex Corporation suit,
designated the XMC-2-ILC, and a David Clark Company suit,
identified as XMC-2-DC. This was an improvement over earlier
designation systems.

A more important improvement was the suits themselves. Yet
Program XMC-2, despite its later success, started its race from
the wrong pit. The first suit of the program was introduced at a
Pressure-Suit Symposium cosponsored by the Air Force and the
Navy at Philadelphia, Pennsylvania, from the first to the third of
February 1955. This was an experimental space suit that the David
Clark Company had put together from available components of
partial-pressure suits in its Massachusetts fabricating shop. A few
design flourishes were added to tie up the loose ends in the garment
and make it a full-pressure suit. After retesting by the manufacturer,
the suit was renovated. The second version of the suit was returned
to the Aero Medical Laboratory and was tested early in 1956.
Upon inflation, the suit stretched out along the subject's body so

*In 1956, the U. S. Air Force had again begun to concentrate on the
development of an effective full-pressure suit, working with
a number of civilian contractors. Shown here are front and side views
of the XMC-2-DC full-pressure suit. It was a prototype built by
the David Clark Company. Helmet was the MA-1 by the Bill Jack
Scientific Company. This suit almost cost the life of one experimenter,
an Air Force volunteer. When it was inflated, the suit stretched
violently upward along his body, causing the neck ring and helmet to
rise and almost strangle him. But the "bugs" were finally swatted
out of the Clark suit design and it was developed into an
effectve garment for pilots of the rocket-powered X-15 aircraft.*

Courtesy Don Bowen, Group Leader/Pressure Suits, 6570th Aerospace Medical Research Laboratory, USAF

violently "that the upward pressure of the helmet and neck-piece threatened to strangle its wearer."

Here again was the old problem that had exasperated the famous Wiley Post. Twenty-two years earlier, Post had laid out the guidelines for all future space suits. Such suits had to pressurize the entire body and head of their wearers, yet permit the free movement of limbs and fingers.

This kind of pressurization with mobility was absolutely required if men were to survive and perform useful work in their aircraft or spacecraft. Space suits also had to be reliably safe and lightweight. The second David Clark full-pressure suit *was* lightweight and mobile as well as being safe enough—until it was pressurized. Then it almost killed a man.

The Aero Medical Laboratory and its civilian contractors tried one approach after another to define and solve these problems. Yet they were icebound by a basic law of physics: any gas sealed into a closed container equalizes its pressure throughout the volume of that container. This is true both of a pure gas, like oxygen, and of a mixture of gases, like air. Space suits, or full-pressure suits, are closed containers.

So what was the great problem? Couldn't the gas pressure inside a suit be kept low enough so that its wearer could move around freely? Wouldn't this simply solve the problem of mobility? A human being in a space suit would soon collapse if his suit-pressure were dropped for any length of time below three and one-half pounds per square inch (psi). Below this level there is not enough pressure to push oxygen or air into a man's lungs. With uninflated lungs, he could not exhale a by-product waste of respiration—carbon dioxide gas—which would settle heavily in his lungs until he died of a combination of oxygen starvation and suffocation.

The cardinal dilemma, then, for the scientists and engineers working at and with the Aero Medical Laboratory was how to achieve a space-suit gas pressure that would remain a constant three and a half psi or higher, while permitting suit mobility. The dilemma was compounded by a side effect of that same basic physical law: any container made of a flexible material which is inflated with a gas or air has a tendency to form a spherical shape.

Space suits are made up basically of an interconnecting array of cylindrical and domelike forms that match the general contours of the human body—the limbs, thighs, trunk, and shoulders. These forms cannot be sealed off from each other to permit mobility of the joints—ankles, knees, elbows and shoulders—without unacceptable complications. Each sealed-off area would require its own valve system and hoses to circulate the life-supporting pressurized gas. Each would also demand its own gas-flow regulator system. In effect, it would be like designing a dozen miniature space suits into one. This would vastly reduce the reliability of the suit, because the larger the number of component self-contained systems, the greater the chance of failure of any one of them. Besides, between each sealed-off component would be an unpressurized area—where the lethal effects of abnormally low pressure would take their toll by incapacitating the wearer of this kind of suit. He would have the mobility of his joints for a few seconds before those joints were paralyzed by extreme swelling, or worse.

Yet the only way to go, it seemed, was also an impossible way. The entire body had to be pressurized to keep a man alive and doing useful work either in the upper atmosphere or in space. Thus a full-pressure suit had to be a long-term protective garment, not just a device to maintain life for a quarter- to a half-hour in emergencies, when aircraft or spacecraft cabin pressurization failed, so that crewmen could safely descend to a livable part of the atmosphere. In fact, if the cabin pressure failed in a spacecraft orbiting the earth, it would—depending upon the orbital altitude—take several or more hours to bring that craft back to a landing place where it could be recovered reasonably fast. If the spacecraft were orbiting the moon, in the same emergency situation, its crew members' full-pressure suits would have to keep them alive for several days before they could be recovered on earth.

Still, during those experimental struggles of the latter 1950's, when a full-pressure suit was inflated all of its cylindrical and dome-like forms tended to merge into one huge balloon, thoroughly immobilizing the suit's wearer. Even at three and a half psi, the surfaces of the suit stretched stiffly until they became as hard as metal. Trying to twist or turn inside such a suit was like trying to move your arms, trunk, or legs inside an Iron Maiden.

Going back to the fundamental law of physics that was the nemesis of full-pressure-suit experimenters in those days: gases, like all the tangible materials of nature, are made up of molecules. In a gas, these molecules move more freely than they do in a liquid, such as water, or in a solid, such as a wooden plank or a sheet of steel. The velocity of molecules increases proportionately with an increase in temperature. Gas molecules dart about in straight lines, until they strike another molecule or the walls of a container in which they are confined. Striking against the container walls and each other, they are either speeded up or slowed down from the impact.

In other words, the molecules of a gas—trying to escape confinement in a closed container—beat against the internal walls of the container, bounce back, collide with other molecules heading for the walls from all directions and spread out into a seething mass of motion that balances itself into a quivering three-dimensional

Three views of an advanced XMC-2-DC show successively: (a) the basic suit with underwear covered by a pressure-containing layer, a ventilation layer (note plastic tubes for cooling, most evident as spidery lines along legs), an anti-g layer over torso (outlines can be seen as heavy seams moving up from armpits to shoulders and down toward crotch and around upper thighs) and an over-all restraint layer of link net; (b) an antiflash layer covering the entire inner suit—this is an aluminized material to reflect away heat and protect against fires; and (c) side view of whole assembly, including full-pressure helmet. Helmet is still another version of the MA-1.

Courtesy Don Bowen,
Group Leader/Pressure Suits,
6570th Aerospace Medical Research
Laboratory, USAF

"jelly" that is uniformly dense between every wall. It is the tension of that "jelly" expanding against the walls which creates pressure within the container.

If the container is made of a rubberized fabric or some other airtight flexible material, every time any portion of it is bent or twisted the result is a compression of gas molecules at those bending or twisting points. These molecules are moving at the same speed as before, but they are now confined to a smaller volume of space. Hence there is a much larger number of molecule-wall collisions per unit area than before, causing greater pressure.

In a space suit, if the gas pressure becomes greater at the joints when these are activated, how can its wearer move freely to perform urgently necessary motions? Actually, he becomes more immobile the more he tries to move his limbs by bending or rotating his joints.

Obviously, to achieve mobility for its wearer, the full-pressure, or space, suit must maintain a constant volume and equal pressure throughout every component area, including every joint and movable part. Yet in the early experimental space suits, when an arm was bent at the elbow the effect was the same as pinching an inflated toy balloon across its whole diameter. Volume was radically compressed at the pinch point and explosively expanded above and below that point. Simultaneously, within the pinched volume, air or gas pressure was increased tremendously.

Now suppose the space suit is built of a rigid material, such as a hard plastic like fiber glass. The volume of the suit will remain constant and thus so will the pressure within it, because it's not easy to pinch or compress fiber glass. For the same reason, this kind of suit would also be immobile. How would you move an arm or a leg, encased in this rigid armor? Of course, cleverly designed rotating joints can be built into it, robotlike. Yet the systems that activate robots are not as vulnerable to the death-dealing hazards of space as are the vital systems in humans. Every joint built into the armor-type space suit provides a possible egress for pressurized life-maintaining gas, a welcome vent for the gas molecules that are always so eagerly trying to escape confinement.

So the soft flexible suit concept and the hard-plastic suit concept both confounded the scientists and engineers of the Aero Medical Laboratory at Wright Field in their attempts to design and build a full-pressure suit. But they continued their stubborn search for a practical method to contain the oxygen gas at one constant pressure level without distorting the volume of the suit to a degree where it would become unmanageable for its wearer.

One of the earliest attempts at a solution of the space-suit constant-volume problem was inspired by a creature called *Protoparce*

*Here Scotty Crossfield, first person to fly at twice the speed of
sound, models prototype No. 1 of the X-15 suit. Again the helmet is a
modification of the MA-1. The suit, again, is designated the
XMC-2-DC. All of the Air Force full-pressure suits during the 1950's
were classified under Project XMC-2, and the contractor was
identified by his initials—"DC" being "David Clark." International
Latex Corporation would be identified as "ILC," B. F. Goodrich
as "BFG," and so forth. Crossfield, an engineering test pilot,
was project engineer on the X-15 program for North American Aviation
(now the North American-Rockwell Corporation).*

Courtesy Don Bowen, Group Leader/Pressure Suits, 6570th Aerospace
Medical Research Laboratory, USAF

Several full-pressure suits
and helmets were designed
for the X-15 program
as prototypes. Here is a
later model with an
even later version of the
MA-1 helmet. The outer
flash layer of aluminized
fabric could withstand
2,500 degrees Fahrenheit
before the basic
fabric would melt. Also
an XMC-2-DC, this
suit and helmet were combined
in another attempt to
design the most effective
garment for high-speed
high-altitude escape
from the X-15 if
an emergency should occur
to warrant this.

Courtesy Don Bowen,
Group Leader/Pressure Suits,
6570th Aerospace Medical Research
Laboratory, USAF

quinquemaculata. It is the larva of the sphinx moth. One day past mid-spring in 1943, Russ Colley of the B. F. Goodrich Company became intrigued with the versatile flexibility of *Protoparce*. Colley, who nine years before had built Wiley Post's successful third full-pressure suit, was tending the tomato plants in his garden when he noticed the big fat yellowish green worm casually chewing away at one of the plants' leaves. The bellows like movement of the worm's plump body was accentuated by its pure white stripes contracting and expanding. Suddenly it occurred to Colley that here could be a possible answer to the vexing question of how to achieve mobility in the joints of a full-pressure suit.

If the joints were formed as a series of bellows, Russ Colley reasoned, then they could be bent without reducing the volume in the joint areas. They would function in the same manner as the tomato worm, which moved by expanding and compressing the bellowslike sections of its body. The gas pressure should remain fairly constant around each joint, since the volume of the joint would not be pinched drastically narrow in one side and be widened considerably in the other when an elbow or knee was bent. Instead, the coiled series of bellows would maintain a constant volume and thus a constant pressure within every bellows segment, while only the thin coil loops between the segments would be compressed or expanded.

Using this principle, Russ Colley designed and built a full-pressure garment under Air Force contract. It was dubbed the "tomato-worm suit" (see photograph of this suit in the previous chapter). It was delivered for testing to the Aero Medical Laboratory four years before the Air Force decided to drop all work on full-pressure suits for that time, so that the research effort could be concentrated upon the partial-pressure suit.

The tomato-worm suit *was* more mobile than the earlier space suits, but not enough so to make it combatworthy. At very high altitudes, when it was fully inflated, it could not be worn for any length of time because of extreme discomfort. Ventilation was a major problem. Clumsy and confining, it thoroughly sealed in the wearer's body heat and moisture, to the point where he found it insufferable after an extremely short period.

But the tomato-worm concept was a step forward in conquering the bugaboo of immobility. By 1952, Colley had developed an airtight metal joint that rotated on sealed-in bearings. He combined this with narrow accordianlike pleats, which were a modification of the tomato-worm idea. Considerably more mobility was accomplished with this method. It was incorporated into the design of a full-pressure suit for the Navy. But again, a major shortcoming was lack of adequate ventilation.

Strangely enough, a year before the Air Force officially went back into the space-suit business, a scientist at the Aero Medical Laboratory devised a clever way to ventilate totally enclosed pressure garments. He was Hans Mauch, the German-born chief of the Environment Section at the laboratory. Mauch's system was, in effect, an air-conditioning unit that could be worn under a full-pressure suit. It was a multi-layered liner resembling Long John underwear, but there the resemblance ended. For it contained thousands of pinholes, some tiny and others slightly larger. A blower, which could be connected to the electrical power system of an aircraft or spacecraft, blew air into the liner through the tiny pinholes in an inside layer. This layer was placed next to the skin of the wearer. The larger holes in the outermost layer sucked out the air, creating a constant circulation of air around the wearer's body. A simple hose arrangement, which extended from the belly portion of the liner to the blower, transmitted the air at high speed. The system not only cooled its wearer but also considerably reduced humidity by venting off the moisture of perspiration.

The air-conditioned liner was also successfully tested as a cooling coverall worn over their partial-pressure and g-suits by high-flying, fast-maneuvering fighter pilots and bomber crewmen.

Variations on Mauch's air-cooled underwear were eventually developed, the most advanced being a water-cooled system. This consisted of hollow plastic tubing that was attached in an array of patterns to lightweight loosely knit cotton underwear. An inlet and an outlet manifold allowed water to be pumped into and out of the tubing arrays. Water circulation was not only a simpler but a much more efficient way to cool the man inside a full-pressure suit. It was the method used to cool the American astronauts on the surface of the moon.

An in-between method was used to cool the Mercury and Gemini astronauts. This was also quite simple in its concept: a venting system was developed by NASA to dump the sweat of the astronauts into space. As the moisture of their perspiration was vented, it carried off a portion of their body heat, thus cooling them by causing a drop in skin temperature. Their space suits were further cooled by the circulation of oxygen gas, which would also supply a breathable atmosphere and life-supporting pressure if the cabin were accidentally decompressed.

This double-cooling approach operated with fair efficiency— if the men remained inside their spacecraft. But one of the goals of Project Gemini was to explore the techniques of extra-vehicular activity (EVA), or what was popularly called "space walking." Understanding and overcoming the potential hazards

Front and back views of a full-pressure suit by Arrowhead Products,
produced for the Navy in 1957. Subject is shown wearing the then latest
inflatable life vest over the suit. Helmet was designed and
manufactured by B. F. Goodrich. It was a direct forerunner of helmets
used by the Mercury astronauts. Suit was very lightweight and
comfortable when uninflated. Back view was photographed when subject
was not wearing life vest.

Courtesy Don Bowen, Group Leader/Pressure Suits,
6570th Aerospace Medical Research Laboratory, USAF

of EVA were vitally important if astronauts were ever to step outside a lunar-landing vehicle and walk on the surface of the moon. The suit-ventilation method of Project Gemini caused some trouble during the second of five EVA experiments.

It happened on Gemini Flight Number Nine, launched from Cape Kennedy on June 3, 1966. The EVA program, which was scheduled for a few days after launch, was extremely difficult and lengthy. It was to last at least two hours and included the initial test in space of a new astronaut maneuvering unit (AMU). The first American "walk in space" had been successfully accomplished almost exactly one year earlier, during Gemini Flight Number 4. That EVA was performed by the late Edward H. White II. No serious problems were encountered with the specially designed David Clark EVA space suit—but the so-called space walk lasted only about twenty-one minutes. The basic idea was to prove the reliability of the suit.

On the second EVA experiment, however, unanticipated problems arose that caused the space-suit people to think seriously about ventilation design changes in future EVA clothing. Eugene A. Cernan was the space-walking astronaut in this experiment. His spacecraft Commander was Thomas P. Stafford. One of the doctors involved with the medical side of the EVA mission, who doesn't want to be named, described to me the problems encountered by astronaut Cernan on his long space walk.

"Gene Cernan got into profoundly big trouble," he told me. "He wasn't going to die, but it was a close call. The EVA mission required him to put on his pressure suit, dump the spacecraft pressure and crawl around to the back of the GT-9 [Gemini-Titan Number Nine]. Back there was an adapter unit attached to the spacecraft and on the back side of the adapter unit was an astronaut maneuvering unit—an AMU developed at something like ten million dollars by the Massachusetts Institute of Technology. The setup had been thoroughly checked out on the ground, in the low-pressure and -temperature-chamber at the Manned Spacecraft Center in Houston, Texas. Everything seemed to work fine.

"So Cernan got into his space suit, depressurized his side of the spacecraft cabin, and climbed outside. That took about two and a half, maybe three, hours of work. Up to that time everything was going pretty well. This occurred some three days into the orbital flight mission, as I recall.

"Now when Cernan had been practicing this first part of the EVA in the altitude-temperature chamber at Houston, he had the earth's gravity and friction helping him. He still had friction in his favor out there in orbit, but in that weightless situation it took him a much longer time to crawl along the spacecraft. There were no hand holds on the craft to help him.

"So it took him a much longer time than he planned to move around to the rear of the capsule. This carried him farther away from the sunny side of the world in orbit, much farther away than he would have been if the timing was more perfect. The extra strain of work generated a lot more heat in him than he could get rid of by normal convection, conduction, and radiation. So his body began to perspire excessively. His perspiration could not be effectively evaporated away. And therefore, moisture began to build up all along the inside portions of his suit—including the inside of his helmet visor.

"All of this was going on while he was crawling his way back toward the astronaut maneuvering unit. He finally got there and buckled himself into the AMU—which takes a long time and is very complicated. Understandably, his heart rate was exceptionally high during all phases of this effort—because *if* the EVA pressure suit fails in *any* portion, he's dead, and he knew that. Any number of things *might* have gone wrong. He could have cracked his visor by banging it against a hard surface during his struggles. A leak in one of the gaskets around his wrist could have killed him.

"Anyway, his heart was pumping very fast—a hundred forty to a hundred fifty beats at certain times. After he finally got himself strapped into the AMU, one of the two armrests on the unit jammed before it could be folded all the way down to its operating position. In other words, he was helpless. He couldn't control the little maneuvering rockets on the AMU, because they would only operate when commanded by the throttles on the armrests—and the throttles wouldn't work unless the arms were all the way down in their horizontal operating position.

"On top of this, one of the two access lights failed. These were work lights, so he could see what he was doing in the dark. They were both supposed to be switched on as he and the spacecraft flew over Carnarvon, Australia, and remain on as he moved though the nightside portion of the earth.

"But suddenly, in a matter of thirty minutes, radio communications throughout the whole world really went to hell. Maybe this was caused by an abrupt flare on the sun? Whatever caused the situation, it was striking to all of us on the ground.

"So it was difficult for the command astronaut to communicate with Gemini Mission Control at Houston or with the various tracking stations around the globe. Meanwhile, the moisture was building up inside the EVA astronaut's suit and it was hard for him to see because of the condensation on his helmet visor, or faceplate. Right about now, the communications link between the outside astronaut and the inside astronaut also deteriorated.

"There was Cernan, the EVA guy, out there in space, all alone in silence. His main visor became thoroughly frosted over on the inside. He was still strapped into the AMU, a captive passenger forced to ride through space on the outside of his own capsule—for the AMU was still anchored to the Gemini capsule. The AMU was attached to its adapter unit by a series of explosive bolts. Astronaut Cernan had already armed the powder squibs, getting ready to explode the AMU away from the spacecraft. But now he not only couldn't communicate with his commander for advice relayed from the earth; he couldn't see either. It was a terribly dangerous situation.

"Commander Stafford inside the Gemini capsule was thinking: 'I'm calling the whole thing off, canceling it right now. I am going to order Gene Cernan to get out of that AMU and come right back into this spacecraft—abort the EVA.'

"That's what went through Tom Stafford's mind, I learned later. But there was no way to tell Cernan anything. And even if Gene did unlock himself from that powered-up AMU, how was he going to see to get back inside the capsule? Besides, the AMU had to be disarmed or blown away from the capsule, if the Gemini 9 astronauts were going to be able safely to reenter the earth's atmosphere for a splashdown.

"The first break came in improved communications. Radio signals cleared up—and this made the danger of the situation horribly apparent to everyone. Because even as Cernan was coming back over the sunny side of the world, over Hawaii, his visor was still thoroughly frosted. He was too blind to do anything efficiently, even though now he *could* hear instructions.

"It should be explained that there are two visors on the EVA helmets. The main one is transparent and seals in the helmet's pressurization. It can be an integral part of the total helmet, as it is on the Apollo helmets. Or it can be a separate faceplate set into the helmet and hermetically sealed, as it was on the Gemini helmets. The second is a gold visor that can be raised or lowered over the main visor. The main visor acts as a window, permitting the astronaut to see what he's doing. The gold visor is really a radiation filter and heat reflector. Deposited on it are several very thin layers of filtering and reflecting materials. The gold layer is an extremely effective mirror that reflects away the heat from the sun, while the other layers stop dangerous electromagnetic radiations—such as ultraviolet light—before they can pass through the main visor to injure the eyes and face of the astronaut. Sunlight is so intense in the vacuum of space that even when the gold visor is lowered, an astronaut can see through it. From the outside, it looks opaque—but it is fairly transparent to the astronaut looking out through it from the inside.

"Gene Cernan had lowered the gold visor as he came back

into the sunlit side of the world over Hawaii. I recommended that he raise the visor again, so that the radiant heat coming from the sun would not be reflected away but would rather strike the main visor and melt the frost that had formed inside it. So I sent an urgent telegram to the CAPCOM [Capsule Communicator] at Houston.

"But by the time my telegram was received and processed in Texas, the problem seemed to be solving itself. The frost inside his main visor had dissipated and Gene Cernan completed his EVA mission."

Many important scientific lessons were learned from the crucial EVA situation on Gemini Flight Number Nine. Improvements were made in the EVA space suit that made possible a highly successful space-walking exercise five months later. Astronaut Cernan's actual EVA had lasted two hours and seven minutes. Between November 11 and 15, 1966, Gemini Flight Number Twelve orbited around the earth fifty-nine times. During those orbits astronaut Edwin E. Aldrin, Jr. stepped out of his capsule and performed EVA experiments and useful work for more than five and a half hours. Aldrin thus proved that a man wearing a properly designed EVA space suit and using the right equipment can function effectively outside of his spacecraft.

Less than three years later, on July 20, 1969, the same Aldrin followed his Command Pilot, Neil Armstrong, onto the lunar surface. They were the world's first beings to walk upon the moon— an EVA performance made possible only by the most advanced designs in space suits and life-support equipment.

The basic technology that lay behind the design and construction of those lunar EVA suits was acquired by the dedicated sweat and blood of aerospace medical scientists and engineers during the latter part of the 1950's and the earliest years of the 1960's. Until the closing months of 1958, all pressure- and space-suit research was motivated by military requirements. On October 5 of that year, Project Mercury was initiated by the civilian space agency, NASA. Since NASA itself was then only four days old, it had no technological background in the design of protective space clothing and had to depend entirely on the Air Force and Navy for advice as well as equipment. The Aero Medical Laboratory at Wright Field and the Navy's Aviation Medical Acceleration Laboratory at Johnsville, Pennsylvania, were focal points to develop equipment for and train the Project Mercury Astronauts.

At the time, two basic approaches had evolved in the search to perfect a full-pressure suit that would meet the vital demands of mobility, comfort, and constant volume/constant pressure. One approach was the "soft suit"; the other was the "hard suit." There were advantages and disadvantages to each. The soft suit was naturally more easily stowable aboard an aircraft or spacecraft, but it had a tendency to balloon out of shape in the wrong places. The hard suit was bulky and inflexible, making it difficult to fold up and store when not in use, but it could withstand high internal oxygen pressures and automatically preserved a constant volume and pressure. A major subsidiary problem with either type of suit was making it comfortable to wear for extended periods of time.

The biggest problem with the hard suit was mobility. One solution, proposed by the Boeing Company, was nicknamed the "stovepipe suit."

Another Air Force contractor was also working on the hard-suit problem, with encouraging results. This was Litton Industries of Beverly Hills, California. Litton engineers had designed and built a suit with a hard torso shell. The arms, thighs, and legs of the suit were formed of flexible pleated rubberized material, after the tomato-worm idea, but much refined. On at least one occasion in the late 1950's the suit kept a man alive and working on simulated tasks in an altitude environment of 501,600 feet (ninety-five miles). This was truly a space-equivalent situation, not only for the suit but also for the chamber.

However, no developmental program on the Litton suit was ordered by the Aero Medical Laboratory. NASA, like the Air Force, decided ultimately to take the soft-suit route.

Yet the hard suit—or a hybrid combination of the best qualities in hard and soft suits—must eventually find its place in space exploration. When men are ready to live and work in big orbiting laboratories or on the moon, the hard suit and the hybrid hard-soft suit should come into their own.

The soft suit not only had more immediately desirable characteristics than the hard suit for use by combat crews flying in the stratosphere, but was even more attractive to the pilots in a revolutionary new experimental flight program. From July 9, 1954, when it was first proposed, to October 24, 1968, when it was completed, the X-15 Flight Research Program was the real pioneer in clearing the way toward manned spaceflight.

As a joint effort of NASA, the Air Force, and the Navy, the three rocket-powered airplanes in this program explored for the first time many of the unknown aspects of flight into the void. Unsuspected problems were discovered and solutions to them developed by the X-15 aircraft. In the process, unofficial world records, that still stand for airplanes, were established in altitude and speed: 350,000 feet (sixty-seven miles) above the earth and 4,520 miles an hour (six and seven-tenths times the speed of sound). Several of the twelve test pilots in the X-15 program were awarded Astronaut Wings by the Air Force for having flown one of the rocket aircraft above 250,000 feet, a level of the earth's atmosphere considered to be the edge of space.

One of the X-15 test pilots was Neil A. Armstrong, whose name should be familiar to everyone as the first earthling to set foot upon the surface of the moon. If the X-15 Flight Research Program had never been initiated, that first step onto an alien world would still be in the faraway future.

The three X-15 aircraft provided an economical way to penetrate the mysteries of manned space flight, since they were re-usable vehicles and thus could perform a wide range of experiments over and over again. Total cost of the program was about $300 million, a mere pittance when compared with the price of the Saturn V rocket launch-vehicle program—where each flight of the giant launching rocket is a one-shot affair. The late Dr. Hugh L. Dryden, an outstanding aeronautical scientist and former Deputy Administrator of NASA, had called the X-15's "the most successful research aircraft ever built."

Over-all, the X-15 rocket airplanes more than helped to develop advanced, vitally needed aeronautical and space-flight systems. New flight techniques, new materials, and new instruments were contributed to NASA and the military by the X-15 experiments. Not least of the contributions was the development and testing of comfortable, long-term, mobile and constant volume/constant pressure soft space suits.

The space suit that was developed at the Wright Aero Medical Laboratory for test evaluation and improvement suggestions by X-15 pilots led in a straight line to the full-pressure clothing later worn by Project Gemini astronauts. It also provided the basic knowledge to modify the Navy's full-pressure suit into a space suit for the Project Mercury astronauts. Deep in the X-15 suit-development program was Dr. Edwin G. Vail, then project officer of the program. He told me:

"The first operational-type test-suit for the X-15 program was wrung into the mill about 1955. It came from a basic development we started in 1953 at the Aerospace Medical Research Lab [in those days, of course, called the Aero Medical Laboratory].

"Then about 1958, after we had it in operational shape, the X-15 suit was procured in quantity. The first powered flight of the X-15 was still roughly a year away. In fact, we had the suit ready even before the rollout of the first X-15 at the North American Aviation plant in California.

"We also had begun another suit project with International Latex." This involved experimenting with the molded-convolute system as a fundamental characteristic to obtain better limb joints,

Here are front, back, and side
views of a 1958 space suit made
for the Air Force by
International Latex Corporation,
designated XMC-2-ILC. It is shown
in the uninflated state.
The arm and leg portions of
the suit contained many
fine rubber coils, and the
shoulder and thigh areas had
much wider coils. All
of the coils had indentations
molded into them at right
angles to the coil direction.
When an arm or a leg was
bent or a thigh lifted, these
indentations contracted or
expanded out of phase with the
contractions or expansions
of the coils, compensating for
any shift of volume within
the suit and keeping
its internal gas pressure
constant. This suit
was a precursor of the first
state-of-the-art prototype
space suit for the
Apollo astronauts. The helmet
was produced by International
Latex, but was based on ideas
from the Bill Jack MA-1 helmet.

Courtesy Don Bowen,
Group Leader/Pressure Suits,
6570th Aerospace Medical Research
Laboratory, USAF

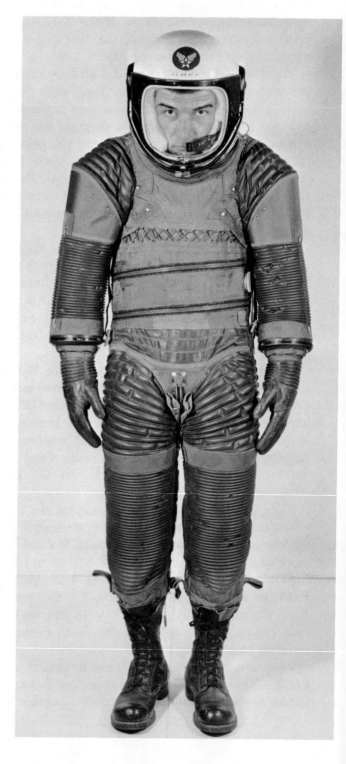

better volume-to-pressure control, and better over-all performance in the suit. (See illustration.)

"We worked on that International Latex program until we had a prototype suit ready to fly in late 1959. About this time—NASA was now well underway—the Air Force ran into some small budget problems and NASA picked up this suit program and continued it right on to an Apollo suit-configuration."

Even as the X-15 Flight Research Program was swinging into action, the Air Force established an X-20 project. It was popularly called DYNA-SOAR, for "Dynamic Soaring." Its purpose was to develop a rocket-boosted vehicle that would perform both as a manned spacecraft and as an airplane. The idea was to shoot it into orbit around the earth for special experimental missions and then have the pilot guide it back to the ground at a landing field of his own choice. Naturally, a specialized space suit was required for the X-20 DYNA-SOAR. Although Project X-20 was primarily military in nature, NASA again benefitted from it.

Dr. Ed Vail summarized this to me as follows: "The X-20 suit was derived from the X-15 suit. As a space-suit development program, the X-20 had an interesting evolution and program relationship with NASA. The X-20 program provided the original prototype suits that were later to become the prototype space suit for Project Gemini. At the time we were working on the X-20 suits, Gus Grissom was Project Officer for NASA on the design and evaluation of the Gemini capsule crew station. We worked closely together on adapting a suit to the crew station. And it was that suit—an X-20 suit—which we developed that NASA used subsequently as a Gemini flight prototype."

The problem of constant volume/constant pressure and mobility in the Gemini space suit was solved uniquely with a fish net. Actually the system only resembled a fish net, although it did at first employ forty-pound-test Dacron fishing line. Later on, Teflon cord was used. Both of these synthetic materials in their stranded form have smooth, slippery surfaces. When either of them is woven into a network of loose interconnecting links, it becomes a mobile chain of mail, so to speak, resembling the flexible metal armor worn by knights and warriors centuries ago. Of course these materials are much lighter in weight than metal links would be. This was the big advantage of the link-net system: light weight with great strength and mobility.

In the Gemini EVA space suit, a link net was carefully fitted to follow the body contours of its wearer. Underneath the net was a rubberized fabric bladder. When the bladder was inflated with oxygen gas to pressurize the body, the net restrained the bladder from ballooning in any direction. Since the net itself had

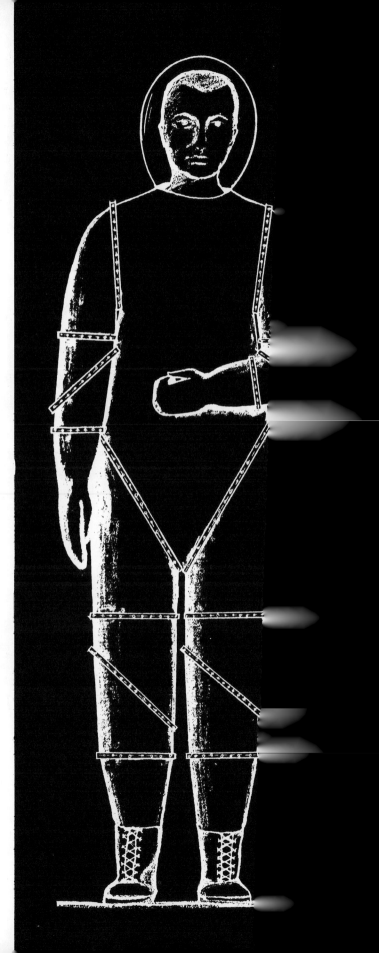

All of the pressure suits shown in this chapter thus far were of the so-called soft-suit design. But in 1961, the Boeing Company, following NASA's lead at its Ames Research Center, proposed a hard suit. It was dubbed the "stovepipe suit," since it would be built entirely of hard segments resembling sections of stovepipe. The sections would rotate on big metal ring bearings. Such a suit had its advantages: it could be pressurized to as high as sea-level air pressure (15 pounds per square inch) without ballooning or shifting its volume-to-pressure ratio; and the various sections could flex with the movement of an elbow, wrist, or shoulder to solve the problem of mobility. Disadvantages were the chance of pressure leakage through the joint bearings and the difficulty of storing it in the confined quarters of a spacecraft. Drawing here is the original Boeing concept presentation.

Courtesy Don Bowen,
Group Leader/Pressure Suits,
6570th Aerospace Medical Research
Laboratory, USAF

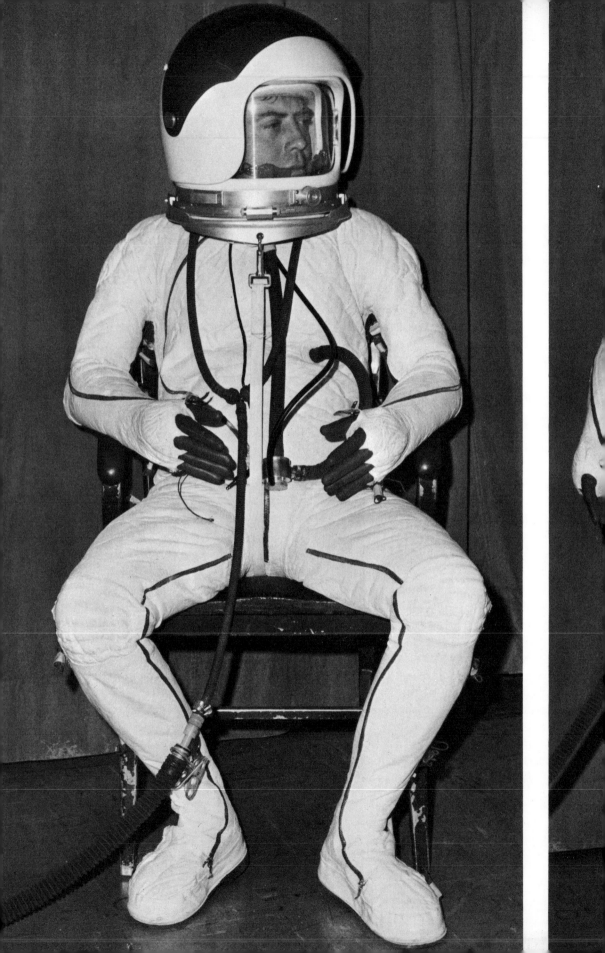

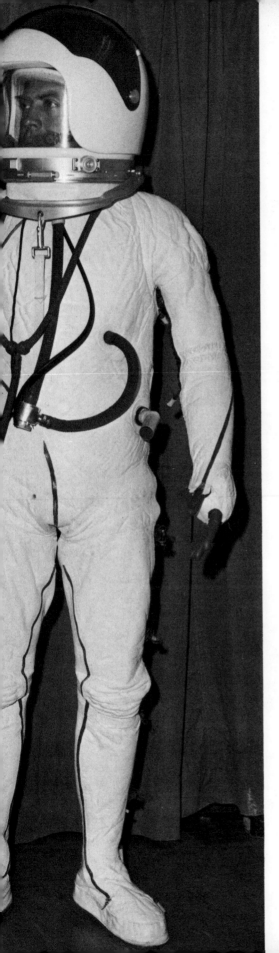

The unique pressure suit shown here in two
views was the result of experimental research
by the Mauch Laboratories, Inc. of Dayton, Ohio,
who carried out the first phase between
April 1959 and April 1960 and the second phase
between January 1961 and January 1962.
Purpose of the experiments was to develop (a)
"a new concept of pressure protection
based on the known principle of mechanical
restraint [the capstan-tube partial-
pressure suit] but eliminating the shortcomings
of past suits based on this principle" and
(b) " a new approach to the problem of
thermal [temperature] control of a space suit
based on the utilization of the human
sweating mechanism in conjunction with controlled
evaporation [of sweat] by providing low
absolute pressure on the skin surface." Principal
investigator in the experiments was
Hans Mauch, who had earlier developed an
air-conditioned undergarment for space suits
when he was chief of the Environment Section at
the Wright Aero Medical Laboratory.
Mauch's new principle for pressurizing the body
employed neither capstan tubes nor gas-
inflated full-pressure clothing. His method was
passive, rather than active. He designed
the space suit so that "the body swells into
the suit." In effect, the suit's fabric
and structure was its own pressurizing agent.
Therefore, it was lightweight and highly mobile.
Its helmet, which had good visibility, was
pressurized separately with oxygen.

Courtesy Don Bowen,
Group Leader/Pressure Suits,
6570th Aerospace Medical Research
Laboratory, USAF

This prototype space suit for X-20 DYNA-SOAR pilots was built by the B. F. Goodrich Company and is being tested here in a chair structured of foamed plastic. Although uninflated in photo, its mobility should be apparent. Gerry Goodman, then of the Air Force and now at NASA's Manned Spacecraft Center, Houston, was the test subject. He was wearing a white cushion liner under the bubble-type experimental helmet. Purpose of liner was to protect its wearer's head from bumping directly against helmet shell during the high-g phase of rocket-booster lift-off.

Courtesy Don Bowen, Group Leader/Pressure Suits, 6570th Aerospace Medical Research Laboratory, USAF

give in every direction, the suit wearer could move his shoulders,
arms, torso, and legs without causing a change in volume or
pressure within his suit.

Made by the David Clark Company, the Gemini link-net suit
was extremely light in weight and very comfortable in its uninflated
condition. It was also more comfortable when inflated than any
other full-pressure suit built up to that time.

Its helmet was another matter. Evolved from the Air Force
MA-1/MA-2 series of helmets, the Gemini headgear was a close-
fitting device which wasn't all that its wearer might wish for in the
way of comfort. Its entire weight had to be carried on the wearer's
head. But it served its purpose well after several modifications.
It was one aspect of the X-20 DYNA-SOAR space suit that was
not adopted by NASA until later.

Dr. Ed Vail himself had felt that an intimately fitted helmet
was the best type, although he did not overlook other possibilities
during his X-20 suit experiments. One of these was a fishbowl-type
helmet that rested on its wearer's shoulders, allowing complete
freedom of movement for the head. It took a terrifying incident
to convince Dr. Vail that the latter type of helmet was superior.
But let him tell the story in his own words:.

"Dan Folger was testing our X-20 suit and survival equipment
by simulating ejections from the DYNA-SOAR spacecraft. We had
set up a DYNA-SOAR ejection seat near the back door of a
C-124 Globemaster. Dan, wearing all of the equipment, including
the survival kit, would roll off a rack in the ejection seat and fall
out the open back door of the C-124. Usually we were at about
eight thousand feet of altitude when he did this."

On his fifth jump, Folger rolled out of the ejection seat in an
unusual position that threw his body off its normal center of
gravity. He fell into a very bad spin. His main parachute was
damaged, and he could not get the auxiliary chute to open until
just before he hit the ground. Folger was not seriously injured,
and his accident was instructive.

"The most important thing discovered, from our point of view
at the Wright Aerospace Medical Research Lab," said Dr. Vail,
"was involved with space-suit helmets. Dan Folger made all his
jumps with a full-head helmet. That is, a fishbowl helmet that
was not padded close around his head—it only had a cushioning
pad system between his head and the fishbowl, plus earphones and
a microphone—and he could move his head around inside it. It did
not move with his head, as the other helmets did.

"We were quite amazed by the fact that Dan had very few
head problems. The fact that the helmet was fastened to his space
suit at the shoulder area meant that he didn't have its weight

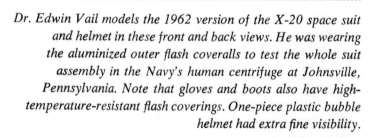
*Dr. Edwin Vail models the 1962 version of the X-20 space suit
and helmet in these front and back views. He was wearing
the aluminized outer flash coveralls to test the whole suit
assembly in the Navy's human centrifuge at Johnsville,
Pennsylvania. Note that gloves and boots also have high-
temperature-resistant flash coverings. One-piece plastic bubble
helmet had extra fine visibility.*

Courtesy Dr. Edwin G. Vail,
Hamilton Standard Division,
United Aircraft Corporation

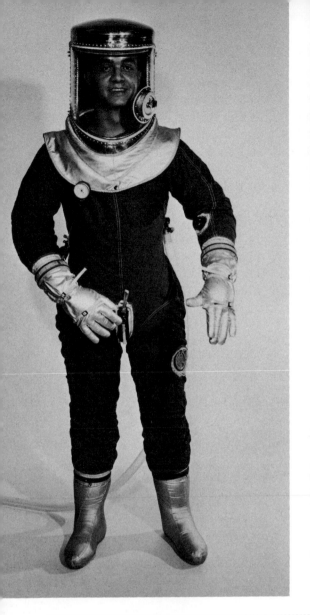
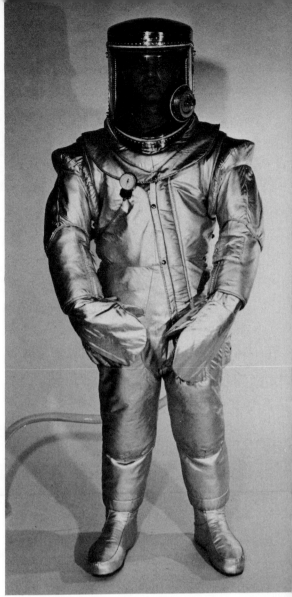

An experimental suit for walking in space or on the moon.
These two views illustrate the pressure suit proper and its protective
outer garment, which was evolved to resist the impact of high-
velocity meteoroids and nuclear particles as well as both visible and
invisible electromagnetic radiations from the sun. During the
research-and-development phases of this suit, many special materials
were tried out, and much was learned that would apply to
the requirements for a safe and mobile extravehicular space suit.
The suit experiments were carried on between July 1962 and April 1964
by Mr. Norman H. Osborne of the David Clark Company and
Mrs. Lee C. Rock, Project Engineer/Pressure Suits at the Aerospace
Medical Research Laboratories, Wright Field. The suit itself was
royal blue in color, and the complete suit assembly, without
its environmental-control system attached, weighed about
twenty-five pounds. It could be donned by a trained wearer in
less than five minutes.

Courtesy Don Bowen, Group Leader/Pressure Suits, 6570th Aerospace Medical Research Laboratory, USAF

pressing down on his head. So those jumps without any head complications led me to suspect that our basic idea which said we've *got* to have an intimate-fit helmet, even on our high-performance fighter pilots today, might be in error. In terms of man-to-aircraft or spacecraft performance, it might be much wiser to take the helmet weight off a crewman's head and put it on his shoulders—where he's got a lot more body strength and structure to carry the load."

This observation of Dr. Edwin Vail on the X-20 program led NASA and the industrial contractors involved to adopt a modified fishbowl-type helmet for the Project Apollo space suits. In fact, when Neil Armstrong and "Buzz" Aldrin first stepped upon the moon in the Sea of Tranquillity they were wearing just such helmets atop their lunar EVA suits.

Chapter 8

MINISUITS FOR ASTROMONKS AND ASTROPUPS

When the first man steps onto the surface of the planet Mars he shouldn't be surprised to find a simple slogan traced by paw in the red Martian sands: "Sam Space, Jr., was here." He'll know immediately that again a monkey has beaten the human race in the exploration of outer space.

Animals, birds, and reptiles are the real pioneers in conquering the hazards of flight through outer space. Dogs, cats, monkeys, apes, mice, rats, goats, rabbits, opposums, turtles, and pigeons have been used in an immense variety of experiments intended to solve the known physical problems of space flight and to discover others undreamed of. Among the experiments have been those concerned with gravity acceleration (increase of weight), zero gravity (weightlessness), high altitudes (low oxygen and pressure), vision, weariness, muscle motor mechanisms, tolerance to toxic gases, fainting mechanisms, and radiation. If these creatures had not been used in laboratory tests on earth and actual rocket flights into the unknown, the science of aerospace medicine would still be a promise of things to come, and the modern space suit that protects astronauts on the moon would not yet be ready to wear.

Many people have forgotten an epic flight made in a missile by two monkeys during the late spring of 1959. Their names were Able and Baker, after the first two letters of the old international phonetic alphabet. The toughness of Able and Baker is remarkable. Together they weighed a total of six pounds eleven ounces.

During their 1700-mile journey downrange from Cape Canaveral (now renamed Cape Kennedy) in the nose cone of an Army Jupiter Intermediate Range Ballistic Missile, they were forced to experience a mighty tug of war between themselves and the pull of gravity. They also fell through space in a weightless condition for the greater part of their journey.

At lift-off of the rocket, in its initial stages of acceleration, the forces pulling against their small bodies were fifteen times as great as normal gravity. This means that the harder their rocket tried to accelerate away from gravity, the mightier was the clutch of gravity trying to accelerate them back to the earth. The same situation was, in a sense, reversed as they decelerated coming back into the atmosphere at the end of their journey. Only it was worse. As the atmosphere slowed down their capsule by friction against the tug of gravity, the force applied against their bodies was thirty-eight g's—thirty-eight times the accelerating force of gravity.

Atmospheric friction also caused the nose cone in which they rode to glow like a white-hot star. Its temperature finally reached 5,000 degrees Fahrenheit. Yet the two little monkeys survived the violent speed, the extreme temperature changes, and the disorientation of weightlessness—with no apparent ill aftereffects.

How could they survive?

The answer to this question covers not merely the physical stamina of a six-pound rhesus monkey and an eleven-ounce squirrel monkey. It encompasses many things—the careful planning of NASA; the fine cooperation between Army, Navy, and Air Force; the ingenuity and imagination of many scientists, engineers, and technicians, both civilian and military; and twenty years of research and development in the fields of rocket-propulsion systems, airframe design, aviation medicine, space biology, environmental testing, high-altitude physiology, psychology, anthropology, electronic instrumentation, electronic and optical tracking systems, and even clothing design.

In other words, the epic rocket flight of Able and Baker was historically important because it brought together all the scientific and engineering disciplines of space technology—and proved that man himself was ready, physically and mechanically, for space flight. By studying the evolution of the physical structure of apes, monkeys, and humans, life-scientists have been able to develop techniques that vastly reduce the shock of acceleration, among other things.

One of the monkeys, Able, was strapped into a form-fitting cradle, called a "contour bed." Such a contour device is useful for men as well as monkeys. It was first thought of by anthropologists working with acceleration scientists at the Air Force's Wright Aero Medical Laboratory, as a means for absorbing the shock of acceleration and deceleration. These contour devices were later adapted for use as form-fitting couches by the Mercury, Gemini, and Apollo astronauts. The protective clothing worn by Able and Baker and the pressurized chambers that kept them alive inside the rocket nose cone came out of know-how acquired through years of research by cooperation between respiration and clothing specialists and, again, anthropologists.

Inside the Jupiter missile was an electronic guidance system that placed its nose cone in the water with excellent accuracy, only about five miles from where the Navy tug *Kiowa* was waiting. The cone itself did not burn up from atmospheric friction because of a special technique developed mainly by civilian research. It carried an outer shell of layers of an ablative material that peeled away as heat was generated, thereby taking away the heat energy from the nose cone proper. As the tug *Kiowa* came abreast of the floating nose cone, Navy frogmen defied three sharks hungrily orbiting around it and swathed it in a net of ropes so it could be hauled aboard ship.

Able and Baker were found to be in good physical shape as the cone was opened. This was not equally true of another biological experiment—a small glass tube containing whole human blood. The blood was donated by an Army medical corpsman, Captain William Augerson, to discover if the violence of rocket flight would have any effect upon human blood cells. The cells were ruptured. The blood-cell experiment was an attempt to discover if whole blood could be rocketed to Army troops in the field or to disaster areas for transfusion purposes. Another experiment that failed was the attempt to fertilize the eggs of sea urchins in conditions of weightlessness. Neither failure, however, had any deleterious effect upon the future of manned space flight.

Several cosmic-ray experiments also accompanied Able and Baker on their historic flight. These included the skin of onions, mustard seeds, spores of mold, grains of corn, yeast cells, and the larvae of *Drosophila melanogaster,* the common fruit fly, sometimes called a vinegar gnat. If any of these were struck and seriously damaged by the heavy primary particles of cosmic radiation, the effects would show up in various ways.

Since fruit flies are exceptionally fast breeders (whole generations of them develop within a few weeks), the hereditary results of radiation exposure may be quickly studied. The genetic effects of exposure to weightlessness may also be observed quickly in succeeding generations of fruit flies whose ancestral larvae have flown through space. Scientists further wanted to know what the combined effects would be of radiation damage and zero gravity. On the brief, though epic, flight of Able and Baker, there was not much hint of damage from either source.

But on much longer later flights in earth-orbiting satellites, bacteria, seedlings, and insects showed remarkable changes caused by radiation strikes in combination with weightlessness. Bacteria, protozoa, and viruses flown on the Biosatellite II mission reacted in various ways—which often could not be explained by scientists.

Frog eggs were also carried aboard Biosatellite II. Six tadpoles were later hatched on earth. None of them showed any ill effects from their long ride in a zero-gravity state.

Wheat seedlings aboard the satellite, however, displayed a total dependence upon the earth's gravity for normal growth. Without such gravity their leaves, stems, and roots grew in a variety of directions opposite to the norm. The leaves of on-board pepper plants did almost the same thing. Normally, pepper-plant leaves grow straight out from their stems. In weightless space they curled and twisted themselves in a downward direction.

But most spectacular of all were the effects of radiation in combination with weightlessness upon the common fruit fly. Some of the fruit flies that made the space journey produced eggs that hatched into flies with half a thorax, with the stump of a wing, or with a wing entirely missing. Such odd genetic effects occurred, fortunately, in only one out of every ten thousand fruit-fly eggs. This holds out a hope for not too great a danger to the future generations of humans whose ancestors made space voyages.

Other insects flown aboard the biological satellite were mutated genetically in various ways by the interactions of zero gravity and radiation.

The report on Biosatellite II was summarized as follows:

Since [all] living things have much in common, the results are contributing to [an] understanding of life processes. To biologists studying

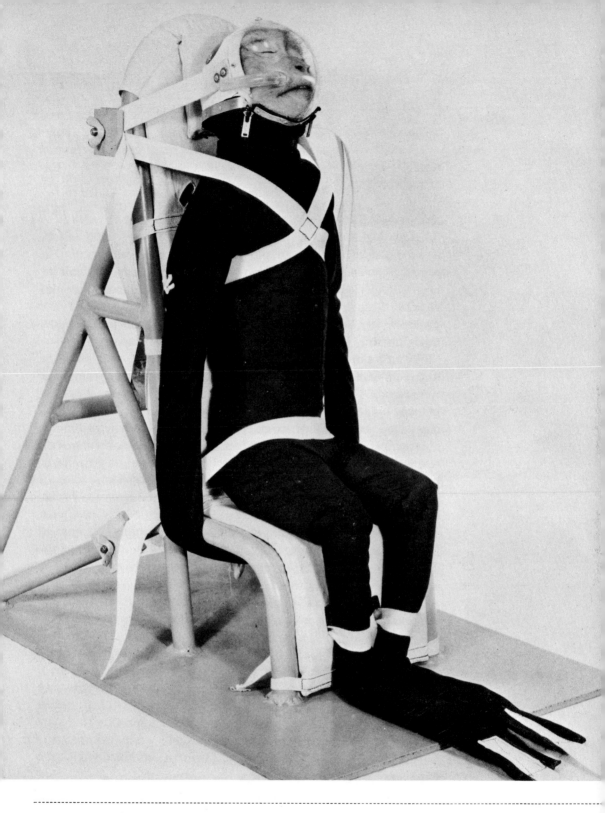

*Exact replica of full-head pressure helmet in miniature
is worn by anesthetized monkey for altitude-chamber test.
Note plastic tube on left side of helmet next to animal's
mouth to feed oxygen into helmet.*

Courtesy Air Force Film Depository

such diseases as cancer where mutant cells compete with normal cells, for example, the fact that lowered or absent gravity can slow down the activity of damaged mutant cells may be significant. Much more experimentation and study will be required, of course, before its significance can be ascertained.

Scientists also caution that Biosatellite II experiments were with relatively simple organisms and the findings cannot be transferred directly to man. For example, forty-five hours of weightless flight for some of these organisms is the equivalent of years to a human being. But the Biosatelilte II experiments and others to follow are adding a new dimension to man's knowledge about life.

Nevertheless, because of the vast differences in biological time between insects and man, the biosatellite experiments at least do not rule out the possibility that human beings can endure extended voyages through space with little chance of physical damage. For instance, three weeks in terms of fruit-fly time could be analogous to six hundred years of the human biological time span.

A much more pertinent experiment related to extensive long-term flights of man in space was Biosatellite III. Launched from Cape Kennedy on June 28, 1969, it was intended to carry a pigtail monkey—known scientifically as *Macaca nemestrina*—on a thirty-day space voyage. This would have been about twice as long as any astronaut had previously flown in space. But something went wrong with the monkey's physical condition, and it had to be brought down after only eight and a half days in orbit.

When Biosatellite III was successfully recovered from the Pacific Ocean, the little astromonk, named Bonny, was in very poor condition. His brain temperature had dropped more than three degrees from normal and his heart rate had fallen sixty beats per minute. The small spacemonk was also about twenty percent lighter in weight due to fluid loss. He was flown to Hickam Air Force Base in Hawaii for medical treatment. Six hours later he had made a remarkable recovery, approaching the normal, but another six hours after that he abruptly expired.

There was some speculation in the press that his untimely death proved that zero gravity, or the weightless condition of space flight, was a killer. Men would not be able to voyage through space on long expeditions without facing the grim possibility of extinction —or so the news stories claimed. But the fact remains that men had already flown on long journeys through space, without any serious damage to their physiology, much before the flight of the pigtail monkey.

Zero gravity may well have been a factor in Bonny's deterioration and death, but there were other factors involved as well. The cabin temperature of Biosatellite III remained at least six degrees below normal throughout his eight-and-a-half-day space flight. Also, his diet was restricted to a single type of protein—cassein—to avoid the development of urinary problems, a condition unique to certain species of monkeys when they eat other kinds of protein. At any rate, the space doctors are not as sure as the press that it was weightlessness in space that caused Bonny's demise.

Scientists had hoped that the thirty-day biosatellite flight would provide more medical data on space-flight conditions for humans than all of the manned space flights combined up to that time.

Pigtail monkeys, despite their small size, are not only manlike physiologically and emotionally; they even act like human beings. Two problems encountered during their training period on earth and one encountered in actual space flight illustrate this. While they were being trained to sit patiently in their form-fitted seats for thirty days, their space suits were zippered to the seats to hold them in. As soon as a medical attendant turned his back or walked away from them, they unzipped their suits and jumped out of the special space chairs. Finally, out of sheer frustration, the training personnel had to have all of the monkey space suits remodeled. This also meant remodeling the seats. The zippers were removed and relocated in the back of the suits, at a position out of reach of the monkeys. Bonny was finally chosen as the lucky one to fly in space.

After the first day of his flight in orbit, Bonny discovered a way to outsmart his human experimenters. He was supposed to receive an extra food pellet automatically every time he successfully performed one of the zero-gravity orientation tests. At last he noticed that the food pellets would pop out of their bin during certain intervals whether he performed the test or not. So he skipped the test and just sat there waiting for a "free" pellet between his regular meals.

Able and Baker, unlike Bonny, didn't have the time to figure out angles on their brief flight of nine minutes, but it was a much greater landmark than the flight of Biosatellite III. The one ironically tragic aspect of the historic project was the death of Able. The rhesus monkey did not die because of any bad aftereffects from the rocket flight. She (here both monkeys were female) was instrumented with electrodes to radio back to earth her pulse rate and respiration rate. To remove one of these electrodes imbedded in her chest, the Army surgeons—it was an Army-supervised project— gave her an anesthetic. Almost at once, Able expired. General anesthesia given an animal after extreme stress can cause death if lung hemorrhages are present. But no hemorrhage was found in Able during the autopsy. So her demise is an ironical mystery.

Able's skin has been mounted by a taxidermist and she still reminds the world of her ballistic tour through space, on display at the Smithsonian National Museum in Washington, D.C. Ameri-

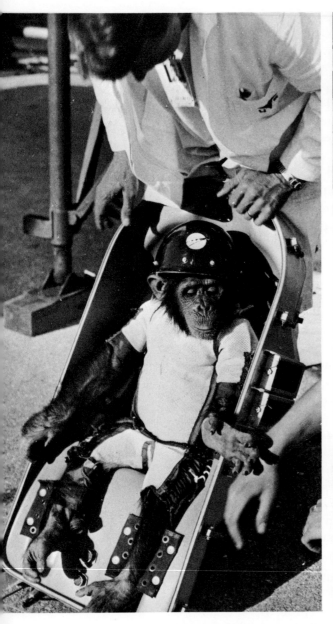

Two of the chimpanzees that were trained for the first "manned" suborbital flight of the Mercury space capsule. The experiment was designed to test the spacecraft's environmental-control and recovery systems. Chimps are shown in their form-fitted couches to reduce shock of high gravity forces during lift-off into space and re-entry into the earth's atmosphere. Both animals are wearing space suits. One poses with a NASA hard hat.

Courtesy NASA

can scientists had launched monkeys in rockets before the time of
Able and Baker—but never so high, so fast, so far, or in a ballistic
trajectory that required high-speed re-entry into the earth's atmosphere. Able was one of two great space pioneers.

The other one, Baker, lived out her days happily in the air-
conditioned monkey house at the Naval School of Aviation Medicine, Pensacola, Florida.

Just under two years after the flight of Able and Baker, another
jungle animal bridged the remaining gap in knowledge to make
manned space flight possible. This time it was a chimpanzee named
Ham who soared out of Cape Canaveral and down what was then
called the Atlantic Missile Range. On January 31, 1961, Ham was
strapped into a Project Mercury space capsule and launched downrange atop an Army Redstone Missile. He ultimately reached a
speed of 5,000 miles an hour during his 420-mile ride through
space. His body was covered with sensors to measure blood pressure,
respiratory rate, and heart functions. The Mercury spacecraft was
also instrumented to record structural stresses as well as skin and
cabin temperatures. Additionally, Ham's facial expressions were
photographed with an automatic 16-millimeter camera.

Ham was safely fished out of the Atlantic after splashdown by
frogmen from the USS Donner. His flight cleared the way immediately for astronaut Alan B. Shepard, Jr.'s suborbital flight
some three months later, on May 5, 1961. Shepard, the first American in space, rode down the Atlantic Missile Range in exactly the
same type of spacecraft as Ham's.

Although monkeys and chimps performed a vital role in the
evolution of manned space flight and the protective clothing required to make such flights possible, dogs, too, played their important part. Dr. Edwin Vail, quoted in the previous chapter,
initiated many of the early canine experiments in high-altitude
physiology. One series of experiments was concerned with aeroemphysema. Dr. Vail defines this serious malady of low atmospheric pressure thus:

"Actually we were investigating the effects of subcutaneous
aeroemphysema. The reason that we call it aeroemphysema is
because it's the best medical term to describe the swelling of subcutaneous tissues—tissues underneath the skin—when the water
there vaporizes. Nobody knew much about this phenomenon, which
was first noted by Dr. Jim Henry when his hands began to swell
up like balloons in an altitude chamber at the time he was developing the partial-pressure altitude suit. So Don Rosenbaum of the
Aero Med Lab at Wright Field and I decided to pin the thing down.
John Kemp at Ohio State helped us with this work.

"We rigged up a series of dog experiments using the university's altitude chamber. We exposed these dogs to a simulated altitude of 75,000 feet, without body protection. After they swelled up, we used a remote manipulator to maneuver a needle and syringe in the chamber to take a gas sample out of the dogs' swollen skin areas. So we could analyze the gas on the ground while the dogs were actually at altitude. Our analysis showed that the swelling was caused by a mixture of gases, most of which was water vapor. There was 85 percent water vapor with small percentages of carbon dioxide and nitrogen mixed in with it.

"Another thing that worried us: would the separation of the skin from the subcutaneous tissue as a result of this gas formation be really detrimental to a human being if he was decompressed while flying at high altitudes? With the dogs, after their first exposure to altitude, their skin hung real loose on them. They looked like their pelts were loose, like they were wearing a fur coat. So we watched the dogs carefully. In about two or three days, their skin recovered its basic elasticity, but it was still loose. After about a month, however, it became pretty well normal again. But we examined them at selected intervals of two, three, and four months. We couldn't find any evidence of physical damage in the dogs.

"Of course the dogs passed out from hypoxia at 70,000 feet. There just wasn't enough oxygen to keep them conscious. But this was no problem, because they recovered easily. We only kept them at altitude for a maximum of ninety seconds. If you expose them for much beyond this length of time, they might not recover. But in our experiments they were back on their feet wagging their tails in something like eight or nine minutes. By then their nervous-system reflexes had recovered and they were fully conscious."

From where did Dr. Vail and his colleagues get their experimental dogs and were any special breeds preferred?

"We took what the dog pound gave us—any kind of a dog," Dr. Vail explained. "It was amazing how many terrier- and beagle-type dogs were loose in the world. We also had a toy collie. When we got the animals they were mostly in a very poor condition, suffering from malnutrition and parasites. Roaming around loose on the town, you know, they couldn't find a whole lot to eat. So we took them into the Veterinary School at Ohio State and kept them quarantined for three months, while we fed them, deparasitized them and generally nursed them back to a very good physical condition. In many respects, these animals were finally in better shape than most household pets."

Dr. Vail feels very strongly about the care and affection experimental animals deserve. "Anyone who uses animals in research and doesn't like animals," he says, "should certainly not be in this field! Pain is just as real to them as it is to us. We're trying to prevent pain in man, and if we don't consider the full health and status of our research animals, the whole value of our experiment is lost."

Referring to the development of an Air Force long-term pressure suit, he adds: "We simply can't take risks with human life. So we have to risk animals. But we pay special attention to see that the suits and helmets they wear are a perfect fit. We don't want anything to happen in either case. And we've never had a serious accident!"

The main purpose of Dr. Vail's experiments with dogs in subcutaneous aeroemphysema were pertinent to the development of Dr. Henry's partial-pressure suit. "We had a great problem with gloves for the partial-pressure suit," he recalls. "We didn't know whether we had to actually pressurize the hands or merely have the wearer of the suit put on tight gloves. We even tried a partial-pressure glove, which consisted of inflatable bladders on the back of the hand underneath a glove. When the bladders inflated they tightened the glove, pressurized the top of the hand and prevented the swelling there. But it was a difficult situation, because this interfered with hand and finger mobility. It was then that we looked into the possibilities of just leaving the whole hand exposed. The dog experiments at Ohio State suggested that in emergency situations the hands could be bare for a brief period without deleterious physiological aftereffects.

"So we asked for human volunteers to fly up to 70,000 and 80,000 feet and expose their hands in an altitude chamber.

"As near as we could tell from both the animal and human experiments, you could tolerate bare-hand exposure at high altitudes for up to thirty or thirty-five minutes. Of course, as your hands begin to swell, your dexterity and ability to manipulate fingers are considerably decreased. But we found that you could still fly your airplane down to a thicker part of the atmosphere in an emergency manner and get rid of the swelling. So it was not actually necessary to wear a specific pressure glove to protect your hands if aircraft cabin pressurization failed.

"Those experiments with dogs and men antedated the supersonic transport programs by almost twenty years. What we learned then will help SST pilots and passengers."

Dr. Vail's experiments were later extended by another project, a series of eighteen tests using chimpanzees. A joint project of the Air Force Systems Command and NASA, the experiments sought answers vital to emergency procedures that might be used after an explosive decompression in space. The questions were: Can a healthy, unprotected mammal survive swift decompression of a pressurized cabin flying through a vacuum? If so, for how long can he survive? How useful will he be after he recovers? What is the time of useful consciousness from decompression to black out? What is the time of total impairment of his central nervous system from unconsciousness to recovery? How long will it take him to get back to normal? And how does his behavior before decompression compare with his behavior after he is brought back to normal atmospheric pressure?

The chimps being tested had an average age of six years and were all from the chimpanzee colony housed at the 6571st Aerospace Medical Research Laboratory, Holloman Air Force Base, New Mexico, where the experiments were carried out in a small altitude chamber. Before being placed in the chamber, the chimps were trained for eight weeks to operate a puzzle of lights by pressing buttons to solve the puzzle. Inside the chamber, starting at 35,000 feet, each chimpanzee was placed on a twenty-two-minute schedule of button pressing with a thirteen-minute break in the middle. Air was rapidly withdrawn from the chamber until its "cabin" atmosphere was equivalent to the near vacuum of 150,000 feet. At that altitude, the chimps were exposed for 5 to 210 seconds (three and a half minutes), then dropped back down to the 35,000 foot level, where they remained for twenty-four hours.

While the time of useful consciousness varied from animal to animal—some blacked out in only 3.6 seconds, but others maintained consciousness for as long as 29.7 seconds, or almost half a minute—it was found by the experimenters that there was a direct ratio between the time, in seconds, the animals were kept at 150,000 feet and the time of total behavior impairment and total behavior repair.

After the tests were completed, the conclusion of the experimenters was: "Chimpanzees have demonstrated they can survive explosive decompression from 35,000 feet to the near-vacuum of 150,000 feet for three-and-a-half minutes without any noticeable residual ill effects after a four-hour recovery time." So the chimpanzee tests set an ultimate limit on how long a human being can survive in the upper atmosphere or in outer space without wearing a pressure suit.

It was generally felt in the years before man actually flew into space that an extended state of zero gravity would seriously incapacitate pilots—whether their ship was moving through space or merely pushing over into a ballistic dive. In fact, even now that men are flying to the moon and back there is some question about how the human body will hold up in zero gravity on very long space voyages of months or years.

In the early days of rocketry, immediately after World War II, the Air Force felt the zero-g problem to be important enough

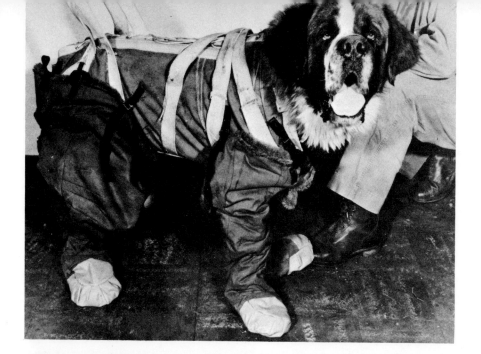

Dogs of all kinds have experimentally contributed to the development
of space suits and other types of protective clothing.
This Saint Bernard was used to test a new approach in survival clothing
for high-altitude pilots whose cabin pressurization failed or who
had to bail out over Arctic or Antarctic regions. Photos show
dog partially dressed and fully dressed in his personal survival suit,
with full-head oxygen mask.

Courtesy Air Force Film Depository

for the initiation of rocketborne animal experiments. White mice were photographed by automatic camera as they went through a gravity-free state in captured German V-2 and American Aerobee rockets. Later monkeys were used in similar tests. The experiments suggested that zero *g* was not as befuddling to the brain and body as had previously been supposed by some experts. But it remained for *Hydromedusa tectifera* to supply more absolute proof.

This is a species of South American water turtle noted for its long S-shaped neck and lightning-like accuracy when striking for food. Floating lazily in the water, it darts out its neck in any direction with the speed of a snake when it sights food. According to zoologists, it never misses.

Quite innocently, the little *tectifera* showed that man does not need a gravity environment in order to operate normally.

The combination of an accident and the curiosity of a South American scientist was enough to make the point. Dr. Harald J. A. von Beckh, former Medical Director of the Argentine State Lines, had been experimenting with the small water turtles during 1949. He is presently chief scientist at the 6571st Aerospace Medical Research Laboratory, Holloman Air Force Base, where he supervised the chimpanzee high-altitude decompression tests described earlier. While in Argentina, Dr. Von Beckh assumed that the little turtles would be very helpful in his then current studies of orientation because of their acute sense of direction, which gave them a lethal accuracy. During those studies he was called out of town for several days. When he returned, he found that the caretaker had forgotten to lower the thermostat in his laboratory. The place was insufferably hot—so much so that the water in the turtles' tanks was near to boiling. Many of the *tectifera* had expired. But one was still alive.

Apart from a permanent injury to the labyrinth of its ear, it was in good enough shape to recover. The labyrinth, or inner ear, controls orientation: it is nature's device for locating position and the relationships of positions in all mammals, including man. Although the *Hydromedusa tectifera* is not a mammal, its labyrinth has developed to an extremely high state of sensitivity. Throughout the next several weeks, Dr. Von Beckh's little water turtle went through some strange gyrations.

It almost starved to death, for one thing. When food was dropped into its tank it would strike just as swiftly, as viciously as always—but it never quite made its target.

One day, after the doctor had given up hope for the small beast's survival, it surprised him by awkwardly reaching its food. This was an amazing phenomenon. It became even more amazing: the injured turtle's accuracy improved with time. Finally it was able to strike its food with the same unerring aim of its normal brothers.

There could be only one explanation for this: out of sheer desperation and the need for survival it had learned to use its eyes alone for orientation.

Dr. Von Beckh became excited. As an aviator, he had always been interested in the effects of subgravity and zero gravity on human orientation. If what he now suspected were true, man, with enough patience and training, could learn to overcome the disorientation normally caused by the effect of weightlessness upon the inner ear.

The doctor loaded a tank with *Hydromedusa tectifera,* including the injured one, which was now completely adapted to its new state of a visual approach to position. With the tank on his knees he took a fighter airplane aloft. Just before he nosed over into a zero-gravity ballistic dive, like an artillery shell, he dropped food into the tank. All of the turtles missed the food—except one. In both the subgravity and zero-gravity states, the injured turtle had a merry feast.

Here was sufficient proof that weightlessness was not incapacitating if a person used his eyes rather than allowing the instinctive machinery of his ears to control his motions and balance.

Of course there still remained the undiscovered psychological effects of weightlessness. But these, as well, have since proved not to be disorienting. Following Dr. Harald von Beckh's experiments, the Air Research and Development Command (now known as the Air Force Systems Command) carried out a series of zero-g tests with top-notch pilots. Scotty Crossfield, first man to fly at twice the speed of sound, made thirty-odd ballistic dives in a jet. The first five times he felt confused. After that, he had complete control of the airplane by using visual references. Scotty flew his jet in both the upright and upside-down manner during the subgravity and zero-gravity tests in order to make the experiment as thorough as possible.

It is a mistaken notion of the average person that to achieve a no-gravity situation one must be beyond the earth's atmosphere and pull of gravity. Altitude is not important. As was suggested earlier, by pushing an airplane up and over the top of a ballistic curve a situation is created whereby the inert weight of the craft creates enough centrifugal pull outward to balance exactly the inward pull of earth's gravity. At this point everything in the aircraft floats. Subgravity states are those which approach zero gravity. A slight lift or suspension is felt for a moment, rather than an extended floating sensation.

I first experienced full zero g in 1954 at Edwards Air Force Base while aboard a B-25 bomber of the Experimental Flight Test Pilot School. One of the stability performances then required of every student at the school was a pushover into zero gravity. The student on this particular B-25 flight pushed the airplane over so hard that I abruptly found myself floating straight up from the deck. A moment later my head nudged the top bulkhead of the cabin. I remained suspended like this until the airplane pulled out of the dive many seconds afterward.

A month later, at Wright Air Development Center, I persuaded the commander of the center, Brigadier General Homer Boushey, that it would be a fine idea to photograph men floating freely in zero g. Such photos had never been made before. Permission was granted, provided I could find men willing to volunteer as subjects. This was not so easy to do, but finally Lieutenant Paul Maier volunteered as subject; Lieutenant Art Harris as pilot; and Sergeant Robert Frazier, crew chief of the C-47 cargo airplane, went along— because he had to—under protest.

Before the flight was touching down on the runway at Wright Field, Harris had made fifteen zero-g pushovers and Sergeant Frazier, watching Lieutenant Maier floating about the C-47 cabin as if he were swimming through the air, apparently in enjoyment, began demanding that he be taken as a volunteer subject also. I shot a dozen photos, two of which were quite clear. They were published in an earlier book of mine called *Space Flight* (Fawcett Publications). However, a photo of men floating in zero gravity to test their space suits does appear here in Chapter 5.

Those photos were also made in an airplane flying through a ballistic dive above Wright Field. Quite unwittingly, I had been responsible for the initiation of a program at Wright Air Development Center to study the effects of weightlessness upon human beings in flight. The program was much refined by the time that Project Mercury was preparing American astronauts for space flight. They and all other astronauts following them were and are being trained to function normally in zero gravity at Wright Field.

The sensation of zero g is actually pleasant, unless you try to fight it. Then tension and fear create a physical condition not unlike seasickness. Dizziness and disorientation immediately precede the sickness. But if you are psychologically primed to accept weightlessness, the experience is exhilarating, somewhat like diving from a high board, as Lieutenants Maier and Harris and Sergeant Frazier discovered. Most importantly, zero gravity is not seriously damaging to the body in any permanent manner—at least not on space flights of up to two weeks. Future, much longer flights in a zero-g condition may change the picture. But animals will pioneer those lengthier space voyages, so man can follow them with confidence.

Baboons, for example, have pioneered a unique adaptation of the space-suit principle to save the lives of heart-attack victims

right here on earth. After the baboon suits were thoroughly tested,
prototype pressure suits working on the same principle were built
for human beings.

The new suit is made of rubberized nylon with a zipper down
the front to allow easy and rapid fitting. It also has a clear-plastic
helmet into which oxygen may be pumped. But the basic principle
behind the suit is a pulsating pressure system that relieves the
heart of its workload. Bladderlike cuffs inside the suit surround the
arms and legs of its wearer. The cuffs are inflated and deflated
to provide a series of pressure pulses to compress and release the
blood flow of the arteries in exact timing with a patient's heartbeat.
The system includes an electrical contact attached to his chest that
senses his heartbeat and triggers a timing device that controls
the sequence of external arterial counterpressures. The sequencer
operates in milliseconds, or thousandths of a second, to control
pressures within the cuff bladders. When the heart is at rest, the
cuffs are inflated to squeeze blood through the arteries. When the
heart begins its next beat, the cuffs are deflated so that it can pump
the blood normally.

After it becomes operational, the heart-attack suit could be a
boon not only to emergency cases but also to persons who are
bedridden for one reason or another. By wearing the suit for a
few hours daily, they would be able to give their heart a rest and
perhaps in this way speed up recovery.

Baboons may have led the way to a boonful (pun intended) use
of space suits on earth, but their cousins and other relatives
showed that space suits could actually be used in space.

America's hero of the week during the closing days of November
1961, now sadly forgotten, like his female colleagues Able and
Baker, was an adolescent chimpanzee from Cameroon in western
Africa. About eight months earlier he had been shipped from his
tropical homeland to an aerospace medical field laboratory, managed by scientists of the Air Force Systems Command, amid the
mountains and deserts of New Mexico. There someone christened
him Enos the Astrochimp.

On November 29, 1961, he became the first anthropoid ape in
simian history to orbit the earth successfully. Enos was shot into
the sky from what is now Cape Kennedy inside a Project Mercury
spacecraft atop a modified Air Force Atlas D-model intercontinental
ballistic missile at 10:07 A.M. EST. Twenty-eight minutes after he
left the Florida coast, he was soaring over his native jungles at
17,500 miles an hour. But he may have been too busy pushing
levers, as he was trained to do, to care.

Enos made two swift trips around the globe before a radio signal
from Point Arguello, California, knocked him out of orbit and

dumped him by parachute into the Atlantic Ocean off Bermuda. There he was safely retrieved by scuba divers from the Navy's destroyer *USS Stormes*. His planned three-orbit trip had been cut short because of several minor malfunctions of devices in the Mercury spacecraft that were too much for a chimp—but not for a man—to handle.

Project Mercury scientists were elated as they later observed the astrochimp in perfect health, blithely munching bananas. Technical information was what the United States sorely needed in that period. No true scientific data on the space flights of the late Yuri Gagarin (April 12, 1961) and Gherman Titov (August 6, 1961) had been released by the Soviet Union. But Enos the Astrochimp supplied information freely, and the United States program to orbit men through space got under way in earnest.

Correlating the scientific data acquired from Enos' flight with that of the two manned suborbital flights by Alan B. Shepard, Jr., and the late Virgil I. Grissom, earlier the same year, scientists and engineers of both the NASA and the Air Force Systems Command were convinced that Project Mercury would be successful. NASA people now knew that the spacecraft was feasible for manned orbital flights. The Systems Command's management experience in launching and tracking large space vehicles as well as missiles would make the boost phase of the Mercury flights almost routine.

The Mercury space capsules in which Enos, the earlier chimp Ham, Navy (then) Lieutenant Commander Shepard, and Air Force (also then) Captain Grissom rode were all essentially the same. Their protective clothing was almost the same. Just as Able, Baker, and Ham had preceded Shepard and Grissom in a suborbital flight that lasted minutes, so Enos preceded Marine Lieutenant Colonel John Glenn, the first American to orbit the earth, in an orbital flight that lasted hours. All of these flights were a part of Phase One of the United States program to land a crew of men on the moon's surface and bring them back safely to earth before the end of the 1960's.

Chapter 9

SILVER WAS THE RAGE THAT YEAR

Comparatively crude, the Project Mercury capsules were to space flight what the Model T Ford was to the automotive industry. Their objective was to determine the physical and mental effects of orbital flight on human beings. They were controlled automatically, from launch through almost every phase of the flight. The astronaut had no control over his orbital plane and altitude. He had no control of his own safety during launch. If a serious malfunction occurred, an electronic computer made the decision to blast him and his capsule away from the booster rocket.

Although the Mercury astronaut had plenty of experiments to perform while in orbit and many things to keep him busy during the re-entry period through the atmosphere, it was planned from the start of Project Mercury that he be a "passenger." He was such a good passenger that he ultimately proved not only that he was physically and mentally capable of flying through space, but that he could also perform useful work in the process. Once this was made evident, the Mercury program had more than accomplished its original purpose.

The Mercury space suits were as crude as that program's capsules. Compared with the modern "moon suits" of Project Apollo, they were an unsophisticated compromise between giving the Mercury astronauts an emergency backup system in case of cabin decompression—and hoping that there would be no such decompression emergencies. But the Mercury suits were colorful. They were coated with a silverlike spray which served the double purpose of a heat buffer and a radiation shield. In case the cabin of the capsule became overheated, say, during the re-entry phase of a flight, the suit coating would act like a mirror to reflect heat away from the astronaut's body. Not exactly silver, the aluminized coating also provided a thin metallic outer layer that could to some extent absorb and decelerate particles of nuclear and electromagnetic radiation.

Weighing only twenty pounds, the suit was (to quote the B. F. Goodrich news release) "a dazzling aluminum-coated nylon-and-rubber creation." Glittering and lightweight the Mercury spacesuit was indeed. But it certainly was not flexible and comfortable. More specifically, the suit consisted of a modified Navy Mark IV pressurized flight suit of rubber and nylon with an undergarment of double-walled rubber for ventilation. The ventilating system was developed by the Air Force at the Wright Aero Medical Laboratory. It came out of the experiments of Hans Mauch in the Environmental Section.

The double walls of the undergarment had tiny perforations to allow the pores of a Mercury astronaut to "breathe." Air was pumped into the suit through a hose connection at its waist. The air then circulated through the undergarment and was exhausted by way of a pipe in the helmet. The stale air, carrying impurities

A cleverly dramatic photo to demonstrate the mobility of the Mark IV full-pressure suit, this was released by the B. F. Goodrich Public Relations Department soon after that company was awarded the NASA suit contract. Caption read, in part: "On the moon, the weak gravity would mean that a normal earth-type home run would travel about a half-mile." But please note that these suits are not inflated.

Courtesy B. F. Goodrich Company

such as moisture from sweat and carbon dioxide, next was fed into an air-conditioning system underneath the astronaut's form-fitting couch, where it was purged of impurities, cooled, and re-circulated through the suit.

Mobility of the suit was good—when it was not pressurized. When it was pressurized during ground tests, inflation of the suit forced the astronaut into a bent-over position, somewhat like the position of a fetus in its mother's womb. Arm and leg movements were quite restricted. However, extreme mobility was not required of the Mercury astronauts. If their capsule sprang a leak and their suit automatically inflated in flight, they would only have to sit back and ride out an extra orbit or so until they could be brought safely back to earth by the computers. Happily, however, not once during the six Mercury manned flights—two suborbital, four orbital —did the suits have to be inflated. There were no cabin decompressions on any of those flights.

The Mercury space suit got around the problem of a constant volume-to-pressure ratio in a simple manner. Restraining cords were sewn about its elbow and knee areas. The cords were inelastic, that is, they could not be stretched when the suit inflated. The idea was to give the joints a limited mobility by compressing the volume around them into a series of sections. In effect, it was like stringing together a series of small balloons, each of which would have constant volume and pressure, while the squeezed-in points— where the cords prevented ballooning—could be bent against the "balloons." At right angles across the joint-circling inelastic cords were attached lateral "wires," also inelastic, to restrain the balloon series in a lengthwise direction. These lateral restraints made it possible for a Mercury astronaut to bend an elbow or knee because they would force the sleeve or trouser leg of the suit to follow the movement, since they would not stretch but stiffly moved with the astronaut's joint movement.

Obviously, a great amount of effort was required of the astronaut to move his limbs when the Mercury suit was inflated. Even with the circumferential and lateral restraining network, the suit would bunch together in various areas, thus increasing the internal pressure by reducing the suit's total volume. To bend his elbow fully so that his hand could touch his shoulder would have demanded of the Mercury astronaut almost the effort needed to bend an iron bar double.

As things stood, the Mercury space suit when inflated curved broadly over the elbows and knees of the astronaut, rather than performing the ideal action of bending sharply to follow the natural movement of the joints themselves. In other words, the suit joints did not move as hinges. They resisted movement in the manner of a sausage-shaped toy balloon if an attempt was made to bend it in half—only much more so.

Regardless of its limitations, the Mercury space suit was not an idle choice by NASA. A six-man Suit-Selection Board, which included astronaut Walter M. Schirra, first decided on the basic qualities wanted in a full-pressure garment. These were compactness, reliability, resistance to temperature, pressure integrity, ease of getting into and out of the suit, and mobility. Although this last quality was quite limited, it was adequate for the purpose.

Rigorous suit-evaluation tests were carried out at the Wright Aero Medical Laboratory and the McDonnell Aircraft Corporation (now McDonnell-Douglas Astronautics Company), NASA's prime contractor for the Project Mercury space capsule. Members of the testing team spent as long as twenty-four hours in various suits to evaluate how well they met the standards set. In heat chambers, team members wore the suits for more than two hours at a time at temperatures up to 180 degrees Fahrenheit—more than twice the temperatures that the Mercury astronauts were expected to encounter inside their capsules during orbital flight. Tests of the suits also included wearing them in human centrifuges that developed eight times the pull of gravity, and in aircraft performing zero-*g* dives to cancel out gravity's pull. Noise-reduction features of the suits were also carefully evaluated.

Finally, the Navy's one-piece Mark IV high-altitude full-pressure suit was chosen as the most desirable then available for modification to meet the predetermined standards. The suit included a full-pressure helmet. Already noted was NASA's choice of an Air Force ventilating undergarment to be worn beneath the suit.

NASA originally contracted with the B. F. Goodrich Company for twenty Mercury space suits at a cost of about $75,000, which set the unit price at $3,250. These were suits to be used in test evaluations. The ultimate flight suits worn in orbit by the Mercury astronauts cost $10,000 apiece. The reader will recall that the same company a quarter-century earlier had budgeted Wiley Post's first full-pressure suit at $75—and finally built it for $15 less than that.

The major purpose of Project Mercury was to discover whether a man could survive a full twenty-four hours in space without any ill effects from the flight. On May 16, 1963, L. Gordon Cooper, Jr., then an Air Force captain, exceeded that goal by more than ten hours. Launched the day before from Cape Kennedy atop a modified Atlas missile, he made twenty-two orbits of the earth in his Mercury capsule *Faith 7*. His time from lift-off to splashdown was thirty-four hours nineteen minutes and forty-nine seconds. So the Mercury program had met its final objective.

This is the Mercury space suit as modified from the Navy's Mark IV.
NASA announced on July 24, 1959, that "the astronaut suit will be silver-coated. Underneath this outer suit will be a double-walled ventilated rubber garment which will be perforated to permit the body pores to 'breathe.'"
Actually, the silver coating was an aluminized fabric to reflect away heat.

Courtesy NASA

The Mercury "silver" space suit is shown here undergoing an inflation test to 3.5 pounds per square inch, the minimum pressure required to keep a man alive in space if his cabin pressurization fails. The suit's restricted mobility is evident from the bent-over position of its wearer's torso, elbows and knees. However, it was adequate for its job at the time—which was strictly an emergency backup device to protect the early astronauts if their orbital capsule lost its pressure.

Courtesy NASA

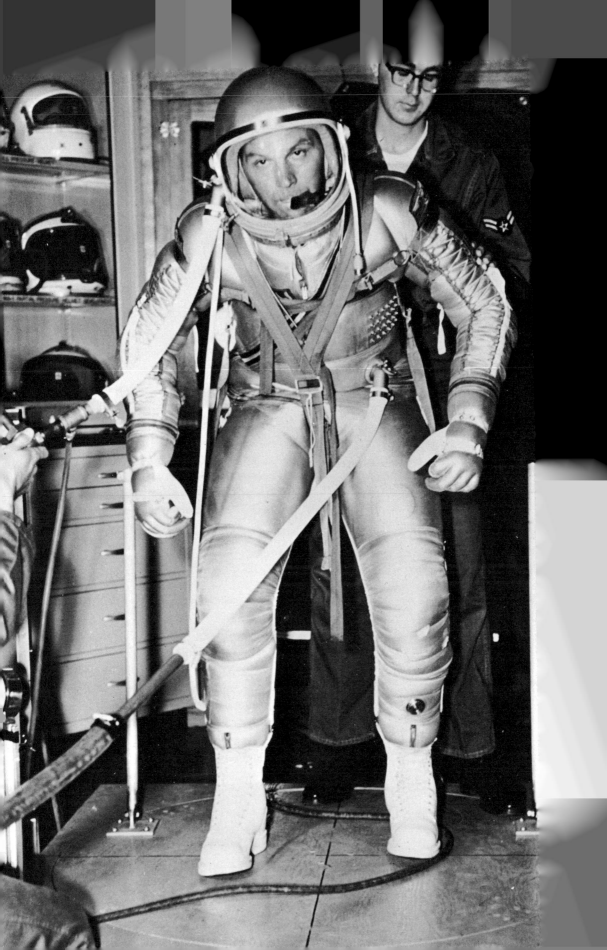

But it was only a beginning. The next question was, Can men live and work in space for much longer periods than this? To answer that question not only required a more advanced space suit and capsule, but it posed two subquestions: How do you support human life for, say, two weeks in space? and, What can you do with a man's body wastes throughout such a long period?

Chapter 10

DIAPERS UNDER DUNGAREES

On very long manned flights through space, there is the problem of what to do with certain human waste products. This was no problem, really, in the early short lived flights of Project Mercury—but it became quite serious on the much longer two-man Gemini flights.

As of this writing, the world's longest manned space flight still remains that of Gemini Mission 7. Despite the fact that men have landed on the moon and explored its surface, the seventh flight of a Gemini spacecraft presently holds the record for sheer length of time that men have lived and worked in space. Launched from Cape Kennedy, Florida, on December 4, 1965, the GT-7 capsule made 206 orbits of the earth. The splashdown occurred on December 18, 1965—very close to a full two weeks of space flight for Lieutenant Colonel Frank Borman of the Air Force and Commander James A. Lovell, Jr., of the Navy.

But what about waste management—as NASA politely calls it—during such epic flights? Certainly the astronauts on long missions can't step out the back door of their spacecraft to use an outhouse.

You probably never suspected that astronauts wear diapers. They do. The diapers are sophisticated, of course, but they wrap around in the same way as baby diapers and are worn underneath the outer space clothing. Their purpose is to collect urine, which is then transferred by hose to a waste-management control system—a genteel phrase to describe spacecraft latrines—and later dumped overboard. The diapers are made of rubberized nylon.

During the Gemini flights, a new word was coined—uriglow—because in the intense cold of outer space, the urine froze almost immediately into ice crystals and would travel in orbit along with the spacecraft. When the craft headed toward a sunrise, the solar glow would illuminate the urine crystals, causing them to look like bright stars—brilliant enough to be photographed by the astronauts.

In the Apollo program, the urine flow overboard as well as the dumping of excess water from the water supply system is restricted to paced intervals. This is to prevent the formation of ice in the nozzle of the liquid overboard dump system. Heaters around the nozzle also help to prevent ice formation.

According to Thomas W. Herrala of the Hamilton Standard Division of United Aircraft Corporation, the problem of waste disposal has not yet been solved in a way that could be called the most comfortable situation in the world for astronauts. Tom Herrala has been working for a number of years on the design and development of modern space suits that would be very reliable, mobile, *and* comfortable.

Regarding the disposal of feces, Herrala had this to say: "There actually isn't a way of handling it without making a guy *really* uncomfortable. It's a very challenging problem. Chemical toilets have been proposed, as well as incinerators—a disposal system where you burn the stuff down to ashes. None of this seemed acceptable to use in a zero-g environment.

"NASA handled a good part of this problem by developing low-residue diets for their astronauts. In fact, in some of our associated laboratories we have people working on the development of a balanced diet that is purely liquid. This is an attempt to cut all the bulk out of a man's diet—at least in terms of the mass that he would normally defecate. But the defecation problem is not at all easy to solve."

The solution that NASA came up with for the Apollo program—apart from a low-residue diet—actually appears to be the most comfortable compromise. It was derived from a similar method used in the Gemini program. Fecal odors, like urine, are dumped overboard into space, but the feces themselves are stored in specially designed bags. These are called "blue bags" by the space men. They are actually two bags in one, with pouches containing a germicide and a skin-cleaning towel. The inner bag contains a rim coated with a cement-like substance that is protected by a plastic strip. When an astronaut has to go, he peels off the plastic strip, which exposes the sticky substance. He pastes the inner bag onto his buttocks and performs the necessary duty. After he's through, the germicide is inserted into the inner bag and the outer bag is sealed over it. The combined blue bag is then kneaded to flatten it out and stored in a waste-stowage compartment that can hold up to thirty bag assemblies. The compartment has a special split-membrane trap that allows the bags to be inserted into it while preventing them from floating back out through the space-ship cabin when its door is open again for stowage of freshly loaded bags. This was an ingenious solution to a problem that *had* to be solved, because, as the reader already knows, in a condition of no gravity everything not tied down or restrained in some way, floats aimlessly about.

One bathroom luxury the Apollo astronauts do enjoy: they use pure three-ply Kleenex backed with a polyethylene plastic sheet for cushioning support instead of ordinary toilet paper.

Of course, in order to eliminate bowel wastes by the method described here, the Apollo astronauts must take off their space suits. But this is no problem when they are flying in their command module, where normally they are dressed in a minimum light-weight suit known as a "constant-wear garment" that resembles long john underwear beneath ordinary coveralls. Only at lift-off atop the giant Saturn V rocket and during re-entry into the earth's atmosphere are they required to wear their full-pressure garment assembly. The same situation prevailed earlier with the Gemini astronauts.

The lunar module crewmen, however, do have a problem. For throughout their mission to and from the moon's surface they must always be dressed in a full-pressure suit. While they are exploring the lunar landscape and performing scientific experiments, they have additional protective clothing to wear constantly on top of their lunar-module space suits.

As Tom Herrala puts it: "When you place a man in a full-pressure suit, you've got him canned in a very isolated and intimate environment. If you want him to defecate normally, you've got to put a wide tube into his anal canal. Even then, the action of defecating might push out the tube. So you have to design something that can't be pushed out—which isn't easy. You need a really

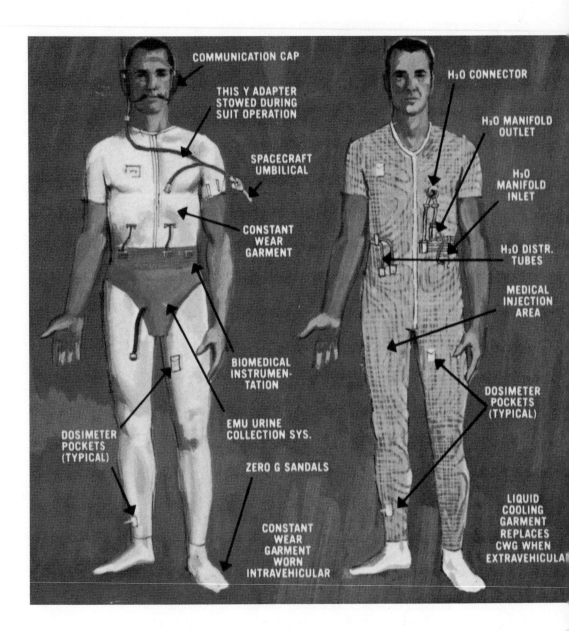

*These diagrams illustrate the progress made in crew-comfort clothing for
the Apollo astronauts while they are working inside and outside their spacecraft.
At left the men are wearing 1965–1966 versions of an intravehicular and
extravehicular undergarment. The intravehicular suit is called a constant-wear
garment (CWG). Here it looks like flannel Long John winter underwear.
The CWG is intended for wear in extended orbit about the earth or during the
long coast periods to the moon and perhaps, someday, to the planets.
The extravehicular (EVA) undergarment is cooled by water
through an array of plastic tubes next to the astronaut's skin. It is worn*

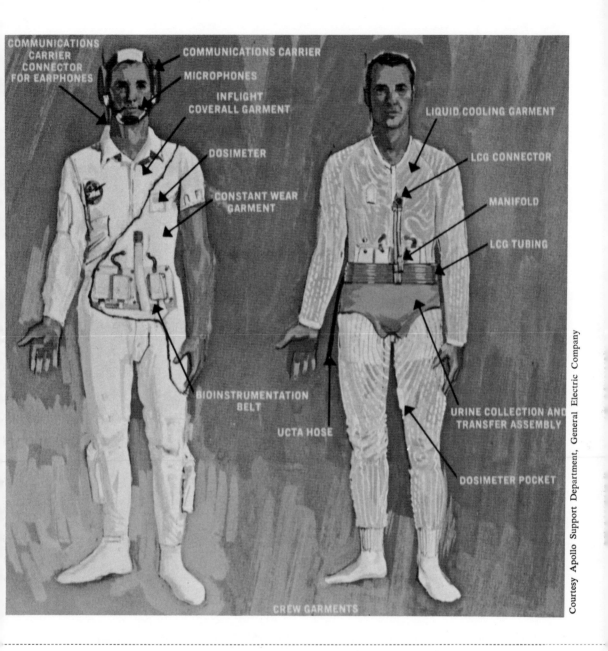

beneath his EVA space suit to remove excessive body heat caused by confinement in the cocoon-like suit. Water is fourteen times more effective than air as a heat remover. At right the men are wearing the 1969 versions of the CWG and EVA water-cooled underwear. Note the differences. Most obvious is the CWG, which now looks like a comfortable loose-fitting suit of flight coveralls. Compare also the communications headgear, the LCG (liquid-cooling garment) connectors and inlet tubing and the positions of the UCTA (Urine Collection Transport Assembly) hoses. The word *dosimeter* in the diagram refers to an instrument that measures radiation dosage—in other words, a "dose-meter."

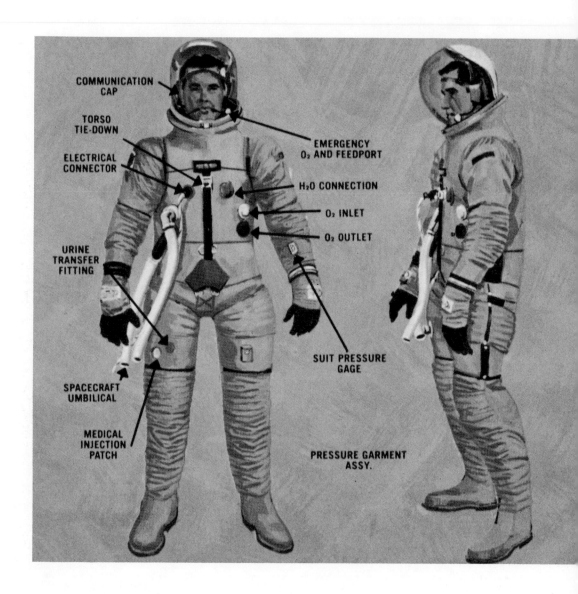

COMMUNICATION CAP

TORSO TIE-DOWN

ELECTRICAL CONNECTOR

URINE TRANSFER FITTING

SPACECRAFT UMBILICAL

MEDICAL INJECTION PATCH

EMERGENCY O₂ AND FEEDPORT

H₂0 CONNECTION

O₂ INLET

O₂ OUTLET

SUIT PRESSURE GAGE

PRESSURE GARMENT ASSY.

Diagrams here show the differences between the 1965–1966 and 1969 astronaut life-support equipment, which include the entire space-suit assembly and the oxygen-supply, gas-recycling, cooling, and electrical systems. Shown are only the space-suit assemblies. These suits are worn mainly for protection during the lift-off and re-entry phases of a space flight—except

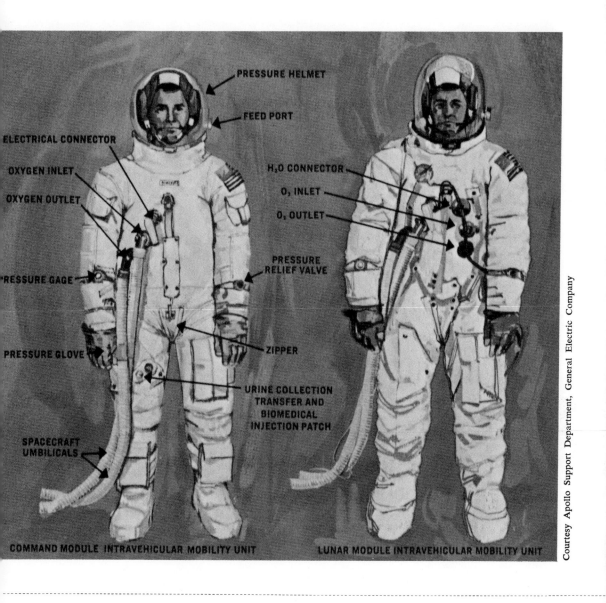

PRESSURE HELMET

FEED PORT

ELECTRICAL CONNECTOR

OXYGEN INLET

OXYGEN OUTLET

H₂O CONNECTOR

O₂ INLET

O₂ OUTLET

PRESSURE RELIEF VALVE

PRESSURE GAGE

PRESSURE GLOVE

ZIPPER

URINE COLLECTION TRANSFER AND BIOMEDICAL INJECTION PATCH

SPACECRAFT UMBILICALS

COMMAND MODULE INTRAVEHICULAR MOBILITY UNIT

LUNAR MODULE INTRAVEHICULAR MOBILITY UNIT

Courtesy Apollo Support Department, General Electric Company

for the lunar module intravehicular suit, which is called a
"mobility unit." It is pictured at far right. Observe the vast differences
between the earlier and later models of the operational Apollo
space suits. Even the color was different: the suits were blue in 1966,
they were white when the first men landed on the moon.

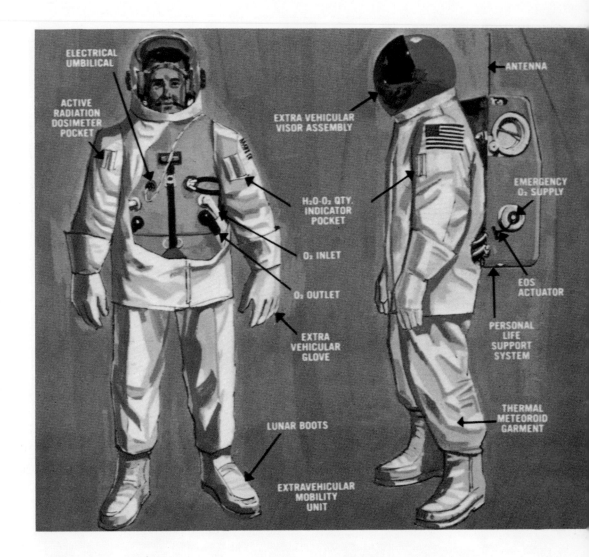

The differences between the lunar EVA protective coverings were vast.
At left, the early coverings were a two-piece affair—dungaree-like jacket
and trousers—with gauntlet-type gloves and inadequately insulated boots.
The gold visor to filter out or reflect away damaging radiations was attached
to the helmet on pivots for lowering or raising it. At right, the later
EVA version is essentially of a single piece. Gloves are still the gauntlet type,
but boots are much better insulated. The filtering shield against radiation
is no longer a visor, but a full-head shell that fits over the helmet.
In the 1966 lunar EVA concept, the two-piece outer suit was insulated against
meteoroid punctures and radiation with various layers of metal-wire

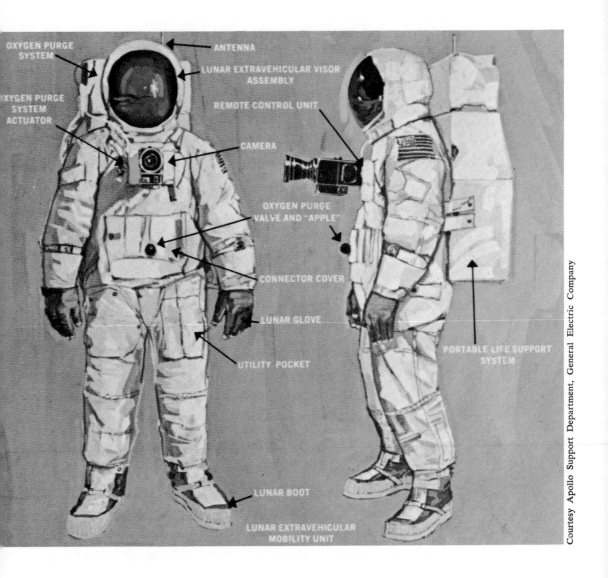

OXYGEN PURGE SYSTEM

ANTENNA

LUNAR EXTRAVEHICULAR VISOR ASSEMBLY

OXYGEN PURGE SYSTEM ACTUATOR

REMOTE CONTROL UNIT

CAMERA

OXYGEN PURGE VALVE AND "APPLE"

CONNECTOR COVER

LUNAR GLOVE

UTILITY POCKET

PORTABLE LIFE SUPPORT SYSTEM

LUNAR BOOT

LUNAR EXTRAVEHICULAR MOBILITY UNIT

Courtesy Apollo Support Department, General Electric Company

*mesh and special fabrics. It was called a "thermal meteoroid garment" (TMG).
When two men actually walked upon the moon in July 1969, their TMG was
not a separate garment—it was built into their space suit. On top of it
was the outer covering shown at right. Another difference was the location
of an emergency oxygen supply (EOS) tank. In the early version it was fitted
inside the personal life-support system. In the later version it was
attached to the top of the portable life-support system, which permitted a much
larger O_2 tank to be carried for emergencies. Note that even the names
of the life-support systems have been changed. The total EVA outfit, in both
cases, was called an EMU, or "Extravehicular Mobility Unit."*

wide tube, so that no gas or muscular pressure can overlap its rim and thus push it out. I've heard that NASA was using special diapers for this kind of elimination as well as for urine collection. At least it could be a good interim answer to the problem of a man in a space suit—but I'm sure he isn't overjoyed with the situation."

The ultimate answer to the problem on long space voyages by men is a combination of two vital systems that are now more or less separate aboard spacecraft. These are the already described waste-management system and the life-support system. To bring the two together requires a closed-loop system in which each is an integral part of the other.

Such an interdependent system has been in the minds of scientists and engineers for many years. That it can be made to work was demonstrated at the 1960 Annual Meeting of the American Medical Association in Atlantic City. In the Convention Hall there was a display of a "closed gas system."

Four white mice sat nonchalantly inside a hermetically sealed plastic sphere. No outside air could get into their small domed world. Nor was there an oxygen tank visible anywhere, inside or outside the clear plastic globe. A small tank of green *Chlorella,* an algae cousin of the green scum found floating on stagnant ponds, was the only source of life for the mice. The *Chlorella* absorbed the carbon dioxide they exhaled and by a process of photosynthesis released breathable oxygen. It also produced carbohydrates and proteins by synthesis, so the mice could have nourishing food. Finally, it even made use of the rodent body wastes, nourishing itself and growing on feces while it purified urine into water so the mice would not go thirsty or become dehydrated. All that the system required to function was a source of light that set the photosynthetic mechanisms in motion. Monkeys have also been kept alive indefinitely, sealed inside tanks with similar systems.

While such closed gas systems may upset the squeamish, they are actually in a miniature way almost exactly the method by which the earth itself supports life on a grander scale. Successfully miniaturizing the system is a notable scientific achievement.

Using larger algae tanks to meet a man's requirements for waste disposal as well as of oxygen and food, a space pilot could live indefinitely inside a hermetically sealed capsule in the vacuum of the interplanetary void. The tanks would not have to be prohibitively large either. Out of the Air Force research at the University of Texas, it was found that about five pounds of *Chlorella* per man would do the job.

But although the use of algae to turn fecal matter and urine into nourishing food and potable water was a starter, even more efficient methods are being explored today. In terms of an astronaut's food

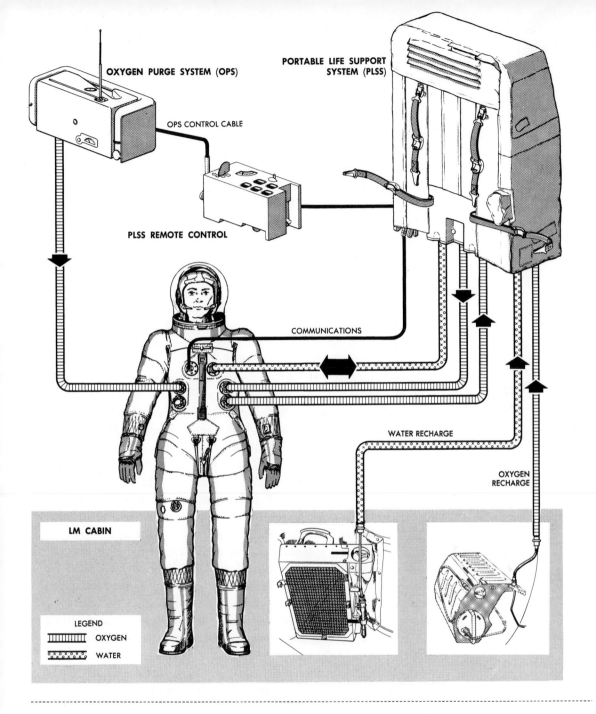

OXYGEN PURGE SYSTEM (OPS)

PORTABLE LIFE SUPPORT SYSTEM (PLSS)

OPS CONTROL CABLE

PLSS REMOTE CONTROL

COMMUNICATIONS

WATER RECHARGE

OXYGEN RECHARGE

LM CABIN

LEGEND

OXYGEN

WATER

Here is a diagram of the portable life-support system (PLSS)
for space-walking on the moon. It is self-explanatory.
Worn as a pack strapped onto the back of the astronaut, the PLSS weighs
84 pounds (14 pounds on the moon) and costs $200,000 per system.
The system is self-contained; here the method of recharging
its oxygen and water supplies from stores in the lunar module is illustrated.
On a single charge of O_2 and H_2O, the PLSS can keep
an astronaut alive for four hours on the lunar surface or in free space.

Courtesy Grumman Aerospace Corporation

This simplified diagram of a combined closed-ecology and waste-management system illustrates an experimental life-support arrangement that was conceived and is being developed by engineers and scientists at the Grumman Aerospace Corporation. Based on the aerobic process, the system shows great promise for the future as a means to transform the body wastes of astronauts into clean breathable air, potable water, and nourishing food. It would weigh comparatively little and keep astronauts alive on long space voyages. There would be no need to carry extra supplies of oxygen and food because it is a recycling closed-loop system.

Here's how it works: Body wastes from the toilet bowl (3) are pumped (1) into the first stage of the aerobic digestion chamber (4), called the "comminutor," where they are mixed with water and broken down into smaller particles. The second stage (5) oxygenates the flow of material with O_2 under pressure (7). Next the fluid wastes stream into the third stage (6), where they are digested by millions of bacteria, protozoa, and rotifers that live on several pounds of crushed bark from the California redwood. The cleansed stream then leaves the aerobic digestion chamber and enters a heat exchanger (8), where it is cooled before it enters a tank of scavenger fish (9). The fish eat any microorganisms that may have escaped from the chamber into the stream, which goes on to flow into a diffuser (10), where silicone membranes further filter out whatever toxic agents remain. On the exit side of the membranes, the products are water vapor and carbon dioxide. These are blown into the greenhouse (11), where they are absorbed by green leafy vegetables, which in turn are flooded with fluorescent lights that encourage photosynthesis to transform the carbon dioxide into carbon and oxygen, while the plants are being fed moisture from the water vapor. The oxygen is pumped from the greenhouse into the spacecraft cabin to give the astronauts a life-supporting atmosphere. Clean water not filtered through the diffuser's membranes circulates back to the pump, which passes it into a storage tank or accumulator (2) for drinking.

Excess clean water passes by the accumulator and is flushed through the toilet bowl to mix with other liquids and solids, so that the whole cycle can begin again. Water from the fish tank that cannot enter the membrane diffuser because it is overloaded flows into the greenhouse to irrigate the vegtables and supply them with nourishing chemicals and minerals that have been separated from urine and feces, but still remain in the clean water. As the vegetables and fish multiply, they are eaten by the astronauts. In this way, the astronauts supply food and an atmosphere for the fish and plants even as they supply food and an atmosphere for the astronauts.

Courtesy Grumman Aerospace Corporation

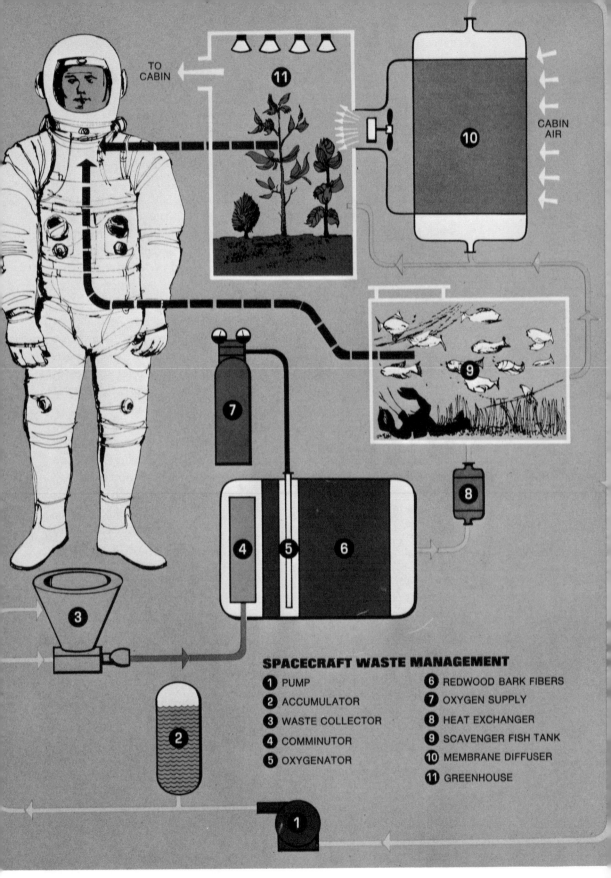

TO
CABIN

CABIN
AIR

SPACECRAFT WASTE MANAGEMENT

1 PUMP
2 ACCUMULATOR
3 WASTE COLLECTOR
4 COMMINUTOR
5 OXYGENATOR

6 REDWOOD BARK FIBERS
7 OXYGEN SUPPLY
8 HEAT EXCHANGER
9 SCAVENGER FISH TANK
10 MEMBRANE DIFFUSER
11 GREENHOUSE

supply alone, the TRW Systems Group has discovered that a certain species of bacteria is an even better source of nourishment than *Chlorella*. The Principal Scientific Investigator in this research is Bernard H. Goldner of the group's Biosciences Department. He has been working with a bacterial species known as *Hydrogenomonas*. The particular bacterium isolated for his studies is called *eutropha*.

According to biologist Goldner, "To grow, the bacteria simply take urea—the result of human protein metabolism—and convert it back to protein. . . . Large cultures of *H. eutropha*—which consist of 70 percent protein and are capable of storing carbohydrates and lipids [fats]—would be harvested and treated to produce a dry, tasteless substance. Using food additives, it can be processed into a palatable food, such as a biscuit or cracker."

"Results of this research," in the view of Goldner, "will not be limited to the space program. With the predicted rate of increase in world populations and pending food shortages in many parts of the world, there is a real need for finding additional sources of food for mankind. *H. eutropha* may eventually represent one of these sources."

A much more ambitious system for keeping space men alive and in good health during extended voyages through the void is being investigated by biological scientists and engineers at the Grumman Aerospace Corporation. They call the system "closed-loop ecology." In biology, an ecological system is one in which there is an interdependence between living organisms and their external environment. For example, the entire earth is a closed-loop ecological system. All animal, including human, metabolism is supported by oxygen from the atmosphere. A waste-product result of animal oxidation is carbon dioxide, which is absorbed by plant life and transformed back into oxygen through photosynthesis. During the transformation process the plants produce nourishment for themselves. To them, the oxygen is a waste product. Many vegetable plants are eaten as food by animals, which in turn eliminate the unused portions as excrement and water—both of these then provide the basis of food for plants. The interaction of air with the seas, lakes, and rivers of the world creates rain—to provide potable water for animals as well as plants and replenish the water basins used for irrigation in agriculture. The sea itself not only provides food for animals in the form of fish and other marine creatures, but it also teems with scavengers that keep its own ecology balanced.

Admittedly, the foregoing paragraph is an oversimplification of an extremely complex interrelationship between all forms of life on earth as well as their interrelationship with the minerals and chemicals that are the nonliving aspects of nature. But it at least provides an idea of what the Grumman scientists and engineers are trying to duplicate in miniature for future astronauts.

Manned space stations orbiting the earth with astronaut-scientist teams remaining aboard in shifts of from one to six months are a real possibility of the near future. Manned voyages to Mars and other planets of the solar system will take from more than a year to several years per round trip—unless a revolutionary rocket-propulsion system is developed to shorten the time of travel. Colonies of scientists living on the moon for extended periods are equally a not-too-far-off possibility. In every case, a closed-loop life-support system should be mandatory.

The scientists and engineers at Grumman Aerospace Corporation explain that at present there is no international legal agreement to prevent astronauts from dumping into space either their liquid or solid body wastes. But the problem is: what would happen if such waste products were dumped from a spacecraft in large quantities during a long space voyage, including an extended orbit of the earth? Would they be carried throughout the solar system by electrified plasmas from the sun (known as solar winds)—or would they congeal into a kind of celestial garbage, to endlessly orbit the earth or the sun?

At Grumman this problem was evaluated and a solution to it presented in terms of research already accomplished by the company's engineers and scientists. (See illustration.)

Undoubtedly, Grumman as well as other industrial aerospace laboratories will refine the closed-loop-ecology waste-management system until it becomes a foolproof operational unit that can be carried easily aboard any long-voyaging spacecraft. In this they will be substantially aided by biological research accomplished in scientific laboratories of the military and various universities.

Such a system would have been welcomed by the astronauts of Project Gemini, who proved that man can live for moderately long periods in space, but who were provided with relatively primitive waste-management systems.

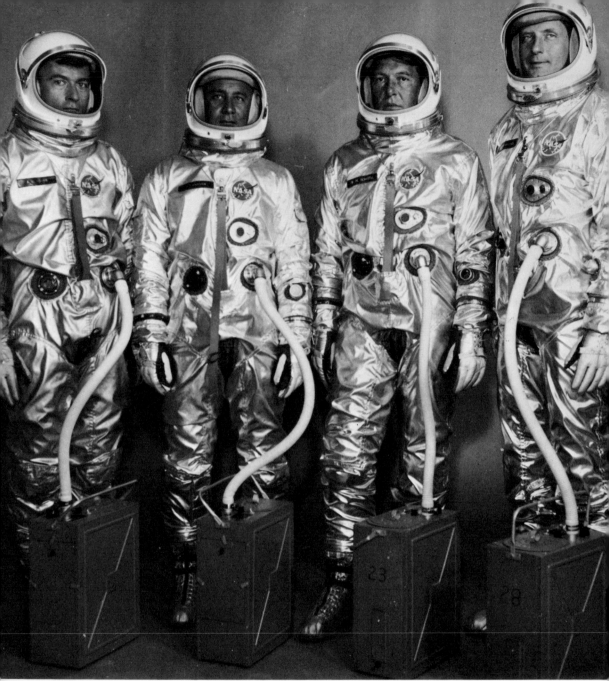

It would be hard for an untrained observer to determine immediately that these were Project Gemini space suits. At a quick glance they appear to be carbon copies of the Project Mercury suits. But the resemblance is only superficial. The Gemini helmets were entirely different from the Mercury helmets, and the Gemini suits, when uninflated, hung more loosely on their wearers. Their restraint layers (not shown) were also completely new. This photo was released in April 1964 and pictures, from left to right, Astronauts John W. Young, Virgil I. ("Gus") Grissom, Walter M. Schirra, and Thomas P. Stafford. Young and Grissom were the prime crew of GT-3, America's first two-man flight, while Schirra and Stafford were the backup crew.

Chapter 11

THEN THE STYLE WAS TWINS

Phase two en route to the moon was Project Gemini. In that program, the two astronauts who rode around the world in their single spacecraft were intended to be pilots, not passengers like the Mercury astronauts. Gemini was, at the time, a central terminal for the United States in its planned future manned explorations of not only the moon but the planets and perhaps, someday, of the closer stars.

It was a critical project, even more so than Mercury, because it was a commitment to manned space flight on an operational level. Such a commitment demanded absolute certainty of their skills on the part of tens of thousands of persons—scientists, engineers, astronauts, industrial managers, NASA managers, the managers of the Air Force Systems Command, and the indispensable technicians. Safety and reliability were two prime requirements.

Whereas the space suits of Project Mercury were backup devices to save the life of an astronaut in an emergency situation of cabin-pressurization failure, those of Project Gemini were designed to be work clothes—as well as emergency backup garments. They not only had to be reliable and moderately comfortable but they also had to be fairly mobile when inflated and sufficiently protective to keep a man alive when he went outside his spacecraft—where the raw high-energy radiations, the possible micrometeoroid or larger meteoroid impacts and the vacuum of free space were never-ending threats to him. In this sense, the extravehicular astronauts of the Gemini program were performing a dress rehearsal for the moon with the clothing they wore.

Tom Herrala, pressure-garment designer at Hamilton Standard, has called the Gemini EVA (extra vehicular activity) garments "the first true space suits." As he explains it: "The Mercury suit, for example, was nothing but a Navy Mark IV suit. It was a high-altitude airplane full-pressure suit with special outer coverings—and maybe an attempt at a little more mobility than the original airplane suit had. The first suit that diverged radically from the air-craft emergency pressure suits was the one that Ed White wore when he left the capsule to float in free space on the Flight of Gemini Four. That was the link-net suit made by David Clark Company."

David Clark, it should be noted, built all of the Gemini suits and helmets, redesigning them for improved efficiency as their performance data were analyzed after each flight.

Shortcomings had been noted in the EVA suits and their life-support systems as well as in the spacecraft during excursions through free space on Gemini flights 9, 10, and 11. These discrepancies were overcome with engineering changes. For instance, handholds, both fixed and portable, were incorporated on the spacecraft after astronaut Gene Cernan's struggles with his EVA mission. The handholds permitted later Gemini astronauts to have an ease of maneuverability for practicing useful work while they were outside their spacecraft.

Cernan's Gemini 9 flight EVA excursion also indicated that something was wrong with his space suit, since he was perspiring profusely from his efforts and the perspiration in good part remained inside the suit, fogging, and finally freezing over, the main visor of his helmet. The problem was finally solved with an improved ventilation system for the EVA suit. This was evident on the twelfth and final flight of the Gemini program. Edwin "Buzz" Aldrin, Jr., was the EVA astronaut. During more than five and a half hours of exposure to free space he experienced no fogging or freezing over of his helmet faceplate, nor did he feel uncomfortable because of excessively collecting perspiration inside his space suit.

*Rear view of early Gemini space suit
that was worn by Young and
Grissom on the first manned flight.
Outer coveralls were fabricated
of a heat-resistant material. By this
time the Mercury-type aluminized
silvery coating was dropped.
Suit was designed and built by the
David Clark Company, which made
all Gemini suits and helmets.*

Courtesy Dr. Edwin G. Vail,
Hamilton Standard Division,
United Aircraft Corporation

And he was working hard at practicing the use of tools in an EVA condition.

He did have his problems, however. While performing a simulated repair job on an outside panel of the spacecraft, in the Gemini adapter section, Aldrin removed a bolt and washer that slipped away from him and floated in under his helmet, against his chest. He finally managed to ease them out in front of him again, where he grabbed them and replaced them in the panel as part of his job. But although they were floating in zero gravity, they might have, if impelled to a high enough rate of acceleration, punctured a layer of his suit or cracked one or both of the visors of his helmet. In either case his life would be endangered.

Aldrin also reported an uneasy situation to his command pilot, Jim Lovell: While he was working outside on a daylight pass above the world, he could feel the strong heat of sunlight against his back and when he experimentally pressed himself against the rear inner wall of the inflated suit, he almost burned his skin before he leaned forward again. An external zipper was located in that area and its metal parts had become intensely hot from absorbing raw solar radiation. The situation was noted and compensated for afterward on the Apollo EVA suits.

Apart from its vitally important EVA functions, Project Gemini had two other equally significant basic goals: the gathering of experience in the rendezvous and docking of two orbiting spacecraft. The project provided actual conditions for pilot-proficiency training in the interception of targets in space and docking with them. It also provided an intimate familiarity with the conditions of living and working in space. Without the biological, engineering and piloting experience that the Gemini program provided, men could have neither reached nor landed upon the moon.

Front views of the early Gemini space suit on the morning of actual GT-3 launch. Astronauts Young (foreground) and Grissom have just left the suiting trailer van (in far background) and are walking up the ramp to enter an elevator that will carry them to the so-called White Room atop the Gemini-Titan launching rocket. There, final checkouts of the space suits and spacecraft systems were made before the Titan servicing tower, containing the White Room, was lowered prior to time zero. America's first two-man space flight was made on March 23, 1965. It lasted for three orbits of the earth: four hours, fifty-two minutes, and thirty-one seconds.

Courtesy NASA

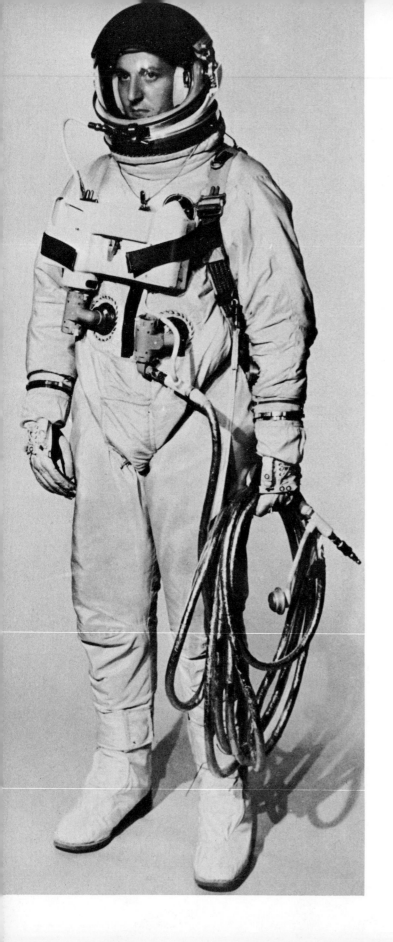

The first Gemini EVA space suit is modeled here by a NASA technician. He was wearing an emergency oxygen supply strapped to his chest and was holding the coiled twenty-five-foot gold-coated umbilical cable, which connected the suit to the spacecraft's life-support and communications systems. Coated with gold to reflect away the solar heat, the cable also included a safety tether. Note that helmet now has a visor, which acts as a neutral density filter to shield the EVA astronaut's eyes and face from intense solar radiations. It, too, was gold-plated.

Courtesy NASA

Side view of a later Gemini space suit. This one featured a bubble-type helmet protected with fabric which was an integral part of the coveralls that protected the space suit proper. The wrist rings, as always, were colored to match corresponding attachment rings on gloves: red for right hand, blue for left.

Courtesy Dr. Edwin G. Vail, Hamilton Standard Division, United Aircraft Corporation

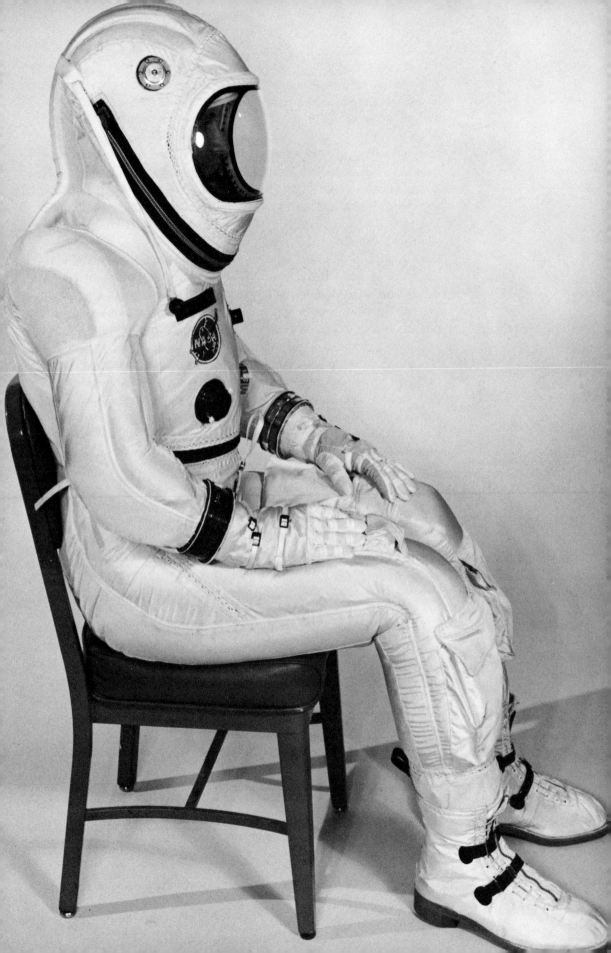

Project Gemini was named after a pair of twin stars, well known to amateur and professional astronomers, in the autumn-winter constellation of Gemini. They are stars of the first magnitude, brightest in that constellation, and are called Castor and Pollux— twin boys from ancient Greek mythology. There were twenty astronaut twin boys who flew in the Gemini program (the first two of the dozen Gemini space flights were unmanned). Of these, thirteen of the "twins" were chosen to use their Gemini experience in the first five critical manned flights of the Apollo program.

Project Apollo was Phase Three in the United States effort to land men on the moon and bring them back safely to earth before the close of the 1960 decade. That goal was surpassed by almost a full half-year, thanks in large part to experience gained from Project Gemini—which in turn could not have been launched without the cruder experience supplied by Project Mercury.

The first manned flight in the Apollo program was Mission 7. If that number bothers you, remember that there were unmanned flights in the program before it and one horribly tragic fire on the launch pad that killed three fine Apollo astronauts inside their space capsule. On Mission 7, Wally Schirra was the command pilot. He had been in space earlier, on both Mercury and Gemini flights. His two companions on the mission were rookies Donn Eisele and Walter Cunningham. The purpose of Mission 7 was to make an engineering test flight of the three-man command and service modules (CSM), or the space ship and its power plant, in earth orbit.

Mission 8 carried Frank Borman and Jim Lovell, both veterans of the Gemini program, plus rookie Bill Anders to the moon and back. Their purpose was circumnavigation of the moon to check out the CSM systems and space suits in lunar orbit as well as during the round-trip voyage through far-out space.

On Mission 9 were Gemini veterans Jim McDivitt and Dave Scott with rookie astronaut Rusty Schweickart. Their flight, also,

Closeup view of the GT-8 space-walking assembly, which was never used on the flight of GT-8: it is being tested here on the ground by Fred Spress of NASA's Crew Systems Division at Houston. He is holding the hand-held self-maneuvering unit (HHSMU) and wearing the full life-support regalia. The backpack later evolved into the Apollo personal life-support system, which led to the much advanced Apollo portable life-support system.

Courtesy NASA

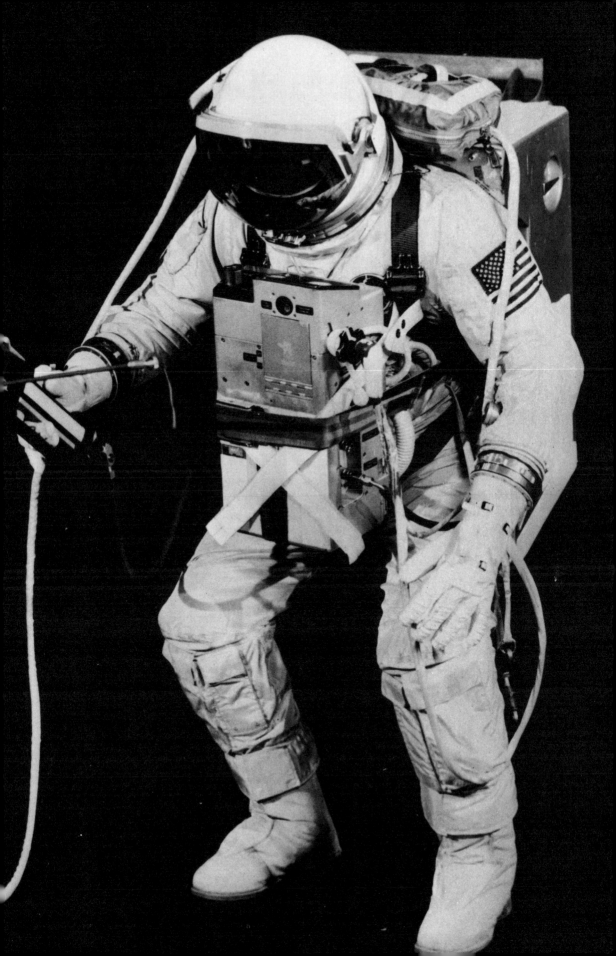

was in earth orbit, but this time they carried with them another spacecraft, the lunar module (LM), or the moon-landing vehicle. Their purpose was to prove out the reliability and maneuverability of the LM in a rendezvous and docking exercise with the CSM.

All three pilots on Mission 10 were former Gemini astronauts. They were Tom Stafford, John Young, and Gene Cernan, and their purpose was to take the LM to the moon, where they could check out the systems, procedures, and space suits in a lunar environment. There was no intention on this mission to fly the moon-landing vehicle down to the lunar surface. Instead, it was a kind of repeat performance of Mission 9—except that the LM was piloted to within 50,000 feet of the moon, where it surveyed a landing site, before returning to the CSM mother ship for a rendezvous and docking procedure in a gravity situation that was only one-sixth as strong as the earth's gravity. All maneuvers were made in exactly the way they would be if there had been a lunar landing —without the actual landing.

Mission 11 was the crowning event of the Apollo program. Again, the three astronauts were old-timers from the two-man Gemini program. Everybody by now should know their names: Neil Armstrong, Buzz Aldrin, and Mike Collins. They flew the CSM, with the LM in its nose, to the moon, established a lunar orbit while Armstrong and Aldrin crawled into the LM, pressurized it, and checked out its systems, and then detached it from the mother ship for a lunar descent and landing. Everything was critical, especially their space suits, when they stepped out of the LM and down its "front-porch" ladder for a restricted exploration of the moon's surface and the collection of lunar rocks and "soil." Thus they swept the highway clear for more extensive explorations, sample collecting, and scientific experiments. At the time, there were nine more moon landings programmed into Project Apollo.

One manned Apollo mission had slipped smoothly into another, because as design discrepancies were discovered on one flight they were fixed or improved for the next flight. This was true not only of mechanical and electronic systems, but also of the space suits. It was parallel in this way to the logical progression of Project Gemini.

Progressive modifications of the Gemini space suits should be self-evident from the photographs illustrating this chapter.

Chapter 12

WARDROBE FOR THE MOON

Symbolic of the design complexity and extra safeguards that had to be built into an EVA suit for moon walking is a comparison of its cost with the price of a Gemini EVA suit for use in free space. The Gemini EVA suits were each priced at $80,000. The Apollo moon suits each cost $400,000.

The total cost to develop and perfect the Apollo-program space suit was $150 million—a small enough price to pay when you consider the $24 *billion* spent on the whole manned space program. Those billions went into the development of the huge Saturn V rocket launch vehicle, the Apollo mother ship and lunar-landing vehicle, as well as into the purchase of launch vehicles and spacecraft for the Mercury and Gemini programs. So they can be called well spent. The prime contractor for developing and building the Apollo suits is the International Latex Corporation of Dover, Delaware. Their Government and Industrial Division is contract manager. The division not only designs and produces space-suit helmets along with the suits themselves but it also makes helmets for industry, the military, and underwater use.

The International Latex Corporation designers and tailors have accomplished a remarkable success in the development and building of the Apollo space suits. The crewmen of Apollo 11 wore two versions of the suit. One was the intravehicular garment assembly and the other was the extravehicular garment assembly. Basically, the two versions are identical—except that the EVA version includes an additional outer suit called an integrated thermal micrometeoroid garment. It is essentially a coverall suit to protect astronauts on the lunar surface from intense solar radiations, both visible and invisible, as well as from the high-speed impacts of micrometeoroids that might otherwise penetrate deeply through a space suit's fabric to cause a fatal loss of pressure.

Underneath the inner and outer space suits, the EVA astronauts when they walk on the moon wear a special liquid cooling garment next to their skin. The ultimate version worn by Armstrong and Aldrin when they made man's first lunar exploration was tailored of a knitted nylon-spandex fabric, on the inside of which was attached a network of plastic tubing. The tubing was connected to a manifold that circulated water through it. Water is fourteen times more effective as a cooling medium than any gas or combination of gases, such as pure oxygen or air. The liquid-cooled undergarment is worn by astronauts only during an EVA excursion. When they are inside

The basic objective of America's Project Apollo is achieved as astronaut Edwin E. Aldrin, Jr., climbs down ladder of the lunar module to become second human to step upon the moon. Photo was made by Neil A. Armstrong, first on the lunar surface. No one was there with a camera to take his picture, although his foot was photographed as if seen through a knothole by an automatic camera in the lunar module's descent stage. The historic moment when his foot touched the moon was clocked at 10:52 P.M. Eastern Daylight Time on July 20, 1969. Purposes of Apollo Mission 11 were the landing of two men on the lunar surface for exploration, the collection of rock specimens, and the setting up of three scientific experiments. Details of Aldrin's backpack portable life-support system and lunar overshoes can be clearly seen in this photo. Note the solid black shadows and bright flat white highlights, caused by a lack of atmosphere to diffuse sunlight.

Courtesy NASA

the command or lunar module it is replaced by the standard constant-wear garment.

Water is supplied to the cooling garment from a portable life-support system (PLSS), essentially a large backpack worn like a Boy Scout's camping knapsack, but attached much more securely to the astronaut's back and shoulders. The PLSS performs several other essential EVA duties and will be described in detail farther on in this chapter.

The basic intravehicular garment assembly, which is worn in the command module during lift-off and reentry and in the lunar module at all times, consists of six layers and weighs 35.6 pounds. Starting from the inside out, there are a comfort layer made of Nomex—a high-temperature-resistant nylon, a neoprene-rubber-coated nylon pressure bladder, a nylon restraint-layer (to prevent ballooning under pressure), another layer of Nomex and two layers of Teflon-coated Beta cloth. The significance of the Teflon and Beta-cloth layers will be described later.

Ten layers make up the covering suit for lunar EVA. These comprise an inner liner of two layers of neoprene-coated nylon, seven layers of Beta cloth interleaved with Kapton spacers and an outer layer of Teflon-coated Beta cloth. Kapton is an effective insulating material.

There are also, to complete the moon walker's wardrobe, a lunar EVA visor assembly, EVA gloves, and lunar overshoes.

The visor assembly consists of a polycarbonate shell that fits over the main full-pressure helmet for protection against the impacts of meteoroids. Two visors are attached to the shell. These are optically coated with materials that filter out specific wave lengths of electromagnetic radiation, such as ultraviolet and infrared light. The coatings also reflect away the radiations of heat energy from the sun.

The EVA gloves are built of an outer shell of Chromel-R, a metallic fabric, and thermal insulation to protect a lunar astronaut's hands when he is handling extremely hot or cold objects. Silicone-rubber fingertips allow the gloves to give him more sensitivity of touch.

The lunar overshoes, unlike the gloves, are an integral part of the EVA suit. They have thirty-three layers of insulation to protect the moon men against extremes of temperature found on the lunar landscape—roughly between plus two hundred and fifty degrees and minus two hundred and fifty degrees Fahrenheit—as well as against micrometeoroid impacts. Special features of the overshoes are ribs on their soles made of a metal-woven fabric, somewhat like chain mail, in combination with silicone rubber. The ribs not only help to prevent slipping but they also protect the soles, keep the overshoes rigid, and provide general traction.

Built in two sections the lunar overshoes employ a variety of exotic materials for insulation. The inner section is made up of thirteen layers of Teflon-coated aluminized Kapton plastic, which are separated by twelve spacing layers of Marquisette, a glass-spun kind of taffeta, and Beta glass-fiber felt. The outer section includes not only two additional layers of Beta felt underneath the silicone-rubber and metal-fabric soles but also employs at least sixteen layers of materials used in the EVA suit itself.

Both the lunar overshoes and the EVA gloves are a bright blue in color, which should produce a handsome tailored effect against their white space suits as the moon men stroll across the brownish gray landscape in the low sunlight of an early lunar morning.

Taken altogether—including the water-cooled underwear and the portable life-support system—the moon man's wardrobe is called an EMU, or extra vehicular mobility unit. Total weight of the EMU is 183 pounds—in terms of the earth's gravity pull. On the moon, where the pull of gravity is six times weaker, it weighs a mere thirty and one-half pounds.

Considering the apparently cumbersome array of items in his wardrobe, the lunar explorer has an almost fantastic amount of mobility. He can reach as high as six feet and work at a maximum height of five and a half feet. His downward reach is as low as twenty-two inches and his minimum working height is twenty-eight inches. With exceptional efficiency, he can work best between an optimum range of thirty to forty-eight inches above the lunar surface.

Materials almost magical in their qualities are incorporated into the Apollo space suits. All are fairly recent developments from American industrial or scientific research. The main full-pressure helmet that the moon men wear underneath an outer protective shell is made of Lexan, a trade name of the General Electric Company. Lexan is a clear polycarbonate with a peculiar stubbornness: it won't crack, break, or shatter. You can hit the Apollo pressure helmet with a baseball bat—and the bat will bounce back at you—spraining your wrist, if you've put enough zap into the blow. However, it has never been tested against a high-velocity meteoroid in the actual vacuum conditions of space, so the helmet engineers decided that for lunar exploration an additional protective shell of Lexan wouldn't do any harm. Besides, it was a convenient way to add the double optically filtering visors.

One of the new materials used in the space suits proper was introduced because of the horrible deaths of three astronauts selected as the prime crew to fly the first Apollo manned mission. They were Lieutenant Colonels Virgil I. Grissom and Edward H. White II of the Air Force and Lieutenant Commander Roger B. Chaffee of the Navy. Commander Chaffee was a rookie astronaut.

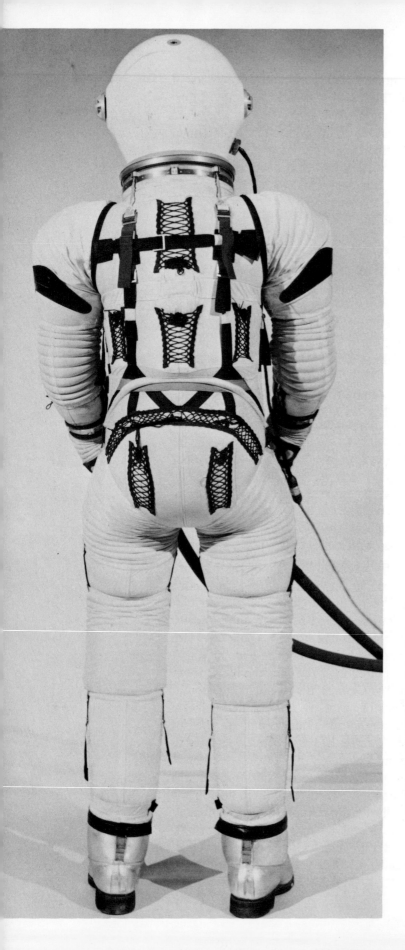

An extension of the 1961 suit was this 1964 state-of-the-art Apollo space suit, shown in back view. It had aluminized-coated boots for thermal protection, a different helmet and different lacings, but the joint-mobility bellows were about the same.

Courtesy Dr. Edwin G. Vail,
Hamilton Standard Division,
United Aircraft Corporation

The other two were veterans. Ironically, they were practicing a routine countdown in their spacecraft atop a Saturn I rocket which was on the ground at Pad 34, Cape Kennedy, when the accident occurred on January 27, 1967. They were locked inside the Apollo spacecraft, as they would be during a live countdown before an actual launch, when a high-intensity fire enveloped them. The 100 percent pure oxygen atmosphere of the spacecraft cabin intensified the heat of the flames to as high as 2,500 degrees Fahrenheit. The exact cause of the fire is not known to this day. But after an intensive investigation of the accident, NASA replaced all flammable materials in the Apollo spacecraft—among many other design changes—with fabrics made of Beta fibers. This included the astronauts' space suits.

The term "Beta," when applied to glass fibers, is a trademark of the Owens-Corning Fiberglas Corporation at Toledo, Ohio. Beta yarns are fireproof, and even when they are heated to their melting point of some 1,350 to 1,500 degrees Fahrenheit, they will not burn. They are woven of pure glass fibers that are only one-sixth as thick as fine silk filaments. These glass fibers are the finest textile filaments known to mankind. Because of this, the Beta yarns have a surface texture that feels like a soft, closely packed, smooth fur. They are not only fireproof but also have extraordinary insulation qualities. In addition to being used as fabric and insulating material for the Apollo space suits, they are used aboard the spacecraft for sleeping bags, medical-accessory kit bags, coverings for oxygen tubes and electrical cables, the oxygen tubes themselves, and a variety of harnesses and equipment bags.

Later, to guard against flaking of the finely woven glass fibers in a vacuum, the Beta yarn used in the Apollo space suits was coated with a fluorocarbon substance. The coating also protected the suits against abrasion. Known to housewives as Teflon, the substance is also used to line the inner surfaces of cookingware, such as pots and pans, because it will not scratch easily and can bear up under high temperatures, and nothing will stick to it. Teflon is a trademark of the E. I. du Pont de Nemours & Company, Incorporated; the substance is widely used in industry for its unique qualities.

The redesigned Apollo space suit, in addition to being fireproof, is much more comfortable and mobile than earlier models. Pressure points—which irritated the astronauts by pressing down on their shoulders, pushing up under their arms, and bearing in on their thighs—have been eliminated. The thermal-meteoroid protective garment for EVA work has been integrated into the suit, where before it was a separate cumbersome two-piece affair that had to be donned over the suit.

Even the outward physical appearance of the Apollo space suit

EXTRAVEHICULAR MOBILITY UNIT

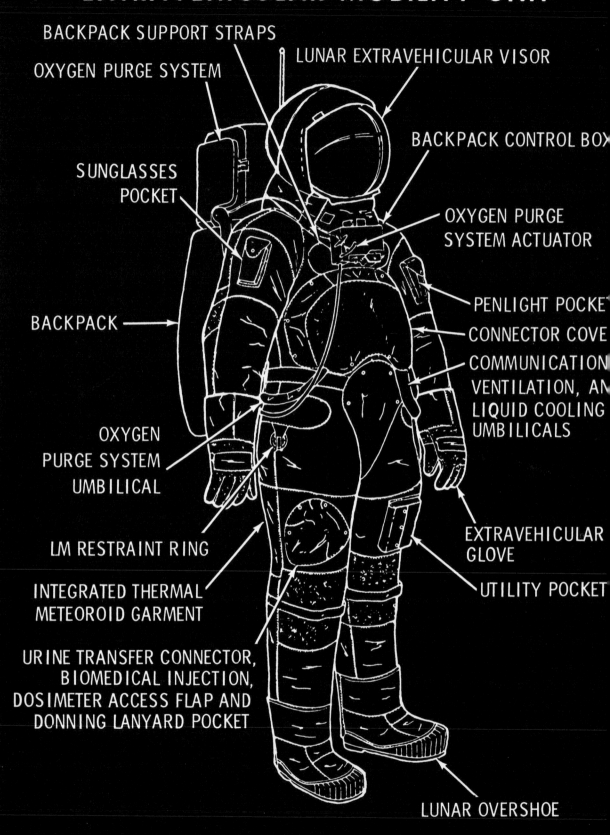

BACKPACK SUPPORT STRAPS

OXYGEN PURGE SYSTEM

LUNAR EXTRAVEHICULAR VISOR

BACKPACK CONTROL BOX

SUNGLASSES POCKET

OXYGEN PURGE SYSTEM ACTUATOR

PENLIGHT POCKET

BACKPACK

CONNECTOR COVE

COMMUNICATION VENTILATION, AN LIQUID COOLING UMBILICALS

OXYGEN PURGE SYSTEM UMBILICAL

LM RESTRAINT RING

EXTRAVEHICULAR GLOVE

INTEGRATED THERMAL METEOROID GARMENT

UTILITY POCKET

URINE TRANSFER CONNECTOR, BIOMEDICAL INJECTION, DOSIMETER ACCESS FLAP AND DONNING LANYARD POCKET

LUNAR OVERSHOE

has been changed. The former operational suit was colored blue. The suit worn on the lunar surface by astronauts Armstrong and Aldrin was white. The same color change was made in the PLSS, or portable life-support system.

Designed and produced by the Hamilton Standard Division of United Aircraft Corporation, the PLSS provides a livable atmosphere inside the Apollo space suit during EVA excursions either on the moon or in free space. Connected to the suit with umbilical hoses and electrical cables, the PLSS backpack worn by the lunar explorers permits up to four hours of EVA. Future modifications should extend its effective time for life-support purposes.

In its present form, the PLSS can be refilled with fresh equipment three times from extra supplies carried aboard the moon lander, or lunar module. Including the original PLSS equipment, this makes it possible for each of the two lunar module astronauts to make a total of four EVA's—an exploration time of sixteen hours each. The extra supplies are oxygen tanks, water reservoirs, batteries for electrical power, and lithium hydroxide canisters.

---

*The ultimate Apollo space suit worn by the first men on the moon
is diagrammed here. By that time—July 1969—cost of the developmental
program had increased tenfold. The actual suit was not merely
a piece of protective EVA space clothing but a coordinated array of
components to keep the lunar astronauts alive. It was called an
"extravehicular mobility unit" (EMU) because it included
communications and life-support equipment in a self-contained package.
Incorporated as a built-in part of the full-pressure suit was
a thermal-meteoroid garment (TMG) that shielded the astronauts against
solar heat, lunar cold, and high-speed metal or stone fragments from
the space debris shaken out of orbiting asteroids and comets.
The TMG part of the suit assembly also shielded them against those
high-energy nuclear and electromagnetic particles that speed
throughout the universe and would have a deadly effect when they strike
human tissue if there were no atmosphere to slow them down or
stop them. Added to this one-piece outfit were extra items of wear—
EVA gloves, lunar overshoes, and a lunar EVA visor, really
a shell that fits over the full-pressure helmet. Made of a resilient
plastic trade-named Lexan, the shell not only filters harmful
radiations before they can reach the astronaut's eyes and face, but it
also has enough "bounce" to reject meteoroids as if they were
tennis balls hitting a racquet. All of these extras must be donned
before astronauts open the hatch of their lunar module to
climb down a ladder onto the moon's surface.*

Oxygen recirculating back through the PLSS from the space suit passes through a lithium-hydroxide cartridge, where the carbon dioxide gas exhaled by an astronaut is trapped. The oxygen then continues onward through a bed of activated charcoal, which removes trace contaminants, including body odors. So an Apollo astronaut on an EVA mission stays fresh, bright-eyed, and bushy-tailed—thanks to the PLSS.

The PLSS backpack not only supplies oxygen for breathing and suit ventilation, but it also provides refrigerated water for body cooling. It pressurizes the space suit to a life-sustaining three and nine-tenths pounds per square inch and is equipped with a radio communications-and-telemetry set.

The radiotelemetry system informs Mission Control at Houston, Texas, of the astronaut's physical status as well as the status of critical conditions in the space suit itself. The radio transceiver system makes possible voice communications between the astronauts on the lunar surface, the astronaut in the command module mother ship orbiting the moon, and the people at Mission Control about a quarter of a million miles away. The PLSS also contains controls for an astronaut to operate the communications-and-telemetry set as well as signal devices with which the astronaut can monitor the set's functions.

Also on the PLSS is a separately operated emergency or backup oxygen-purge system that can supply an extra half-hour of oxygen.

The life-support backpack, with its controls and shielding, weighs eighty-four pounds—fourteen pounds on the moon, zero pounds in free space. Its power source is a silver-zinc battery that supplies sixteen and four-fifths volts. As protection against meteoroid impact, it has a cover of Fiberglas. On top of this is a thermal insulator made of fire-resistant Beta yarn and aluminized Kapton. A similar insulator covers the emergency oxygen-purge system. The purpose of the insulation is to prevent the leakage of heat into or out of the PLSS, regardless of the moon's temperature that might cause such leakage.

A precautionary by-product of the Apollo EVA space-suit system was the BIG, or biological isolation garment. The BIG was incorporated into the Apollo moon-landing procedures because some scientists felt that harmful bacteria or other microorganisms dangerous to life on earth might exist in the lunar surface.

So the BIG was designed as an available countermeasure to prevent the introduction of lunar germs into the earth's atmosphere. It was an interim device to insulate the bodies of the returning lunar explorers—which might carry an infectious-disease-breeding bacterium—before they left their spacecraft after splashdown. This would be long before they could be properly isolated in more thor-

Armstrong photographed Aldrin as he was setting up the seismometer,
known as the "passive seismic experiments package." He had
already deployed the cluster of prisms, designated "Laser ranging
retro-reflector," to measure precise distances between the
moon and the earth. It can be seen in the background, almost directly
in line with the seismometer and diagonally to the left of
the lunar module spacecraft.

*Appropriately looking like creatures from
another world in their new finery, the first men
back from a walk on the moon, along with
their spacecraft pilot, leave their
rescue helicopter to step upon the deck of
the* USS Hornet. *They were immediately locked up in
an isolation van to begin a three-week period
of biological confinement. The suits they wore when
this photo was made are called BIG's, for
"biological isolation garment." But not even a
microflea was found on the moon rocks that
they brought back to earth. During repeated tests
of their blood and continuous medical
observation of their respiratory and circulatory
systems, no symptoms were discovered of any
alien disease. Yet to play it safe, the BIG style
in space clothing was not discarded.
Apollo Mission 12 astronauts also had a wardrobe
fitted out with confinement tailoring.*

Courtesy NASA

oughly sealed quarters for medical observation and scientific testing during a sufficiently long quarantine period.

The procedure was to have a Navy frogman, wearing a BIG himself, open the hatch of the Apollo command module as it floated in the ocean and toss three BIG's in to the astronauts for donning before they left their spacecraft. Prior to this action, they were to vacuum-clean the interior of their craft, collecting the swept-up material in airtight canisters which contained chemicals to kill any bacteria that might be mixed in with it. Then they were sprayed with a liquid decontaminant by the frogman, who in turn was sprayed by an astronaut. Their life raft had already been thoroughly decontaminated, but was also filled with the liquid decontaminant to play doubly safe.

As it turned out, after a period of weeks in quarantine, there was no evidence that the moon-walking astronauts had brought back any lunar bugs.

The biological isolation garments are made of an airtight lightweight cloth fabric woven of Teflon fibers. They completely cover a wearer's body, from the soles of his feet to the top of his head. The BIG is a weird-looking costume, mainly because of a face mask built into its hood. Hung below the clear-plastic face mask are an air-inlet flapper valve and an air-outlet biological filter. These allow the wearer of the BIG to breathe in uncontaminated air, while the air he exhales is purified before it reaches the outside air. The frogman's BIG was designed in the opposite direction: the air he inhales is filtered of contaminants before it gets inside the suit. This protects him while he is in close contact with astronauts just returned from the moon.

Getting back to the Apollo space suit proper as well as to its integrated EVA suit, the final operational garment that made possible man's first walk upon the moon bears little resemblance to the early space suits designed for that purpose. There have been many design changes during the evolution of a secure, mobile, and comfortable moon suit.

Chapter 13

TAILORING A SPACE SUIT

But how do you actually fit a man into a space suit that will guarantee his safety while he moves and works among the lethal hazards of the moon? You certainly don't trust his life to the deft chalk marks a fine custom tailor draws along your chosen yards of fabric.

The average tailor, no matter how skilled and experienced he may be, does not have to worry about the heat exchange between your body, your suit, and the external environment. Nor will he have to study the variations in dimension of the inner and outer surfaces of your joints when you bend an arm or a leg. He would undoubtedly fling his own arms outward in despair if you told him that before he tailored your new suit he must be familiar with every one of the 206 bones in your body—giving special attention to the long bones of your limbs and the miniature long bones of your fingers and toes.

After that request, if your tailor isn't already thinking that you are on the verge of insanity, you might drop the helpful hint that he take a quick short course in the science of biokinematics—just so he'll be aware of the bone and muscular forces involved in lifting, walking, twisting, sitting, standing, reaching, and even smoking a pipe.

Your tailor is now aghast. He snaps: "Sir, you don't need me to style your clothes. What you want is a team of physiologists and engineers!"

His indignant statement is absolutely correct—if you want to be fitted for a suit that will keep you alive and active in the deadly environment of space. Although originally the conventional tailor played an important part in the early days of space-suit development, his successes were wasteful and thus expensive. He used the cut-and-try method to fit men into their pressure suits. No two suits were exactly alike, despite their general resemblance to each other. Each was custom built to be worn by a specific individual, even though all of the mechanisms and pressurizing devices had to be the same in every suit. Today, the space-age tailor is a new breed of professional. Instead of working with paper patterns, cloth, chalk, and scissors, he makes engineering drawings based on "nude range," "neutral range," "fabric mobility convolutes," and "omnidirectional joints."

A definition of these terms would be a description of the "materials" with which the space-age tailor works. Nude range refers to the range of muscular movements and bone flexibility available to the unhampered nude body. Neutral range deals with the restrictive qualities of any clothing that hampers the nude range. Tom Herrala, a top engineering tailor at the Hamilton Standard Division of United Aircraft Corporation, explains neutral range like this:

"Historically, the pressurized space suit has always tended to go cylindrical. When it was inflated, its urge was to become stiff, straight, and round—because that was the path of least resistance.

"If you continuously have to apply a muscular force against the suit to keep it from springing back to its original shape, then you are depleting your energy for useful work. I want that man on the inside of the suit to be able to assume normal postures without any effort. For instance, he should be able to sit down in a chair and relax. Once he assumes that position, he should be able to hold it without working against the suit. That's the definition of neutral range—the range of motions and positions which can be assumed without fighting to maintain those motions or positions.

"A further example: when a man has to reach up, say, to fix the hatch of his spacecraft, he can't do the job if he has to exert energy to hold his arms in that position. So it's necessary to design

Some space-suit gloves incorporate metal fingernails, so that
mobility of hands can be increased for astronauts. Hamilton-Standard
gloves have these fingernails on thumb and first two fingers,
since these are the three parts of the hand most used for grasping
objects. Technician wearing space-glove here demonstrates
how easy it is to pick up a dime.

Courtesy Hamilton Standard Division, United Aircraft Corporation

This closeup view of lunar overshoe shows insulation over ankle and protective sole to resist high or low temperatures on the moon's surface. The photo here was made of astronaut Neil Armstrong while he was practicing how to place his right foot (left to reader) into lunar module landing foot pad. Such training helped him to maintain equilibrium after he dropped from the ladder of the module onto the moon. Making the overshoes, and also seams apparent in legs of his space suit, require great skill.

his suit in a neutral range. In our latest suit I can bend my arms or
legs and the suit stays in that position. There is no tendency for it
to spring back into a stiff cylinder, simply because it is inflated.
That's because of the neutral range we designed into it.

"We have a man in our department who claims that it is easier
for him to do situps in our inflated suit than it is for him to do them
without the suit. This is because when he starts to do a situp in the
suit and his stomach muscles get a little tired about three-quarters
of the way up, he can rest against the suit, which holds its position
at that point. He then continues on up after a second or so. To an
outsider looking at him, there is no perceptible change in the continuity of his movement.

"We're getting more sophisticated now too. Not only do we want
our suit designs to have complete neutral range, but we also want
them to have the mobility of 100 percent nude range."

As a matter of fact, Hamilton Standard had already achieved a
space suit with 93 percent of nude range before October 1968,
when they demonstrated it before the aerospace scientists and engineers attending the Fifth Annual Meeting of the American Institute
of Aeronautics and Astronautics held at Philadelphia, Pennsylvania.
Live demonstrations of the suit during the week-long meeting at-
tracted wide interest and attention—plus some disbelief. It was
hard for some of the onlookers to believe that so much mobility
could be designed into an inflated space suit. But it was. For the
advanced suit was developed to meet the greater mobility requirements of manned space missions to follow the Apollo moon-landing
program.

The Hamilton Standard suit obviously has considerably more
mobility and neutral range than any of its contemporary space
suits. Unlike existing suits of that time, it also employed a sealing
zipper that runs down the front of the torso so that it can be put
on like coveralls. This frontal entry makes donning and doffing of
the suit much faster in emergencies. Even the advanced Apollo suit
has its entry zipper running from the crotch up the back of the torso.
According to Tom Herrala, the Hamilton Standard suit can be
donned by trained personnel in one minute forty-five seconds—
more than twice as fast as any other pressure suit up to its inception.

Another unique feature of this suit is the nylon-fabric gloves with
built-in metal fingernails on their first two fingers. The gloves are so
tactile and flexible that their wearer can pick up a dime from the
floor—a difficult accomplishment for the wearer of most other
space-suit gloves. But this suit was designed for the workingman
in space, for scientist- and engineer-astronauts who one day will
be living and performing complex tasks in earth-orbiting laboratories and lunar bases.

This workman's space suit incorporates two up-to-the-minute design concepts: a fabric-mobility convolute that is positioned at eleven joint areas—including shoulders, elbows, the waist-hip area, and knees—and an omnidirectional elbow joint. The ultramodern joint concept makes it possible for a spaceman wearing the Hamilton Standard suit to move his elbows with ease in any direction of which he is capable when dressed in ordinary work clothes.

Tom Herrala, who was intimately involved with engineering the unique elbow joint, described to me how it works: "After a whole series of studies we discovered that the best way to get the highest neutral-to-nude range was to make the joint itself one-directional and line it up with the elbow just above the elbow. In other words, this stationary joint allows you to bend your elbow. Then in conjunction with the joint we use a very low torque bearing, which just rotates easily and allows you to turn your forearm in any direction. We've done the same thing with the wrist joint. You can bend and turn your wrist in the suit almost as if you didn't have the suit on.

"Of course, engineeringwise you pay something for a ring bearing like that because it provides a gap in the continuity of the suit and could possibly be a source of pressure leakage from the suit. But after many tests, we are confident that it's pretty secure. It's one of those compromises that you have to face when you design anything. You trade off a little bit of extra weight against achieving a lot more mobility. The same thing goes for the leakage possibility."

Regarding the reason why the Hamilton Standard space suit is the only one to date that zippers up the front instead of up the back, Herrala had this to say: "There are a lot of problems with frontal entry designing. They all have to do with sealing in the suit-pressure. You're bringing together two soft pieces of fabric and hard-sealing them with metal. You have to squeeze them closed in a way that prevents leakage. It's easier to do this from the back of a suit, since the pressurizing gas is fed in from the front, where normally the immediate pressure will be somewhat higher.

"But we felt strongly that the human element was very important psychologically. You don't button up your shirt from the back, for example. In fact anything you put on—your trousers, jacket and overcoat—you button up the front or zip up the front. If a guy's spacecraft sprang a leak for one reason or another, his life would depend on how fast he can get into his pressure suit. . . . If he has to fumble behind him, things are going to be real tough.

"We ran a whole big trade-off study on the situation—something like twelve different zipper-entry concepts that could be considered valid—and decided that for space-suit application the only answer was frontal entry. So we sweated out the design and test phases of this approach and finally came up with something that worked the way we wanted it it to."

Courtesy Don Bowen,
Group Leader/Pressure Suits,
6570th Aerospace Medical
Research Laboratory, USAF

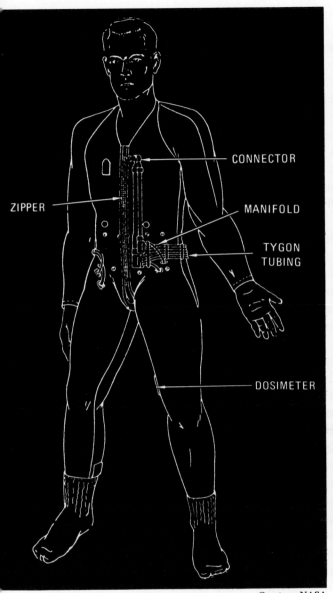

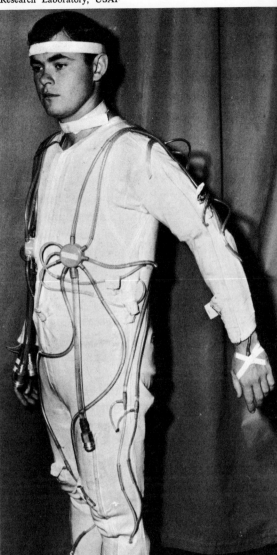

ZIPPER

CONNECTOR

MANIFOLD

TYGON
TUBING

DOSIMETER

Courtesy NASA

*NASA diagram of liquid-cooling garment (LCG) shows basic
tailoring of water-cooled underwear worn next to skin
by Project Apollo moon walkers.*
*The photo pictures a 1963 prototype of LCG about to be tested
in a heat chamber by Airman First Class Epperson, a space-suit
specialist working on an early-type EVA suit at 6570th
Aerospace Medical Research Laboratory, Wright-Patterson Air
Force Base. Epperson, now a civilian, is at International Latex.*

Another aspect of their space suit that the Hamilton Standard engineers "sweated out" was its helmet. Tom Herrala told me: "Our earlier suits used plexiglass visors, which can crack—and if they crack, there goes your pressurization. Today's suits, naturally including the Apollo suit, use Lexan. As a matter of fact, our entire helmet is made of Lexan. It's a big bubble with the back part of it painted white. The paint on the back prevents excessive internal reflections, since it has a flat finish. But we also had problems with the Lexan itself. Yet with Lexan you were buying a material that did not, or would not, shatter on impact. You can put on the helmet and butt your head against a stone wall and it wouldn't shatter or even crack on you. Therefore you can't lose your suit atmosphere through the helmet."

Herrala also pointed out something about the space business that a lot of people overlook: "There's a great big difference between building a 'boiler-plate' model of something and the actual successful production of it. So far as space suits are concerned, there has always been a problem with reproducibility.

"An example of the engineering problem is this: your shoulder comes off your body at a certain angle in a certain position. So you've got to make sure that the shoulder of your space suit comes off its torso at just that angle too. The seam must be in the right position and at the right angle—or every time you move in that suit it's going to hurt. Your movement will be restricted. This is what we call reproducibility. You build, say, two suits and test them side by side—and they both work exactly the same.

"Everything we do in the space-suit business is from engineering drawings. We've trained our seamstresses to read them. One suit consists of more than three thousand drawings. So when we want to put a suit together, we take a stack of drawings that reaches from the floor to the ceiling and send it out to the shop. From that stack the girls can make thirty, forty, fifty, sixty, and even a hundred or more space suits all exactly alike."

I have quoted Tom Herrala at some length to give the reader insight into the problems involved with tailoring a modern space suit and how at least one prominent engineering firm goes about solving them. Obviously, the new look in space suits involves a complex of design features. The numerous details that must be fitted into the suits are self-evident from the three thousand-odd drawings that permanently freeze a suit concept for all time.

Chapter 14

BLUE COLLARS BEYOND THE EARTH

Looking ahead two decades, Dr. Edwin Vail of Hamilton Standard foresees man as a valuable working resource on the moon. He envisions the moon as a place where the original Apollo astronauts have already "completed the preliminary exploration and geological survey of parts of the lunar surface and have identified a good site for a permanent base installation."

That word "geological," Dr. Vail explained to me with a smile, obviously showed that he was still psychologically earth-oriented. "One day we'll all be calling it 'lunalogical,' " he said. " 'Geology' will become 'lunalogy'—a very important aspect of exploiting the moon from a permanent manned lunar base.

"Other new words should also become a part of our everyday **243** vocabulary," he continued. "We'll be talking about moon-moving equipment, such as moondozers, rather than of earth-moving equipment, like bulldozers. 'Geophysical' will be replaced more accurately by 'lunaphysical' to workers on the moon, as will heat sources in the moon become known as 'lunathermal' instead of 'geothermal' sources. The study and measurement of broad areas of the moon will be a science designated by the word 'lunadesy,' as a logical substitute for 'geodesy,' the designation for the same science on Earth. 'Geography' will understandably be transposed to 'lunagraphy.' These are only a few examples."

(Dr. Vail is obviously more partial to Roman derivations than to Greek. For example, the Greek goddess of the moon was Selena, so *selenology* and *selenography* would be equally apt.)

But more immediately, Dr. Vail is seriously concerned with establishing a colony of workmen on the moon. These workmen would include not only scientists and engineers but also miners, farmers, construction workers, surveyors, machinists, riggers, drillers, excavators, electronic-communications specialists, rocket-engine and rocket-airframe technicians, foundry and mill workers, truckers, food processors, mineral processors, plumbers, and lunologist-explorers. This last group of workmen would explore the craters, plains, and mountains of the moon for mineral deposits.

Dr. Vail estimates that "approximately 50 percent of the lunar miner's time will be spent working in the life-support cabs of vehicles, while the rest of his time will be involved in surface tasks that require his wearing of EVA space suits—tasks such as loading a drilled hole for blasting, adjusting, servicing and maintaining mining equipment, and the recovery of drill cores for analysis."

Transforming the crude minerals into refined metals for the construction of shelters, machinery, and rocket components will also demand considerable EVA work in its preliminary stages.

Two of man's major activities on the moon will be never-ending, from Dr. Vail's view. These are exploring and experimenting. "All scientific knowledge that will be obtained about the moon can be considered essential to the successful exploration of other planets in the solar system."

Dr. Vail proposes that the manned exploration of other planets can be efficiently accomplished from a permanent moon base on a self-supporting foundation of mining, refining, and manufacturing. His plan includes a gas-processing and -extraction facility, wherein oxygen and hydrogen are withdrawn from minerals and separated to be stored for use as rocket-engine fuels and oxidizers as well as for the support of human and animal life in the lunar colony. "When the mining and mineral-extraction capabilities reach a level where pure metals are available, then a fabrication facility for the manufacture of all types of equipment will be required. The fabrication and assembly of rocket vehicles for further scientific exploration of the solar system should be emphasized.

"In addition to this important activity, the fabrication facility should have the capability to manufacture new pressurized shelters for living quarters and other workshops as well as replacement components for moon-base equipment. In many respects this facility might be considered a super-model shop. It would be the last step in maximizing the self-sufficiency of the lunar-base complex."

Dr. Vail's lunar-base concept includes electrical and heat power sources from the sun, from isotopic nuclear power plants and from lunathermal sources. Radiations from the sun alone could be harnessed to produce several types of power through the use of solar cells, specially designed spherical and parabolic mirrors, and nuclear-particle as well as electromagnetic-particle collectors.

The Vail moon colony was conceived on the basis of pressurized modules for flexibility and expansion. There would be living-quarter modules, workshop modules, and factory modules. Some of these could be interconnected by pressurized tunnels. Others could be reached by men wearing EVA space suits. The colony would grow in size and sophistication with the expansion of lunar-exploitation activities. New modules would be continually built, fitted, and added to the complex as needed.

Since food production will be a vital adjunct to colony growth, a note about farming on the moon cannot be overlooked. It will be the quality of the food that directly affects the quality of metabolic energy transfer in the lunar workman. "As the capabilities of the lunar base are extended," says Dr. Vail, "farming will become an essential activity. A farm and food-processing facility will probably begin as a separate module from the main life-support shelter. It will initially provide staple green vegetables to supplement the basic food supplies. As the base grows in size, the farming facility will gradually grow until it reaches the level of a balanced closed ecology. At this point, selected animals will be raised within the complex for dietary protein. The workload on the lunar farmers will range from light to moderate. No lunar EVA surface activities are visualized by me for this area, except those activities required for necessary external building maintenance."

How will Dr. Vail get his farm animals to the moon? The answer is: by using rocket-powered support spacecraft sent out from the earth. Eventually, such supply vehicles would be built on the moon and sent to the earth with cargo and men who are being rotated from their lunar jobs to other tasks on their home planet. As Dr. Vail puts it: "When the full capability of the lunar launch complex is attained, interplanetary vehicles will be assembled and launched from the moon to explore the entire solar system."

Finally, Dr. Vail foresees the development of a perfect space

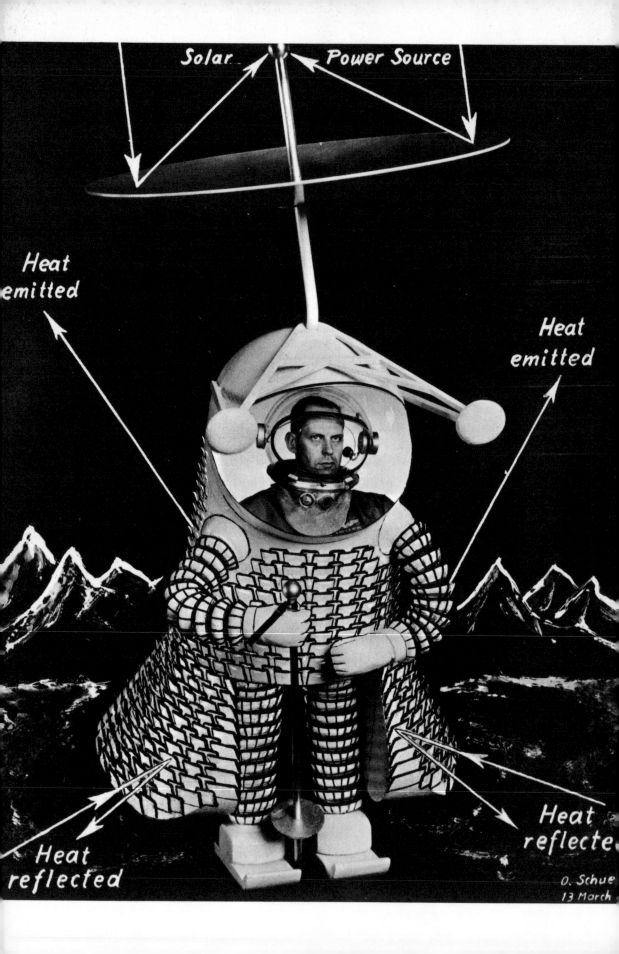

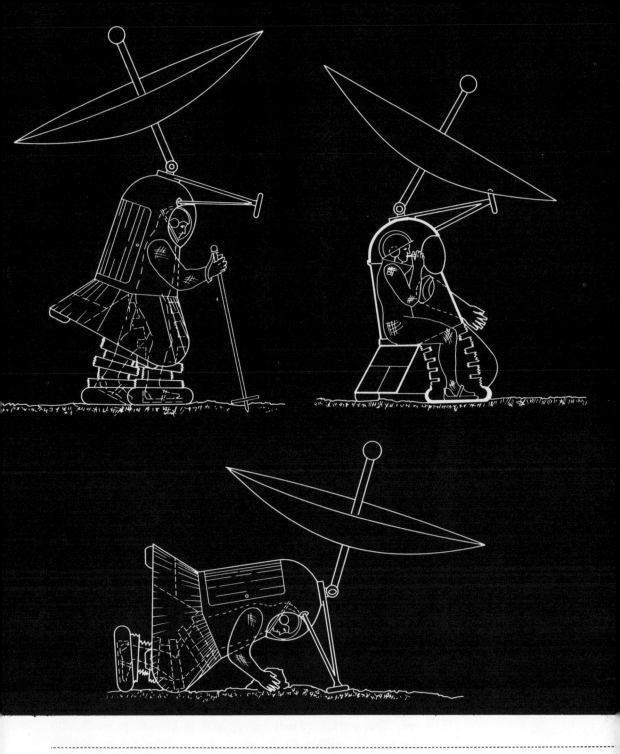

Less than a month after John Glenn's successful three-orbit flight around the world on February 20, 1962, the people at the Air Force's Wright Aerospace Medical Laboratories began to produce ideas for personal life-support equipment that could make possible man's exploitation of resources on the moon. These three drawings and a model dated 13 March 1962 by O. Schueller may appear whimsical, but they are based on valid scientific and engineering concepts.

Courtesy Don Bowen, Group Leader/Pressure Suits, 6570th Aerospace Medical Research Laboratory, USAF

suit within the next two decades: "In the next twenty years, space suits will evolve into well-engineered functional units, with integral life-support systems having a minimum of eight hours' capability. Wearing these suits, man will readily adapt himself to a working environment on the moon."

Dr. Vail has drawn up a chart to extrapolate the nude-to-neutral-range ratio from the best present space suits to those of two decades hence. He finds that 100 percent of the nude-movement capabilities of shoulders, elbows, wrists, the waist-hip area, knees, and ankles will be matched in the space suits of the future. This is a lot better than can be said for the conventional dress clothing worn by the man in the street today.

The self-sustaining moon colony is proposed by Dr. Edwin Vail for activation in the late 1980's. But meanwhile NASA has been working toward two more immediate goals that must surely build the foundation for such a colony during the 1970's. These are continuing advances in lunar exploration by Project Apollo astronauts and the follow-on project known as AAP, for Apollo Applications Program.

By 1971, the Apollo astronauts will have a lunar rover vehicle, which they will carry with them to the moon. This will be a much smaller machine than the type Dr. Vail requires for his lunalogical prospectors, but it will make possible the start of extensive explorations of the lunar landscape. The LRV, as it's called, will have four wheels, weigh about four hundred earth pounds and act as a rugged jeep for two astronauts by transporting them over the rocky terrain of the moon. Space will be provided in the jeep to carry the astronauts' hand tools, the lunar rock samples they collect, and miscellaneous equipment for various scientific experiments. Unlike conventional jeeps on earth, this one will be powered by small rockets, since there is no air on the moon to make possible the combustion of conventional automotive fuels. Research and planning toward the development of a lunar roving vehicle has been going on since 1964 at NASA's Marshall Space Flight Center, Huntsville, Alabama, where the giant Saturn V rocket was developed.

The same NASA center has management and design control over the first manned orbital workshop in the Apollo Applications Program. The workshop will carry what is known as an Apollo telescope mount (ATM) for astronomical observations beyond the earth's distorting atmosphere. The atmosphere hinders the accuracy of such observations from the ground, even atop a high mountain, because it combines the distorting qualities of a huge randomly shaped lens, a giant unsymmetrically formed mirror, and an assortment of great filters which block out certain interesting wave lengths of light generated by the sun and other stars. The ATM, for the

first time, will allow men to make extended unhindered observations
of the Universe.

It will also provide them with a platform to demonstrate man's
ability to perform many scientific experiments in space by operating
high-resolution astronomical instruments. Among the experiments
could be an analysis of the effect of intergalactic gravity forces upon
the shifting of light toward the red or blue end of the visible spec-
trum and a search to discover if the theoretically postulated invisible
neutron stars do, in fact, exist. The results of either experiment
could radically change man's present concepts about how the Total
Universe was born and evolved.

Other experiments aboard the orbital workshop will study man's
physiological and psychological responses to an extended stay in
a gravity-free space environment. They should also supply much
more detailed information about his capabilities to endure long-term
journeys through the void.

The orbital workshop will be launched unmanned in 1972 aboard
a Saturn V rocket from NASA's Kennedy Space Center at Merritt
Island, Florida. Lift-off is scheduled from one of two pads at Complex 39 and the plan is to place the workshop into a circular orbit
some 220 nautical miles above the earth. All equipment, including
the ATM and special telescopes, will be on board the workshop
at time of launch.

About a day later, the first three-man crew will be launched
from Complex 34 at Cape Kennedy Air Force Station in an Apollo
spacecraft atop the smaller Saturn IB rocket. The three astronauts
will rendezvous with the workshop and dock on it, then climb into
their living and working quarters for a twenty-eight-day mission.
After this length of time they will return to earth and other three-
man crews will subsequently fly up to the workshop for longer
periods of habitation.

But even as these plans were being made for a 1972 launch of
the AAP workshop, NASA had already established task groups to
direct the construction and launching of a supremely more ambitious project for the mid-1970's. This project comprises two parts:
the manned space station and the space shuttle. According to
NASA: "The space shuttle is a system of low-cost transportation
from the earth's surface to orbit and return. It will service the space
station and carry out other important space missions at greatly
reduced operating costs."

The manned space station itself will be very much larger than
the Saturn V workshop. It is conceived as a permanent satellite to
house many scientists and astronaut-workmen. As NASA officially
states its purpose: "The space station is a flexible centralized base
of support, permanently operating in earth orbit." This suggests

Litton Industries, Inc., has developed advanced space suits of high mobility. Here are their latest soft suit and hard suit. These suits are an innovation, since no zippers are used anywhere on them, thus minimizing pressure leakage. Both use stovepipe joints, which make use of rotary seals—two aluminum rings grooved to hold plastic ball bearings between them. The joints are made airtight with a wiper seal of Teflon on the inner aluminum ring.

Photos courtesy Colonel Barney Oldfield, USAF (Ret.), Corporate Director, Public Relations and Advertising/International, Litton Industries, Inc.

that, apart from numerous other functions, it could be a way station from which men and supplies would be sent to colonize the moon.

A necessary concurrent development with space-workshops, permanent bases in orbit, and earth-to-orbit shuttles is the "blue-collar" space suit. For the workingman in free space, just as the workman on the moon, will have many EVA duties to perform. Outside maintenance and repair jobs alone will be a continuing requirement for any long-lasting orbital installation or vehicle. Apart from being able freely to use his hands and feet as well as his arms and legs, the blue-collar spaceman must be able to maneuver around from place to place with ease. Therefore he will need either a special maneuvering unit or a space suit that can be maneuvered by itself.

In the latter respect, an experimental space suit with integrated maneuvering rocket thrusters is being developed by the Hamilton Standard Division of United Aircraft Corporation. Although the suit development was sponsored by the U. S. Air Force, the operational suit itself will be readily adaptable to NASA needs. Fabrication of the "functional suit," as Hamilton Standard designates it, will be based upon the already completed design of an advanced suit with a built-in life-support system. Development of this suit, also, was supported by the Air Force's Aerospace Medical Research Laboratory at Wright Field in Ohio. With the addition of the rocket thrusters to the original advanced suit, the second-generation suit has been named by the Air Force an integrated maneuvering and life-support system (IMLSS).

The IMLSS is a hybrid space suit: it brings together the qualities of a soft suit and a hard suit. Its arms and legs are made of a rubberized nylon fabric, but its torso is a hard shell of fiber-glass-reinforced plastic. From twelve to sixteen rocket thrusters are experimentally being tried during the developmental period. These are imbedded in the torso section of the suit and produce one and a half pounds of thrust each. The operational suit will use liquid oxygen as a propellant for the small rockets, but an inert compressed gas is being employed for testing and evaluation of the system.

Four-hour EVA excursions will be possible with the IMLSS suit, which is designed so that an astronaut can replenish his oxygen supply and other consumable materials while he is still outside his spacecraft or station. Lockers on the outside of these vehicles will store the fresh materials in module-like canisters. The astronaut merely substitutes his empty module for a loaded one that he takes from one of the lockers and drops into a receptacle on the torso of his suit.

The distribution of life-support components within the torso are arranged to maintain the body's center of gravity. The torso also contains a radio transceiver for communication with the spacecraft, the space station, or the ground. A microphone and loudspeaker are built into the suit's helmet, which is also equipped with an EVA filtering visor to shut out dangerous electromagnetic radiations and reflect heat energy from the sun.

Other advanced EVA space suits are being developed by Litton Industries of Beverly Hills, California. One of these is a soft suit, the other is a hard suit. Both are pictured in this chapter to show their high mobility characteristics and design aspects. Despite its good mobility, the Litton hard suit looks like a study in pre-medieval armor and is just about as tough. Its plastic outer shell gives added protection against meteoroid strikes. Even if a meteoroid should puncture this outer shell, a sandwich structure behind it would probably splinter and stop the meteoroid from further penetration and thus maintain the integrity of suit pressurization.

Both of the Litton suits have a constant volume-to-pressure ratio, which explains their fine mobility. The disadvantage of a hard suit, as with any suit of armor, is that it cannot be compressed or folded into a small space for stowage. But this wouldn't be objectionable in a lunar colony, where hard suits could be hung on racks in a donning room.

The Litton hard suit is unique in its field: there are no competitors at present. However, there appears to be a more favorable future for the hybrid hard-soft suit, which could combine the advantages of both types and eliminate the disadvantages of each. In this respect, Litton has a good head start in the hybrid-suit business, since that company has already developed a workable hard suit and a practical soft suit.

Litton and Hamilton Standard together were inspired to begin the research and development of space suits because of the growing need for EVA protective clothing that became apparent in the early 1960's. The Gemini program demonstrated that excursions outside of a sealed, pressurized spacecraft were feasible when a space-suit

On the following pages an artist's rendering depicts a space suit with an integrated life-support system that is self-propelled for space tasks. It is a hybrid suit: hard-shell torso, containing the propulsion system and controls, coupled with soft-fabric arms and legs. The suit is being developed by Hamilton Standard under contract with Aerospace Medical Research Laboratories of the Air Force Systems Command. But it should have many future applications for NASA.

Courtesy Hamilton Standard Division, United Aircraft Corporation

design could meet the rigorous requirements of extra vehicular activity.

The civilian space program should make steady progress in the conquest of space as an environment where men can safely live and work. New tools and devices are continually being invented for this purpose.

Dr. David L. Richardson, of Arthur D. Little, Inc., a famed scientific consulting firm, puts the situation in these terms: "The present concept of the space suit will be modified by future mission requirements and spacecraft. As spacecraft evolve into large complex space stations and as more intensive manned space exploration is carried out, the space suit will no longer be adequate for all mission requirements.

"Instead, current space suits will be replaced by completely integrated extravehicular protection systems which are designed for maximum interaction with the particular mission and for maximum astronaut mobility."

Disagreeing with this view of the future is Dr. Charles L. Wilson, Chief Medical Advisor in the Life Support Systems Program Office of the Air Force's Aeronautical Systems Division. Dr. Wilson's attitude is: "Space suits will always be with us, even if only as an emergency backup system, just as life preservers are still with us on boats."

At the very least, space suits will still be in fashion when the first men land on the planet Mars.

INDEX